PRAISE FOR

10X MARKETING FORMULA

"A powerful formula for marketing success; thoroughly modern and proven to succeed. This is a book for marketers that want to win."
> — Jay Baer, Founder of Convince & Convert and Author of *Hug Your Haters*

"Today, most companies do some form of content marketing. Unfortunately, most are failing. It doesn't have to be that way. This book will not only get you facing the right direction, but will give you the insight to truly differentiate your company from the competition. There are no more excuses."
> — Joe Pulizzi, Founder of Content Marketing Institute

"Often, books like this are a disappointment. They're long on ideas, short on actionability. This is not one of those books. Garrett Moon delivers on the promise of providing a blueprint for the most differentiating and results-driven content marketing of your career."
> — Marcus Sheridan, Author of *They Ask, You Answer*

"The *10x Marketing Formula* is the real deal. But what I love is that this isn't theory—it's experience! Garrett Moon and the team he's built at CoSchedule have actually done what he's teaching, and now you can too."

— Pat Flynn, Founder & CEO of Smart Passive Income

"Garrett Moon is one of my favorites to follow because he combines the edge of a fearless startup CEO with the savvy of a marketer who's scaled a successful business. The *10x Marketing Formula* challenges you to rethink your goals and definitions of success and, more importantly, how you employ strategic shortcuts to achieve them."

— Michael Hyatt, *NY Times* Best-Selling Author and Founder and CEO of Michael Hyatt & Co.

"Want a guide to creating effective content that's overflowing with actionable tips? Look no further than the *10x Marketing Formula*. Unlike most books in this space, it's written by a guy who's actually done it. Highly recommended."

— Brian Dean, Packed with Actionable Advice

"The *10x Marketing Formula* is fantastic. No fluff or theory. Real-life practical experience based on what really works. I'm a fan of CoSchedule, and I love what Garrett Moon has put together here. It's a must-read for anyone who wants their content to spread."

— Jeff Goins, Best-Selling Author of *The Art of Work* and *Real Artists Don't Starve*

"It's not hyperbole. This is a proven approach written by someone who's actually done it. If you're looking for a refreshing, and real, guide to making your marketing 10x better—this is it."

— Robert Rose, Chief Strategy Officer at Content Marketing Institute and Co-Author of *Killing Marketing: How Innovative Businesses Are Turning Marketing Cost Into Profit*

"Most marketers today struggle to get measurable reach, engagement, traffic, and sales from their marketing efforts. Savvy marketers know it takes a fresh new approach to get real results. Garrett Moon is one of those savvy marketers! In his new book, *10x Marketing Formula*, he shares the exact steps to creating memorable content marketing that actually grows your business. Read, apply, and watch your results soar!"

— Mari Smith, Premier Facebook Marketing Expert & Social Media Thought Leader; Author of *The New Relationship Marketing* and Co-Author of *Facebook Marketing: An Hour a Day*

"Growth no longer goes to the biggest. It goes to the scrappiest. It goes to the content hackers who find strategic shortcuts. Who's gonna own the future? The marketing teams who embrace this blueprint and learn to think like the agile, lean teams outlined in this book."

— Joanna Wiebe, Copy Hackers by Airstory

"A clear-eyed, real-world, no-bunk look at what it takes to make your content marketing program deliver in spades."

— Ann Handley, *Wall Street Journal* Best-Selling Author of *Everybody Writes* and Chief Content Officer, MarketingProfs

"The difference between a content marketer and a really successful one is the 10x approach that Moon has outlined in this book. If you want to make a giant leap forward in your content marketing this is a must read."

— Ian Cleary, Founder of RazorSocial and Co-Founder of OutreachPlus

"If you think you have to be in Silicon Valley to grow a startup, think again. Moon has done an impressive job from NORTH DAKOTA in growing a successful company. Enjoy seeing the exact marketing methodology he used to do it!"

> — Noah Kagan, Chief Sumo at Sumo Group

"Jammed with actionable advice. Pages of meaningful ideas!"

> — Mark Schaefer, Marketing Consultant and Author of *The Content Code*

"If you're an entrepreneur, read this book. If you're a marketer, read this book. If you're tired of 10 percent growth, read this book. The rules have changed, and *10x Marketing Formula* is today's must-read for businesses desperate for real results."

> — Ash Maurya, Author and Creator of Lean Canvas

"Many content marketers are great at one thing, and it's typically publishing. They don't also plan, execute, or analyze their work, which is why content marketing is often considered a failure. In *10x Marketing Formula*, Garrett Moon shows not only how important it is to do all four, but how easy it is. This is not a theory book you'll read and never do anything about. This is an actionable book that will put your content marketing on fast forward."

> — Gini Dietrich, CEO of Arment Dietrich and Founder and Author of *Spin Sucks*

"Garrett Moon addresses what we've all come to realize: traditional content marketing isn't living up to the hype. If you want to finally stand out and drive real results, *10x Marketing Formula* goes beyond theory and provides the 'how-to' behind the most successful campaigns."

> — Sujan Patel, Managing Partner, Ramp Ventures

"10x marks the spot, and right out of the gate Garrett Moon wisely describes the sticky spot most content marketers find themselves in. They relentlessly pour resources into producing 'copycat' content that accomplishes little or nothing. Moon draws on the results of his company's boundless experimentation and the insights of today's most accomplished marketers to guide you down the path to making your marketing pay. Read *10x Marketing Formula* today or continue burning money tomorrow."

> — Barry Feldman, Online Marketing Super Freak and Author of
> *The Road to Recognition*

"Having lived and breathed actionable marketing for fifteen years, I can assure you that Garrett Moon and his CoSchedule team are the real deal. Based on his team's real-life experience, Moon pulls back the curtains to show you step-by-step how to make your content yield measurable results that keep your business going."

> — Heidi Cohen, Actionable Marketing Guide

"The next generation of marketers are entering at perhaps the noisiest marketplace in history. Unlike the Field of Dreams, if you build it they may not come. To truly stand out, marketers would do well to listen to what Moon reveals in this book."

> — John Hall, Author of the Best-Selling Book *Top of Mind* and
> Keynote Speaker

"Even if your marketing isn't in a do-or-die position, you have a huge opportunity. Imagine your traffic and conversions with 10x results. Just picture it. Then follow Moon's blueprint for getting there. He's laid it out for you here in clear, specific steps."

> — Andy Crestodina, Co-Founder and CMO of Orbit Media and
> Author of *Content Chemistry*

"The *10x Marketing Formula* is a treasure trove of up-to-date marketing wisdom for brand marketers, business owners, entrepreneurs, and anyone who needs marketing help at any level. The knowledge shared inside these pages is easily worth hundreds to thousands in a marketing education. This will become a go-to guidebook for marketing wisdom in 2018 and beyond. Read, get your marker, mark, and reread to catch useful, practical advice from a host of industry leaders, led by a fantastic author, the CEO of CoSchedule, Garrett Moon.

— Julia McCoy, CEO of Express Writers and Author of *Practical Content Strategy & Marketing*

"The *10x Marketing Formula* isn't primarily about marketing—it's about results. And it's the new required reading for every entrepreneur and marketer who wants to achieve tenfold growth. Better still, Moon beautifully lays out simple, actionable frameworks so you can get those results with blinding speed. Read this book, do what it says, and watch your competitors' jaws drop at what you accomplish."

— John Rampton, Founder of Due.com and Calendar.com

10x Marketing Formula
by Garrett Moon

Published by CoSchedule.

CoSchedule and the CoSchedule logo are registered trademarks of CoSchedule, LLC.

www.coschedule.com
ISBN: 978-0-692-04827-6

TABLE OF CONTENTS

FOREWORD

The internet is noisy, and it gets louder every day. The supply of content from people, places, and businesses is a glut, at best. Nobody says "you know, my favorite part of social media is the fact that companies participate!"

We are at a crossroads. Digital and social marketing—the theoretical salve and solution for a traditional, analog approach that declined in effectiveness—is itself working less, and costing more.

If you build it, they may not come. The web is littered with lonely websites, ghost blogs, social media with no audience, and videos viewed by only relatives. It's hard out there for a digital marketer these days.

What is supposed to happen is we publish interesting content >> consumers find that content >> the content builds kinship between customer and company >> that kinship spawns buying intent, and everyone wins.

But here's the thing . . . it CAN still work that way. You CAN still succeed (wildly) with digital and social marketing. But you CANNOT just show up and assume it will naturally occur. You have to MAKE IT HAPPEN, and that's what the *10x Marketing Formula* gives you . . . the recipe for making online marketing succeed in a world where that success is increasingly difficult to harness.

I know and admire Garrett Moon. So much so, that I am an investor in and advisor to his company, CoSchedule. I have been in digital marketing since 1993, when domain names were free. I have worked with hundreds of companies since then as a digital marketing strategist and venture capitalist, and I can tell you firsthand that Garrett and his 10x system are the real deal.

As you'll learn in these valuable pages, 10x marketing success is viable, but only under specific conditions:

. . . *if* you're willing to press reset on your entire concept of marketing.

. . . *if* you're willing to get scrappy and risk failure.

. . . *if* you're willing to relentlessly do only the most important things and say no to everything else.

I'm excited to see this book come to fruition, and delighted that Garrett has chosen to reveal his proven playbooks here.

There's a lot of talk out there about how "content marketing" doesn't work anymore. But it does, and Garrett and his team prove it every day. They went from a standing start, with no audience, and built a multimillion-dollar business solely on the back of providing truly valuable and exceptional content to their audience. And they didn't do it in 2007, when competition was minimal . . . they did it RIGHT NOW, when competition is everywhere.

In my best-selling book, *Youtility*, I proclaimed that the secret to marketing success is to provide information and resources so useful customers will pay for them, if you ask them to do so. Garrett and his team are the living embodiment of that approach. Every day, they produce resources that digital marketers cannot WAIT to download and read. And that's no exaggeration.

The thesis of *Youtility* is that you give away everything you know, for free, one bite at a time. Subsequently, the interest and goodwill you generate produces new customers and keeps those you've already earned. You give away information snacks, to sell knowledge meals down the road. That's the core of the *10x Marketing Formula*: taking the premise of usefulness = eventual victory, and putting it into practice, every single day.

In this book, you will learn to create content so good it makes your competitors look like they didn't even try. Then, you'll go even further. Because most marketers don't simply have a content problem; they have an amplification problem. Launching something into orbit around the blogosphere, no matter how useful, doesn't mean anyone will see it. Or click. Or care.

Here, you'll learn to create AND to promote. It's a skill that is no longer optional.

Can content marketing still work? Without question, yes. But only if you're willing to adopt the mindset, frameworks, and formula in the following pages.

You're going to love this book, and if you read it and follow its teachings, and your business does NOT grow, I'll refund your money myself. That's how much I believe in the *10x Marketing Formula*.

Jay Baer

Founder of Convince & Convert and Best-Selling Author of *The Now Revolution*, *Youtility*, and *Hug Your Haters*

November 2017
Bloomington, Indiana

GET SCRAPPY

Don't worry about failure; you only have to be right once.
— Drew Houston, Co-Founder and CEO of Dropbox

Startups are the perfect model for marketing teams because they have no choice but to get results. This means they're willing to get scrappy, take risks, and fail along the path to success. In Section One, you will learn to press the reset button on your marketing mindset and become a content hacker. Growth is the goal; the *10x Marketing Formula* is your blueprint. It all starts right here.

CHAPTER ONE

THINK LIKE A STARTUP

In the late 1800s a tractor company pioneered a marketing strategy that would catch fire a century later.

John Deere started a magazine called *The Furrow*. It was squarely aimed at their target audience: farmers. The publication was filled with pages of high-quality content that helped farmers solve their unique set of business problems. In fact, the magazine persists to this day and is focused on the same audience.

The first issue was hot off the press in 1895. And by 1912, they had grown to a readership of over four million.* Not a bad audience.

The Furrow is the beginning of content marketing lore. It's become an incredible asset for John Deere over the course of a century. Today, 45 percent of its readers read every word of every issue. Almost half go to the website to learn more about their product lines. One-third of readers buy John Deere as a result of learning about new products and services in the magazine. And 90 percent of its readers say *The Furrow* is their sole source of industry information.† Because of this success, the magazine's story has become a proof-text for content marketing.

---

* https://contently.com/strategist/2013/10/03/the-story-behind-the-furrow-2/

† http://www.contentmarketingworld.com/david-jones-original-content-marketers-john-deere-furrow-cmworld-recap/

APRIL, MAY, JUNE, 1897.

The Furrow

A JOURNAL FOR THE AMERICAN FARMER

PUBLISHED QUARTERLY BY

G. L. SHAUL

Clarinda, Iowa.

AGENCY FOR THE

Celebrated John Deere Plows

Cultivators and Harrows

SPRING ANNOUNCEMENT ♣ It gives us pleasure to announce to our many friends that our stock of

Implements, Vehicles and Hardware

HARDWARE

for the spring trade of 1897 is complete in every department. It is a satisfaction to be able to offer our patrons the VERY BEST in these lines. We have some LEADERS which it will pay you to examine early, and we believe we can suit you in quality and price. It is well to remember that PRICE DEPENDS UPON QUALITY. If you expect to invest anything in farm machinery, vehicles or building material this spring it will be to your interest to examine our stock, as it is generally conceded that the man or firm who sells the

John Deere Plows

has the best in their class, and it is reasonably safe to assume that other lines will be kept up to the standard of these goods. You will make a great mistake if you do not

SEE OUR GOODS AND GET OUR PRICES BEFORE BUYING

C. B.

If it works in agriculture, it will certainly work in the XYZ industry, right?

CAN YOU COPY/PASTE RESULTS?

More recently, another established brand commanded attention with top-shelf content marketing results. The UK supermarket chain Sainsbury's won the "Best Retail Publication" category of Content Marketing Institute's 12th annual Content Marketing Awards. Per CMI:[*]

> *Sainsbury's has elevated foodie content to a multimedia art form. From their widely-circulated magazine to their "hugely successful portfolio of social media channels, sell-out live cooking demonstrations, weekly newsletters, the magazine's Food & Drink Awards, a series of editorial one-shots, and more and you get a level of multi-platform audience engagement that would make any content marketer's mouth water.*

Awards are one thing; results are another. Let's look at their numbers.

Sainsbury's amassed a newsletter list over 50,000 readers strong. They have email open rates of 35 percent and click-through rates of 31 percent. Their social profiles overflow with hundreds of thousands of followers. And the kicker: eight out of ten readers have become paying customers after reading their magazine content.

To be successful like Sainsbury's, then, it makes sense to dissect what they've done and repeat it, right? Or perhaps take a cue from John Deere's enduring marketing magic with *The Furrow*?

The promise is if you do things just like them, you'll get results just like them. So, simply slap their strategies and tactics into your marketing plans. Get cranking and watch the same results pour in.

Only, for some reason, it doesn't work right for us. Our blog posts sit dusty on the back shelf of the internet. Our social media accounts are devoid of engagement. Our email list never reaches that hockey-stick moment.

---

[*] http://contentmarketinginstitute.com/2016/09/content-marketing-success-awards/

What's happened is we're told what to do and shown whom to mimic. But when it comes to *how* to make the same things work for us:

. . . crickets . . .

THE LURE OF CONTENT MARKETING

The dream of content marketing is that it's going to be a magical funnel that drips money into your bank account. Its lure is that it will create an inbound sales machine. And the prescribed formula is:

high-quality content + audience building =
increased revenue and business growth

Step One: Create amazing content and optimize it with some SEO love.

Step Two: Visitors experience this amazing content, falling in love with you and your brand.

Result: Credit cards slide out of wallets while you sleep.

What should you do when it doesn't work like that?

The core concept is that if you provide huge value up front, you'll be swimming in quality leads and flywheel revenue. However, less than half of North American business-to-business (B2B) marketers rate their organization's content marketing as successful.[*]

These quality leads are supposed to come from website traffic. And content marketing should eventually deliver critical mass in driving traffic. Per research, year-over-year unique visitor growth should be 780 percent higher for the best content marketers.[†] Not only that; these same rock-star marketers should also achieve 600 percent greater revenue

[*] http://www.iab.net/media/file/B2BResearch2014.pdf
[†] https://marketeer.kapost.com/content-marketing-stats/

yields from their content.* But pesky reality brings many crashing back to earth.

Lack of Time

Most B2B marketers are too busy to go all the way with content marketing, with 69 percent citing lack of time.† Far from being lazy, they're managing more strategies, tactics, and layers of bosses breathing down their necks than ever.

Producing Content

The core function of content marketing is, of course, marketing content. But 55 percent of B2B marketers report they don't have enough of it.‡ If you lack content, success in this arena is a tough hill to climb.

Inability to Engage Audience

To turn an audience into paying customers, your content needs to be engaging. It has a job to do, and that's to provoke an active response. Beyond likes, clicks, and shares, you need people to buy your products and services as a direct result of each marketing channel. If you struggle here, you're not alone. Because 47 percent of B2B marketers cite that they struggle to produce content that engages their audience.§

LIVING UP TO THE HYPE

Imagine walking into a marketing convention. Thousands of marketers mill about, going from one session to the next. Everyone is here, attending the same keynotes, learning the "new rules of marketing," and furiously

---

* *Ibid.*
† *Ibid.*
‡ *Ibid.*
§ *Ibid.*

jotting notes to execute these novel ideas. (The same novel ideas as the other 10,000 marketers.)

Oh, and one more thing . . . 93 percent of them use content marketing.*

So, if you're using content marketing, you're competing with over nine out of ten peers via the same mediums and methods. This marketing promised land loses considerable luster when we step back and behold reality. Marketers are up against staggering competition. And the numbers tell a story that success is the exception, not the rule. But that's not what the marketing books say.

They tell us, "Ads are dead! Content marketing is a panacea of value that will deliver traffic, leads, and an audience craving your delicious content."

Except, it doesn't happen. Content marketing doesn't live up to the hype. Instead of finding ourselves on top of the leaderboard, we've plunged into the "trough of disillusionment."

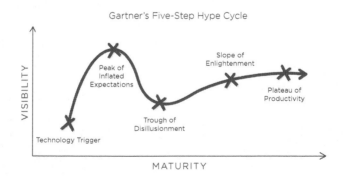

Gartner, leaders in business research and advisement, discerned a pattern in technology adoption for business use known as the "Hype Cycle."† Although it's a cycle of new technologies in business, it applies

---

* http://www.iab.net/media/file/B2BResearch2014.pdf
† https://www.gartner.com/technology/research/methodologies/hype-cycle.jsp

with similar force in the world of marketing—especially with the confluence of marketing and technology known as MarTech.

What happens is something new hits the scene. It could be a new social media platform, strategy, or tactic marketers start using to achieve growth. It gets some press, and the broader market finds out about this new secret weapon.

In reaction, expectations soar with the myriad success stories being blasted across the web. A sizable portion of marketers jump on board and mime the techniques of the innovators. There's big promise because, well, all *those* people got results. The case studies speak for themselves.

(Just look at Sainsbury's!)

Then, crushing defeat. Numbers are stagnant. Leads trickle in at the same pace as before—if they don't dip, that is. And your boss starts asking questions. This new marketing hero fails to live up to the hype. And thus, we find ourselves plummeting into the trough of disillusionment faster than the big drop on a rollercoaster at Six Flags.

It's not a pleasant feeling.

Eventually, the cycle completes itself. Things improve incrementally, and everyone gets on board when the new paradigm is deemed safe. But by then, the advantage has evaporated. Rather than giving an edge, this fancy new practice has become status quo. It's not something you do to stand out—it's something you do because you must. Otherwise you're behind.

This cycle is the story of content marketing. However, this isn't a book pronouncing it dead. Far from it. This is a book designed to help you actually achieve the growth that was promised. How? By equipping you to uncover the hidden path to success. And to get the results you're capable of achieving, but that have been locked inside of you and are waiting to be broken free.

We're not going to do this by working through a formula that helps you copy and paste the success stories. We aren't laboriously crafting a marketing plan. Instead, we're going to lay out the raw material you need to innovate, move fast, and separate yourself from the crowded marketing conference floor. The *10x Marketing Formula* is the secret to unlocking the results that content marketing promised you in the first place.

MARKETING PLANS FAIL, TOO

So, where do these results come from? And how do you know this isn't another book promising Scrooge McDuck-style pools of gold while delivering pennies in return? We're going to avoid the trap of overpromising by starting with a new mindset entirely. Because to achieve growth, we must change both our medium *and* our methods. Growth requires more than subsuming a new channel or tactic into your marketing plan.

You see, marketing plans fail because they assume we know everything at the time we craft them. The truth is, they aren't truly plans—they're guesses. Yet we live, work, and swear by them as if they were truth. In fact, there's a near universal mandate for them.

Universities

College marketing curricula are piled high with plans, strategies, and conventional "musts."

Here, marketers are instructed to take each of these variables into consideration while drawing up an ironclad marketing plan:

> *Planning involves consideration of complex issues covering the whole organization, and the marketer may come across barriers to planning, for example:*
> - *The culture of the organization—is it focused internally rather than externally?*
> - *Power and politics*
> - *Analysis—not action*
> - *Resource issues—money and time*
> - *Skills and technology—may not match customer need*
> - *Ability to challenge existing ideas**

So, per this counsel, five of six elements your marketing plan should address are internal considerations spanning complex organizational dynamics. That's a heavy load for a marketing plan to bear.

Moreover, many classes focus on creating a marketing plan or strategy as the final class project. But, how many greenhorns are going to have the chops to craft such a well-conceived and all-encompassing document?

Leading Publications

Articles from leading publications like *Entrepreneur* tell us:

How to Create a Marketing Plan

Firms that are successful in marketing invariably start with a marketing plan. Large companies have plans with hundreds of pages; small companies can get by with a half-dozen sheets. Put your marketing plan in a three-ring binder. Refer to it at least quarterly, but better yet monthly. Leave a tab for putting in monthly reports on sales/manufacturing; this will allow you to track performance as you follow the plan.*

So, if your company is big, you need hundreds of pages to be successful. And if you're small, you need at least six pages in a three-ring binder to look at every few months.

Governments

Even governments tell us we need a marketing plan:†

Here, we learn that, "The planning process helps you to understand the different factors that may affect your success. Instead of worrying about the future, you can actually have a sense of control over your business and livelihood."

So, they also bestow a sense of security and control on the planner. This level of planning feels like productive work. But planning isn't the work of marketing. In reality, no real work has

---

* https://www.entrepreneur.com/article/43018

† https://www.business.gov.au/info/plan-and-start/develop-your-business-plans/marketing/why-do-i-need-a-marketing-plan

taken place yet. But should a marketing document be granted that much authority and weight to predict the future?

To be clear, I'm not rejecting any of the above ideas as worthless, per se. Smart business, marketing included, is based on wise decisions. Culture is vital, and planning isn't evil. But regardless of how much time we spend on our marketing plans, they're guesses about what will happen in the future. They are big bets based on assumptions that are almost certainly flawed and unaccounted for in the great and powerful marketing plan.

However, the solution isn't as simple as rejecting marketing plans. Even if our organizations don't employ them, there is serious gravity to the same mentality. The danger is that we pick our proverbial horse and ride it without ever looking down. We choose methods based on a set of assumptions without considering the signals our results give us.

ANOTHER TIRED MARKETING METHOD

Another entrenched example is the request for proposal (RFP). I know, because I spent half a decade working at an agency that regularly bid on them—and another five running an agency that frequently ignored them. If you're unfamiliar, an RFP is an open invitation for multiple vendors to submit competing proposals for a project. In theory, they're about vetting companies to find the best fit for the project. But in practice, just like marketing plans, that's not really what RFPs are about.

Instead, they are a self-protective layer snuggled around the decision maker's shoulders. They offer the illusion of due diligence while granting plausible deniability. If you never go out on a limb, you can't get fired. With RFPs, fear of failure is the motivating factor. This means it becomes another tired trope with personal safety at its core. And this will be at the expense of differentiation and results. Why? Because each of these involves risk. They involve sticking your neck out and being personally accountable for growth.

Think of it this way. If a project fails, the person who chose the vendor via the RFP process has a fallback.

"Look!" they can say. "I have seven binders packed with budgets, evaluations, and portfolios. I did my homework just like I was supposed to. *It wasn't my fault.*"

A check-your-own-ass culture is the risk of any profession. Through the likes of mandated marketing plans and RFPs, marketing has fallen victim. This means we spend a lot of our lives pursuing non-failure rather than results. And there is considerable infrastructure built around this pursuit.

We go to school, take notes on the lectures, read the books, and graduate "knowing" how it's done. Then we land our first job and quickly learn the real, unspoken goal of today's marketplace: if you fail, ensure it never looks like your fault. So, both RFPs and marketing plans exemplify the problem with the entrenched mindset. And they reinforce an old saying in Silicon Valley: "Nobody ever got fired for picking IBM."

IBM is big and expensive. It has a strong reputation as an enduring winner. While it's neither cutting-edge nor inexpensive, it's proven to be an incumbent in the marketplace. So, who would ever get in trouble for picking it? It's the safe bet, the one you're *supposed* to make. Thus, we come to the crux of our problem.

Here's an example.

Imagine it's your job to pick winners from losers. Maybe you're buying stocks or picking a new vendor for a project. Or better yet, let's say your job is to run marketing that generates 1,000 qualified leads per month for your sales team.

Did a few butterflies just flutter in your stomach at the thought?

If your marketing sucks, you know the long, bony fingers of the CEO will point squarely at you. Problem is, nothing from your textbooks is working. You stare at a blank whiteboard with your job on the line. It's 1,000 leads per month or you're canned. So, what are you supposed to do?

Nobody gets fired for picking IBM. It's the *right* choice. The *safe* choice. The one you're *supposed* to make. This produces bureaucratic cultures rather than growth-oriented ones. Why, you ask? Because one time someone failed. So, cumbersome processes like marketing plans and RFPs cropped up to make sure no one ever fails again. But the victory is not in avoiding failure. You don't actually have control over failure—but you do have control over how you respond to it. How you learn from it. And how you use it to catalyze growth by different methods and mediums than your competition.

The *10x Marketing Formula* is about looking the 1,000-lead abyss in the face and saying: "Screw 1,000 leads. We're going for 10,000, and nothing's gonna stop us. Now let's get to work."

10X RESULTS

This book's title tips off the premise: we're after 10x marketing results. This means the return we expect, and are resolved to achieve, is ten times greater than what we put in. We aren't looking for 10 percent year-over-year growth; we're laser-focused on blowing the roof off last year's, last month's, and last week's numbers.

To do this requires the mindset shift we've described. You can't expect 10x results from copying everyone else. What worked for someone else isn't a guarantee to work for you. This means drafting a binder full of charts and best guesses and calling it a marketing plan is doomed to fail. The world is too crowded and moves too fast for "copycat" marketing. We'll take a deeper dive into this principle next chapter, but it's worth describing here.

Imagine a sidewalk neatly laid out in a grid. People are intended to follow the intersecting 90-degree walkways to make their way. This represents the broken mindset we've described.

Now, think of this same grid, only instead of an orderly flow of traffic, there are a few people who blaze their own trail. They take off on a dirt path that shortcuts the "planned" course they were supposed to take.

This book is about finding those strategic shortcuts. It's about short-circuiting the path to jaw-dropping growth. You have to find your own way—and the *10x Marketing Formula* is that path.

STRATEGIC
SHORTCUTS

THREE MONTHS TO LIVE

The reason why startups matter to this discussion is because they cannot settle for less than massive growth. Their survival is contingent upon fast, revenue-generating actions. Without results, at some point, funding dries up. Investors want big returns on their money. And the startups that fail to deliver, fail entirely.

While the solution to growth isn't tucked away in the standard tool kit of marketing plans and RFPs, there is a secret found in the startup mentality. And it's simply this: startups have an unlimited tolerance for risk because they have no choice but to grow quickly.

I've spent roughly a decade in marketing agencies. The first five years working for one; and the second running the agency I co-founded called Todaymade. In those ten years, I experienced both extremes.

At the agency I worked for, I trudged through infighting, RFPs, and a never-ending barrage of copycat ads. Really, I had gotten stuck in the cycle described above. I wasn't achieving actual results for clients—I was maintaining a status quo marketing ship. And this is exactly what changed when we started Todaymade.

We focused exclusively on achieving results for clients through web design and marketing consulting services. In fact, we so doggedly pursued results we only took projects where we believed we could make a difference. This was often to the detriment of our pocketbooks. But we thrived on growing revenue and generating real demand for our clients.

The more we helped clients hone their marketing, though, the clearer a problem became: it was extremely difficult to manage content marketing. We were experiencing great results, and so were our clients. But managing the process was frustrating. Our content calendars were a mishmash of spreadsheets, multiple project management apps, and an unwieldy number of usernames and passwords.

After building and teaching an entire course on content and permission-based marketing, we asked: "Wouldn't it be nice to manage and schedule our content and social media messages on a digital calendar?"

This led to: "And wouldn't it be nice to simply drag and drop messages and pieces of content to schedule them?"

Which sparked: "And wouldn't it be nice to do this all straight from WordPress?"

And soon after, CoSchedule was born with a napkin sketch. We knew we had the solution to a major problem. So, we threw up a landing page to validate the demand before writing a single line of code. Overnight, there were interested marketers lining up to check it out. This theoretical piece of software had huge potential. So, we stopped taking on new clients at Todaymade and only serviced retainer accounts.

We were going to build and launch a product in just three months.

Launching CoSchedule meant we made the coveted transition from a service-based company to a product-based company. This was great. But it also meant we literally had three months to live. We were betting it all on CoSchedule with just a few months of runway. At launch day, we had one quarter to go from zero revenue, zero customers, and a small following to a minimum of 300 paying customers and a flourishing audience.

It was 10x growth or lights out.

When you're staring at zeros across the board, and you have both a team and your family counting on you, the stakes are as high as they possibly can be. (Fun fact: my third son was two months old the day CoSchedule launched.) Failure is a real possibility. It becomes tangible, constantly nipping at your heels. So, you either make it happen and generate revenue fast, or you and your entire team are out.

We froze our agency work and launched a startup. When you do this, there's no fallback system. There's no one to pick up the slack. And minimal returns on sales and marketing activities aren't simply a disappointing quarter, they're doom. In a large company, growing revenues, audience, or a similar metric by 10 percent may be acceptable. But in a startup, numbers like that are your death writ.

However, being on the cusp of failure was exhilarating. At Todaymade, we experienced real victories for our clients by generating actual growth for them. So, we knew we could do the same for ourselves at CoSchedule. It simply needed to be fast and furious. This meant the status quo had no place in our company.

The marketing abyss stared us right in the face, and everything was on the line. It was results, or die!

RESULTS, OR DIE!

Consider this scenario. Imagine your boss saying to you: "You have three months to grow our email list from 10,000 subscribers to 100,000, or I have to let you go." Would you know what to do if your job were contingent on achieving 10x growth?

Before you roll your eyes at this scenario, remember, startups fight for survival every single day. And they're not fighting to keep their manager off their backs. They're doing everything they can to stay in business. If they don't win, they die.

I've lived this reality.

Only 5 to 10 percent of startups today will land a second round of funding, because the majority have closed their doors by then. Investors aren't going to pony up the cash unless they think you're the next Uber. They don't invest for double . . . They're hunting for 10x returns.

The only metrics good startups track are growth oriented. Enough money to pay the bills doesn't cut it. Acquisitions and additional rounds of investment only go to those who scale quickly.

RISK VS. REWARD PROFILE

The "Risk vs. Reward Profile" illustrates the dynamic between risk and growth. In the beginning of any new venture, risk is high and reward is low. The potential for reward might be high, but it's unrealized.

Over time, reward increases and risk decreases. You figure out what works and what doesn't. Then, at some point, there is a critical juncture. You can either assume more risk to grow bigger and faster, or you can maintain the status quo. Sure, your risk will decrease, but so will growth.

Risk vs. Reward Profile

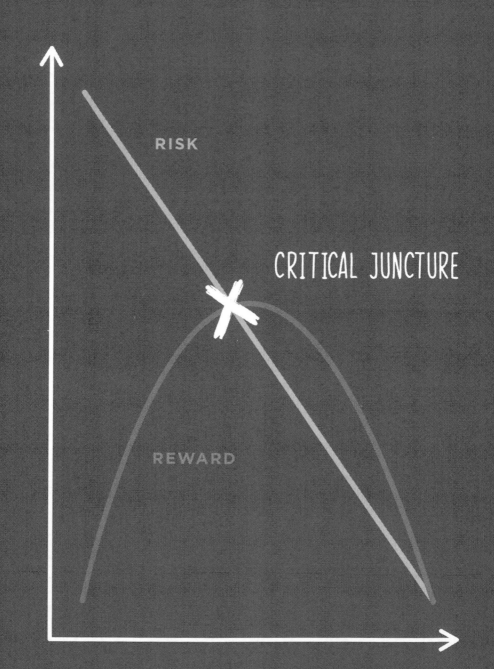

RISK

CRITICAL JUNCTURE

REWARD

THINKING LIKE A STARTUP

The solution is for marketing teams to ditch playing follow the leader and start thinking like scrappy startups. Why? Startups fight for survival at all costs because those are the stakes.

There's no fallback. It's just you and your team. There's no one to pick up the slack, because you're it. The exciting news is this is where the victories live for every marketer today, not just trendy SaaS companies from the Valley. Not simply for the Sainsbury's and John Deeres of the world.

Embrace the reality that failure is a frequent companion to innovation. Like Elon Musk, founder, CEO, and CTO of SpaceX and CEO of Tesla, said, "Failure is an option . . . if things are not failing, you are not innovating enough."* And we're sure he repeats that phrase every time one of his SpaceX rockets plummets into the ocean.

Without innovation, we get stagnation. And innovation only happens when risk is involved. When failure could actually be—*gasp*—someone's fault. When people are responsible for both good and bad results.

So, the first step in the *10x Marketing Formula* is pressing the reset button on your mindset.

RESET: THINKING LIKE A STARTUP

As a startup, it's not simply "ship or die!" It's "results or die!" If you don't get real results with dollar signs and zeros attached, it's the ultimate death march. You die at the end. But those stakes are exactly why startups are the perfect blueprint for marketers.

Most marketing sucks. It looks like marketing, smells like marketing, and acts like marketing—but there are menial returns. It mimes the techniques around them, creating an advertising echo chamber. Everywhere you turn, it's more of the same.

This book is your guide to pressing the reset button and learning to think like a scrappy, results-or-die! startup. Before you read on, adopt the three-month runway position.

---

* https://www.inc.com/john-brandon/elon-musk-on-how-to-innovate-20-quotes.html

In your wildest dreams, what kind of growth could you accomplish in the next quarter? If you had your pick, but could only choose one, which metric would you apply these kinds of results to?

Now, your wildest dream is going to take a risky turn. Put yourself squarely back in the three-months-to-live scenario. Imagine that hitting this 10x metric within the next ninety days will result in staying afloat or going belly up.

What would you do? Where would you start? Who would you go to for advice?

The zero-fluff formula for executing 10x growth is what you'll find in the rest of the book. But before you press on, commit to the paradigm shift of the startup-mentality framework. This results or die! lens is key to achieving serious growth.

Here are the obstacles you are likely to face:

Pushback

Office bureaucracy will rear its head—especially if you work in an established company. You will face pushback to new ideas that are high-risk, high-reward. And will likely hear statements like:

"Our company does it 'this' way. Always have, and it's gotten us to where we are today."

Reset One: Are you willing to fight through to pursue 10x growth via risky, failure-fraught avenues?

Status Quo

Startups that get comfortable are the ones that suffocate from lack of results. Getting scrappy and moving quickly is uncomfortable because it forces you outside of the status quo. Beyond pushback from others, you must embrace taking different actions than ever before.

Here's the truth: to get different outputs, you must try different inputs. Trying more of the same things will not lead to 10x growth.

Reset Two: Are you willing to get uncomfortable and work in radically new ways?

Put Everything on the Line

Thinking like a startup requires that you put everything on the line. In a new venture, there is no fallback system. There is no one else to do the work.

Reset Three: Are you willing to attach your name, reputation, and even career to achieving your 10x growth goal?

Now, let's go.

CHAPTER TWO

CONTENT HACKING

In 2010, Sean Ellis, co-author of *Hacking Growth* and CEO of GrowthHackers, coined the term "growth hacking" in a blog post entitled "Find a Growth Hacker for Your Startup."* Ellis wrote: "A growth hacker is a person whose true north is growth. Everything they do is scrutinized by its potential impact on scalable growth."

He further explained, "An effective growth hacker also needs to be disciplined to follow a growth hacking process of prioritizing ideas (their own and others in the company), testing the ideas, and being analytical enough to know which tested growth drivers to keep and which ones to cut. The faster this process can be repeated, the more likely they'll find scalable, repeatable ways to grow the business."

From its inception, growth hacking has described people whose sole focus is growth. And whose process is a thousand short sprints that test ideas methodically. Keeping what works, and killing what doesn't.

Growth hacking has never been code for being irresponsible and unaccountable. Running fast doesn't mean running without strategy. But strategy in this context isn't traditional fare.

---

* https://www.inc.com/john-brandon/elon-musk-on-how-to-innovate-20-quotes.html

In marketing, growth strategies are confused with fifty-two-page internal documents that spell out how often you're going to blog, publish to social media, and push ad campaigns. The stuff of marketing plans. But think about this. Every second you're not finding ways to directly benefit your customer base and audience is wasted effort. Because once the strategy is submitted, reviewed, and approved by your boss, it's over.

Now, instead of assuming responsibility for the results, you've passed it off on your boss. They now own them, not you. In the bureaucracy, so long as you have a strategy, you're safe. I see this happening all the time. Writing it down feels safe. But the problem with feeling safe is it becomes the goal rather than results.

After you've spent a week or more in documentation mode, all that's left is working the strategy. But in the digital landscape, what's the likelihood said strategy will be viable three months from now? This is the primary fault line in the marketing-plan mindset.

Ready for the good news? You can become a superhuman marketer by merging the best of growth hacking and content marketing.

THE THREE CONSTRAINTS

Growth hacking is about turning clever tactics into fast-paced growth. Content marketing is about creating, publishing, and sharing valuable content with your audience to convert traffic into customers. But as we saw in Chapter One, with its rising popularity, content marketing alone may not be enough. This means marketers need to take a page from the growth hacker's playbook.

We need to become content hackers.

A content hacker is a results-or-die! marketer who merges agile growth tactics with high-converting content to achieve rapid 10x growth. And they never stop doing this.

All you need to start are the three constraints:

One Metric that Matters + Goal + Timeline = Content Hacker

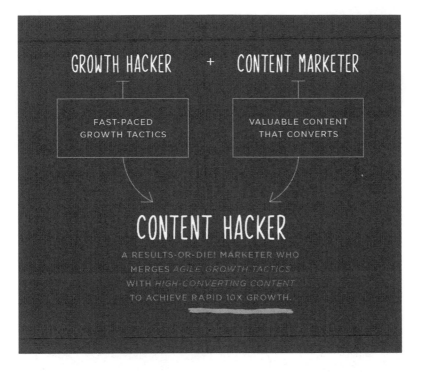

One Metric that Matters

The first constraint is focus. Content hackers doggedly pursue growing one, and only one, metric. It's the gas pedal to slam on—the one metric that will accelerate your business more than any other.

Goal

The second constraint is specificity. Content hackers set specific goals for measuring the one metric that matters. They're not looking for "more" users or "increased" revenue. They are dead-set on a $100,000 increase in monthly sales. Content hackers set hard numbers to reverse engineer from.

Timeline

The third constraint is speed. Content hackers define a clear timeline for when their goal will be a reality. It's a specific month, day, and year. And ideally, it's much shorter than what sounds safe or comfortable.

And there you have it. The three constraints are your new documented marketing strategy; and the tactics and communication between your team remain fluid. People are usually stunned by this. But it's the happy truth. It's neither complex nor gangly. Instead, it's simple, messy in the middle, and effective in the end.

I hope you realize that you can do this too. That doubling your sales, tripling your email list, or increasing users tenfold isn't outside of your grasp. And even better, you can start sprinting toward 10x growth in the time it takes you to drink a cup of coffee.

Thrilling, isn't it?

THE CONTENT HACKER ETHOS

This approach will work for you because the content hacker's primary goal isn't being pretty, clever, or award-winning. Lots of agencies work to make funny ads so they can win advertising awards, not get results. Essentially, they pour their clients' money down the tubes for the thrill of being creative at the expense of the results they were hired to produce. This is not how a content hacker works.

Instead, success is defined by reaching your *one-metric-that-matters* goal within your set timeline. You can let go of every other distraction and focus 100 percent on growth. Working within the three constraints is the framework for getting there. Now, let's look more closely at the journey itself. Because content hacking *will* transcend standard content marketing methodologies and often entails a multidisciplinary approach. Here's the anatomy of the content hacker ethos:

One part marketing, one part engineering, one part high risk, and a whole lot of high reward.

Content hackers are marketers willing to drive in new lanes. Marketers who are more than copywriters, media buyers, content folks, strategists, et al. To succeed in the coming decades, both the mediums and methods must change. The new medium is unequivocally "content + audience," but the methods to engage, convert, and keep them should be ever-evolving.

Content hackers go beyond marketing. They foray into applying disciplines like engineering and data science with ample elbow grease. They aren't scared to try new things while sprinting along the brambly path—and you shouldn't be, either. They're willing to risk failure because they're ready to transcend marketing-plan land, the world of eternal RFPs.

To move quickly, the content hacker understands that new tactics don't have to be expensive or elaborate, or take months of development. For some, it can be just a few words and a hyperlink. Let's peer into the technology vault for a classic growth-hacking example.

P.S. I LOVE YOU

In the 1990s, a couple of guys named Sabeer Bhatia and Jack Smith built a lean working prototype of something called Hotmail. They rolled it out to some friends and family. Which was great . . . but hardly a leap toward capturing market share.

As the story goes, the pair's investor asked them how they were going to market the startup email service. They suggested some traditional, and expensive, marketing channels. But their investor had another idea—and he pushed for it.

He suggested that at the bottom of each email message sent through the service, they append a hyperlinked message that read: "PS, I love you. Get your free email at HoTMaiL.com."

(Yes, that's how they originally spelled Hotmail.)

The theory was that recipients of the emails would see the link to start their own free account, become intrigued, and then sign up for a free email account of their own.

In the startup world, there is something called the viral coefficient. Simply put, it's a measure for how many new users each existing user generates. It's like an accelerated referral formula. Hotmail hit the digital nail on the head. With this small hack, every email attracted new users with viral efficiency. And after about seven months, they had hit two million users.*

Growth hacking is about taking things straight to the users. Because, by circumventing standard channels, you find wonderfully quiet places to get your message heard.

However, it also entails risk. Usually lots of it. For instance, the Hotmail stunt could have easily ticked off thousands of people. After all, they were tossing an ad at the bottom of every email sent. This could have resulted in people abandoning the service just as quickly as they signed up. However, it didn't. It worked.

But consider, even if it hadn't worked, what would they really have lost? With a few clicks, the hack could've been removed. With a few words, they could've offered an apology. In fact, circumstances like those are actually an opportunity to show authenticity to customers and users.

The point is this growth hack wasn't *retroactively* a great idea because it worked. It was great because it was:

1. Simple
2. Low-effort to implement
3. Fast to execute
4. Easy to test
5. And a breeze to revert if necessary

This was the content hacker's three constraints at work. Their one metric that mattered? Customers. Their goal? 1,000,000. Their timeline? Within six months. Content hacking for the win!

USE YOUR REVERTS

That's what a growth hack looked like for a '90s tech startup. With just a few lines of content, Hotmail grew exponentially. But can you imagine if

---

* https://techcrunch.com/2009/10/18/ps-i-love-you-get-your-free-email-at-hotmail/

someone were to include this idea in an established company's marketing plan? What do you think would happen?

Maybe it would get consideration at first blush; but would it actually ship? Not a chance. Fear of pissing off users, decreasing brand value, or getting flagged as spam would prove the stranglehold that put an idea like this to rest.

"Marketers get reverts, too."

Further, this idea would be far too risky for an RFP. They're about slightly bending the knees and knocking the drive straight down the fairway or around the pond. But "P. S. I Love You" looks more like trying to drive the ball straight over the pond. It's the green or the drink. Sure, we'll shave off two strokes, but we may also get wet.

But many of us stand on the tee box and say: "Well, shit, I can't get wet!"

But why not? Pants dry, people.

When you fail, simply delete the proverbial code and let your pants dry. Programmers call this reverting their code. It happens when they launch a new version of something that breaks the application or software product itself. For these programmers, it only takes a single click of the mouse to instantly go back in time to the previous version.

Marketers get reverts, too.

Content hackers can always change their minds. But the marketing-plan mindset is inflexible because it lives and dies by the words, charts, and mission statements chiseled on those fifty-two sheets of paper.

For the marketing-plan marketer, once you make the plan, you work it. That's not how it works for the content hacker. And if you suitably increase your tolerance for failure, you're ready to put unheard-of methodologies to work for you. The things that "just aren't done!" This is how you can 10x your business—and in short order.

What will content hacking look like for you?

"CONTENT HACKING FORCES YOU TO INNOVATE AND TAKE RISKS BECAUSE THERE ARE SUCH HIGH-POTENTIAL REWARDS."

—NOAH KAGAN,
OKDORK

10X MARKETING INTERVIEW: NOAH KAGAN AND THE PROACTIVE DASHBOARD

Content hacking forces you to innovate and take risks because there are such high-potential rewards. However, with innovation and risk comes failure. And lots of it.

In an exclusive interview for the *10x Marketing Formula*, Noah Kagan, Chief Sumo of Sumo Group, explains how his team embraces the failure attendant with growth and content hacking.* Sumo creates tools to supercharge email list growth. The company has grown significantly over the last few years, making it an excellent case study for us.

THE PROACTIVE DASHBOARD

According to Noah, most of your growth attempts aren't going to work. This is why he's adopted a framework for growth that systematically tests ideas, keeping the winners and chucking the duds. His team at Sumo documents these tests using what they call proactive dashboards.

Each week, their teams test a fresh idea and track its results on their dashboard. That means they test fifty-two new ideas each year. From content to ads to email, they're constantly testing. Noah says the regular routine of testing promotions forces his team to find the stuff that works. Imagine what that would look like for your company. How innovative would you get if you forced each marketing team—or even team member—to test a never-before-tried method each week? This kind of consistent innovation fosters growth and helps them avoid the copycat marketing trap.

Here's the thing, though. In the last four months, only two tests have worked. In fact, 86 percent of Sumo's tests haven't worked. So, if you have more than two out of ten attempts succeed, you're sitting pretty. And rather than be depressing, that statistic should actually be encouraging.

---

* You can listen to the full interview for free by visiting https://coschedule.com/10x-toolbox

Failure is the nature of the beast. But every time you learn what doesn't work, it allows you to kill it, and allows room for finding something that does work.

BUILDING OUT THE DASHBOARD

I asked Noah to explain how his teams build their dashboards, and I think this practice is an excellent framework in applying the *10x Marketing Formula*. To begin, every item on the dashboard has to be fully controllable by you and your team. This means that you cannot be dependent upon anything outside of your activities. The problem is that most of the metrics we're looking at as marketers have already happened. So, this dashboard isn't simply based upon past results you cannot change. It's *proactive* in that it's filled with goals you can influence right now.

"Failure is the nature of the beast."

This is a living dashboard that's updated live. Then, as you move forward, you measure against the secondary metric you're hoping to impact. If it doesn't move the needle, you stop doing it. But if it does, it's a keeper.

Noah explains, "We have two proactive dashboards. We have one for Sumo.com and one for each business unit. The idea, and the reason I love them, is that everything has to be completely controllable by you. What does that mean? It means you can't be dependent on anything . . . The dashboard is solely the things we have full control of each week. It's a live-tracking, living dashboard."

Sumo has a proactive dashboard for each marketing team. Here's a breakdown of their dashboards for two of their teams, advertising, and content:

Advertising

Advertising has to spend a certain amount, which is completely in their control. This means they can run as many ad variations as they want within their budget. Each week, they spend $7,560 and run at least five variations.

Key Takeaway: What can you directly control and measure in real time?

Content

The content team measures how many pieces of content they publish per week. And on this content they test things like headlines, email opt-ins, marketing promotion tests, and promotional ad spend. For instance, they tested five weekly posts on Quora for each week. After measuring, however, they saw only 1,000 visitors from each post—which for their team did not merit continuing. The team decided this when they compared it to LinkedIn, which was getting ten times the results Quora was.

Key takeaway: What can you stop doing today that isn't generating results?

DEFINING AND UNDERSTANDING YOUR TARGET AUDIENCE

Implicit in the activities of content hacking is a target audience to which you tailor your content. This makes defining, and deeply understanding, your ideal customer paramount. For Sumo, this was an evolutionary process. As they grew, so did their understanding of who best benefited from their product.

To do this, the Sumo team looked at which customers churn the least, have the highest lifetime value, and are easiest for their sales team to talk to and close deals with. They then worked backward from this group, which made their target audience much more obvious.

They noticed that huge publishers like the *New York Times* were a tough sell. Alternatively, small solo bloggers were also tough because they had such a small budget, and their tiny cashflow made them averse to paying for tools. After some fine tuning and research, however, they found that ecommerce customers were their sweet spot. Why? Because they could directly achieve ROI in proportion to email list growth. In other words, if they could grow their email list by a factor of ten, they could multiply their customer base in the same way.

For Noah, this changed their entire approach to marketing and content. Originally, their blog was all about getting more traffic. This was a fine goal at the beginning. And for other marketers, it's a perfect metric when traffic correlates to revenue or whatever their goal outcome is. However, even as Sumo's content team tripled their traffic, there was no proportional increase in revenue. So, traffic was disconnected from their primary growth goal.

To course correct, they shifted to a metric of qualified leads—specifically, how many ecommerce customers they were converting when they visited their site. Now the content team is responsible for qualified signups, which means every test is aimed squarely at influencing this number. In short, their success is a combination of continual testing of growth ideas and tailoring all content and activities to a target customer. Noah's team is driven by results alone. No big long-term plans, and no grand theories. Noah explains:

> *I don't think I'm actually a great marketer—and I don't even know if I'm that great at running businesses. I think what I've actually done really well is find products that I just love. Then it's my responsibility to go tell the right people in the world about it. That's what I do in marketing, I'm not a genius marketer or anything. I just think, 'Oh, that's a cool product. Oh, that person probably needs to know about it. Now, let me do whatever it takes to make that happen.'*
>
> *I think for other people out there who want to improve their business or marketing acumen, the easiest thing, besides finding a product you love, is to go help people one by one. It's a common misconception I've seen in marketing and in business where people*

Blog Traffic ≠ Revenue
For Noah Kagan

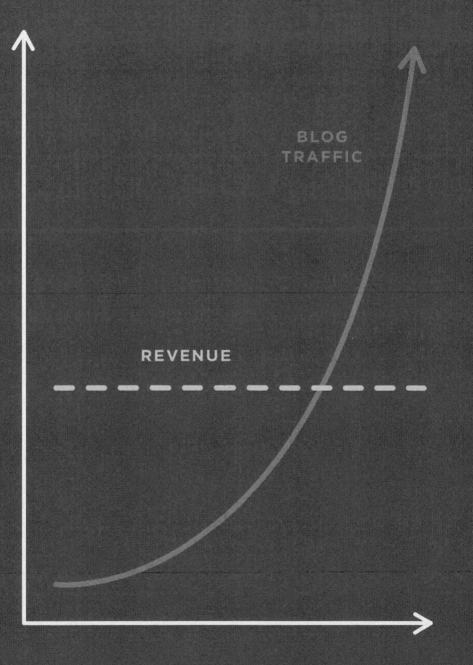

BLOG
TRAFFIC

REVENUE

think: 'I gotta scale! And I'm gonna spin up all these Facebook ads! And I gotta try to figure out Reddit! Or I gotta do content or PR,' or some other thing.

If you come back and just go one by one, either do live chat, do phone calls, do in person, do a manual service, I think that really helps you understand your customers better, and helps you understand your business better. Long term, that'll help you do really well.

Noah doesn't claim to know tons about marketing. He doesn't need to, because he knows how to experiment and shift his thinking to follow the results. That's content hacking. And his team exhibits these same traits. They're willing to take risks and then use their reverts when necessary—even if that means using them for 86 percent of their tests.

THREE CONTENT HACKS IN THE WILD

Without a doubt, real-world examples like Noah's are the best way to cement principles into your marketing. So, let's look at three more real-world content hacks. Now, just like everything else so far, they're not intended as a content-marketing buffet for you to choose from. After all, they've already been done. But they are pieces of world-class inspiration you can use to understand the content hacking mindset.

Write Awesome Headlines

Headlines matter now and forever. And although it sounds like old news, they're one of the most important aspects of your content. If you mess them up, you lose your chance at conversions.

"I already know this! I'm a professional marketer, for heaven's sake . . . " you may be thinking. But are you still writing the same mushy headlines? Ones like:

A unique new Business

April 05,2014

Headline from: http://www.free-press-release.com/news-a-unique-new-business

Or worse yet, clickbait:

Which invite plenty of backlash:

The massively popular media site Upworthy knows a thing or two about headlines. In fact, they've made a science out of them. In their slide deck "The Sweet Science Of Virality," they emphasize the importance of headlines again and again. But first, here's a quick pop quiz to see how well you know headlines. Think hard. Now, which headline do you think will get more clicks?

Headline A: A Journalist Goes Undercover As A Waitress. Guess Which Job Was Harder?

Headline B: Watch A Diner Waitress Explain To A Wall Street Guy How Money Works In America

Answer: Headline B got four times the clicks Headline A did.

Slide 16 in "The Sweet Science Of Virality"

Now, this silly quiz only matters if you're interested in quadrupling your traffic. If you are, let's dissect how Upworthy uses headlines as a content hack. We'll share three key elements:

1. They embrace failure as part of their process.
2. They frame their stories with pitch-perfect headlines.
3. And they use a repeatable process to write super-clickable headlines.

First, they're not afraid to fail. Of this, they say: "Anyone who tells you he can make anything go viral is definitely not telling you the truth. Or is really naive. Almost nothing will. Even if it's great." The 2013 numbers they share tell this story well:

- *66 percent of their posts didn't break 20,000 views*
- *6 percent reached 100,000 views*
- *3 percent reached 200,000 views*

- *1.6 percent reached 300,000 views*
- *0.9 percent reached 500,000 views*
- *0.5 percent broke 750,000 views*
- *And just 11 posts cleared 1,000,000 views (or 0.42 percent)*

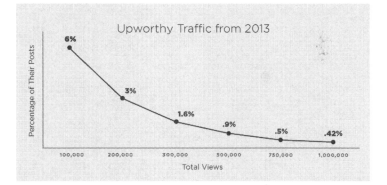

So, they test and test and test again. They fine-tune what resonates with people and immediately stop what doesn't. Most importantly, they never let the fear of failure stop them from testing something that might fall flat on its face.

Second, they're masters at framing their content with their headlines. To do this, they use the "curiosity gap." The idea is to avoid two extremes: vagueness and specificity. If your headline is too vague, you won't generate enough interest to win clicks. However, if your headline is too specific, it may actually give your content away. This means your audience doesn't need to click, because they've already got what they wanted.

Too vague: A Guy Invented This Thing You'll Like

Too specific: Inventor Launches New 3D Printer At SXSW

Just right: The Epic Thinger That Makes The Internet Look Like A Coloring Book

Third, they take all of their learning and bake it into a process. For every story, they write a minimum of twenty-five headlines. Here's their self-described editorial process:

1. *"You have to crap out 25 headlines for every piece of content.*
2. *You will write some really stinky headlines.*
3. *Once you start getting desperate, you start thinking outside the box.*
4. *So you have to write 25 headlines.*
5. *#24 will suck. Then #25 will be a gift from the headline gods and will make you a legend.*
6. *Accept that not every headline will be perfect.*
7. *Then write 25 headlines.*
8. *With practice, you'll be writing 25 in 15 minutes. Then [we] will give you permission to lower your limit.*

So please write 25 headlines."

Then, they A/B test two headlines using cleverly crafted Bit.ly links. One Bit.ly link goes to Headline A and the other to Headline B. When they have a clear winner after a set amount of time (and there usually is one), they launch.

The full Upworthy presentation is excellent and definitely worth a look, a bookmark, and possibly even a printout. It's that good.

Fake Parking Tickets

Y Combinator startup Tripl seized the opportunity to make an impression on more than 200 of the biggest names in tech by placing fake parking tickets on their cars while they were listening to a multitude of product pitches. The tickets read "Violation: You have illegally been subjected to make a big investment decision based on a two-minute demo pitch."

*Image from Content Marketing Institute, "Hacking Content Marketing:
How a Parking Ticket Turned into 40,000 Customers"*

Tripl's Peter Sullivan grabbed a photo of the stunt, which he quickly uploaded to Y Combinator's Hacker News site. Within hours, the story held the top spot and helped guide his startup to 40,000 users in its first year.

Am I endorsing doing something illegal? No . . . But this is certainly a sprint along the dusty growth-hacking trail. And hey, it was content, after all. The point is that many times risky, and seemingly crazy ideas work. All too often, what works is the kind of stuff that never would make it into a marketing plan or RFP. And that's the true risk content hackers teach us to avoid.

GET TRANSPARENT WITH YOUR BUSINESS DATA

When GrooveHQ, a technical helpdesk software company, first launched, they weren't doing so well. According to their head of marketing, Len Markidan, "We had a product, but we didn't really have a thoughtful or effective marketing strategy. We thought we were doing content marketing, but really what we were doing is publishing posts like 'Five Great Things About Our Helpdesk.'"* They were publishing content. But it was stuff nobody cared to read.

"The point is that many times risky, and seemingly crazy ideas work."

Their CEO, Alex Turnbull, knew then it was time for a fresh direction if their marketing was going to work. So, he sent out an email that read simply, "Our blog sucks. Let's discuss." And this came at an especially critical time. They were roughly six months from zero cash day. They were running out of money and had yet to find traction. After meeting, the team decided it was time to take a risk—a big one. They shut down their blog and went back to the drawing board.

Over the next few months, they developed their new blog, calling it, "A Startup's Journey to $100,000 in Monthly Revenue." It would chronicle their successes and failures on the path to $1.2 million in recurring revenue—complete with numbers, warts, and shining victories. The tag line at the bottom of every post read: "From A-ha to Oh Shit, we're sharing everything we learn on our journey from 0 to $100,000 in monthly revenue. We're learning a lot, and so will you."

The results were spectacular. They got more than 5,000 subscribers and 535 trial signups in just five weeks, which generated $3,425 in revenue.† They struck a chord with their target audience. This was

---

* https://coschedule.com/blog/how-to-optimize-your-content-marketing-strategy-with-len-markidan-from-groovehq-amp-051/
† https://www.groovehq.com/blog/100k

because the very people they hoped would become customers were struggling with the same things they were. This radical transparency meant they were talking about content that was wildly interesting to their target audience in a way absolutely no other company could. And today, they're still sharing the journey—though it's grown and evolved. Notice, though, the ingredients present in their secret, content hacking recipe?

One metric that mattered most: revenue. A specific goal: $100,000 in MRR. And a timeline: less than one year.

#RESULTSORDIE

Regardless of metrics, goals, timelines, and tactics, content hackers don't settle for activity; only results. The examples we shared are great inspiration, ranging from the simple to the gutsy to the flat-out vulnerable. But those paths have already been traveled.

So, what are you going to do to get 10x results as fast as humanly possible? Remember, the three constraints are lean enough for a napkin sketch:

One Metric + Goal + Timeline = Content Hacker

One Metric that Matters = your number-one metric for growth.

Goal = the 10x number you're going to hit no matter what.

Timeline = a date on the calendar, not long from now, that you're going to work feverishly to hit your goal by.

Are you the world's next content hacker? You certainly can be.

Your 10x Toolbox

Put this chapter into action with your 10x Toolbox by visiting: https://coschedule.com/10x-toolbox

10x Marketing Interview:

Noah Kagan and the Proactive Dashboard

Founder of Sumo.com and AppSumo, Noah Kagan, and I talk growth hacking, embracing failure, and testing fifty-two growth ideas per year. He explains their team's use of proactive dashboards to track progress against their goal and totally own the process. You will have access to the full audio interview plus transcript.

THE 10X MARKETING FORMULA

You don't learn to walk by following rules. You learn by doing and falling over.
— Richard Branson, founder of Virgin Group

The *10x Marketing Formula* unfolds over four phases: plan, execute, publish, and analyze. At the end, you will understand how to plan high-growth projects, execute them with lightning speed, publish aggressively and promote effectively, and then analyze your results in real-time so you can optimize your work.

Along the way, you will build your own 10x Marketing Toolbox. These are worksheets, templates, and tools to help you put everything you learn immediately into practice. You will also find 10x Marketing Interviews with marketing leaders who have done exactly what we're talking about.

Here's the deal: Nothing is magic about this formula. It won't work just because you've read it. To get the biggest marketing results of your career, you need to put it into action. What will make the *10x Marketing Formula* work is you and your team.

Now, turn the page and become a scrappy, content-hacking, 10x marketer.

"YOU DON'T LEARN
TO WALK BY
FOLLOWING RULES.
YOU LEARN BY
DOING AND
FALLING OVER."

— RICHARD BRANSON,
FOUNDER OF VIRGIN GROUP

PHASE ONE: PLAN

Your 10x marketing journey starts here. In
Phase One, you will outline what your content
will look like and discover exactly how that
content delivers the core value your business
offers to your target customers. This phase
forms the nucleus of your content strategy.

CHAPTER THREE

COMPETITION-FREE CONTENT

When the American Civil War ended on May 9, 1865, the country entered the era of Reconstruction. Much of the US was in shambles, including the economy. However, a major shift was taking place: from a primarily agricultural economy to an industrialized one.*

Peirce College capitalized on this shift. The college was founded in Philadelphia, Pennsylvania, to help returning soldiers transition into the emerging industrial economy. They needed education and training that was both practical and affordable. And that's what Peirce delivered, enrolling 550 students in its first year.†

Over the coming decades, however, Peirce shifted its focus from veterans to the traditional eighteen-year-old student. By the late 1980s, Peirce College was treading water in a sea of similar schools. They were simply another college offering the same things to the same people as everyone else.

Then in 1991 came Arthur J. Lendo, Peirce's new president. Lendo led the school back to its focus on a group of potential students with few alternatives. Rather than claw for the attention of traditional students,

---

* https://www.nps.gov/resources/story.htm%3Fid%3D251
† https://www.peirce.edu/about-peirce/our-history

the college pivoted to a focus on adult learners, military personnel, and prospective foreign students.

To reach this audience, they began offering bachelor degree programs in three venues: on campus, on-site in different cities, and online. No longer was their nontraditional audience limited to associate's degrees from community colleges. Now they had the chance of earning a four-year degree.

In the first year, they beat online enrollment forecasts by 300 percent. And over time, overall enrollment nearly tripled. Notably, the average age of a Peirce student rose from about twenty one to mid-thirties.*

BLUE OCEANS AND RED OCEANS

Peirce College's story is an excellent illustration of how marketers can position themselves today. I learned their story from a case study done by the authors of a business book called *Blue Ocean Strategy: How to Create Uncontested Market Space and Make Competition Irrelevant.*† In the book, authors W. Chan Kim and Renée Mauborgne explain how there are two different oceans in business: a red ocean and a blue ocean.

The red ocean is bloody with competition. In these waters, you're competing with many companies for the same customers via the same methods. Everyone's begging for attention in existing markets. Growth becomes slow, if not outright stagnant. This is where Peirce College found themselves as they transitioned into the mainstream academic market. They were targeting the same students with the same solutions. High competition, low differentiation. This is a brutal scenario for marketers, and one most of us work in today.

Contrast that picture of the red ocean with a blue ocean. These are clear, competition-free waters. It's a place where unique approaches stand out because no one else can compete. In fact, finding the blue

---

* https://www.blueoceanstrategy.com/bos-moves/peirce-college/
† https://www.amazon.com/Blue-Ocean-Strategy-Expanded-Uncontested/dp/1625274491

Blue Ocean
(UNCONTESTED SPACE)

Red Ocean
(BLOODY WITH COMPETITION)

ocean renders competition irrelevant. The extreme upside is that you can capture new demand by doing your best work because you swim in your own waters. And this is where Peirce recaptured success.

THE SECRET TO GENERATING CONSTANT DEMAND

Regular content marketing is just like swimming in the red ocean. It's filled with noise, thrashing, and fierce competition. Everyone's begging for the same audience's attention—and they're doing the same things to get it. They're simply trying to swim faster than the rest. This is what gives us a market bloody with competition and yielding stagnant growth.

You will find your blue ocean through "competition-free content." It's the first step in the *10x Marketing Formula* because, without it, even the best content faces diminishing returns.

Competition-free content is content that adds tremendous value to your customers and audience that *only you* can produce. It's content that stands out through topic, structure, or media type. And it renders competition irrelevant because it exists in uncontested space. This is where you create stuff that stands out while being impactful and meaningful.

Now, why should you embrace and pursue this? After all, producing content is about producing results. The reason is simple. Competition-free content generates constant demand for your product or service.

The coveted inbound marketing funnel is a fringe case for content marketing in the red ocean. There are a few brands that win here, but they are the exception rather than the rule. One of my favorite examples of this is GrooveHQ, a helpdesk software company, which we briefly studied as a content hacking case study in Chapter Two.

DIFFERENTIATION

GrooveHQ found their competition-free content by creating content no one else could. Theirs is a perfect example because only they could talk about *their numbers, their process, and their journey*. Plus, they did more than finding a point of major differentiation. They created stuff that directly interested and benefited both their customer base and their rapidly growing audience.

They didn't simply create content that attracted lots of eyes. They created content that drove results like crazy. You'll learn even more about exactly how to do this in the next chapter. But the intersection between uniqueness and value for your customers is what will qualify your content as competition-free.

"Competition-free content is content that adds tremendous value to your customers and audience that only you can produce."

Consider this scenario.

Let's imagine a marketer who works for a regional clothing retail chain. Her stores have a well-curated selection of clothes, accessories, and more that fits their customers' wants and needs better than any competitor. But here's the problem. Their competitors are huge, with big budgets and voices that dominate the marketplace. They are the big fish in the red ocean of retail.

Obviously, this marketer's job is to do a better job of generating demand than the others . . . (You know, the entire goal of marketing.) But it's a ruthlessly difficult game to win.

While her company provides unique value to their retail footprint, it's tough to get anyone to listen. Her brand only has one part of the equation. Although they provide great value, they have no way of standing out, being heard, and generating that coveted demand because they've been producing nothing but copycat content.

She is the perfect candidate for competition-free content. Her task is finding the space where her brand's voice is crystal clear by being the only voice in its niche. This means she can stop spending her precious time, energy, and budget trying to shout louder than everyone else. If she does this, her competitors become irrelevant. No matter how established they are, they cannot speak with authority in her competition-free content niche. Make no mistake: every company has one. The trick is finding it. So, where can our hopeful marketer begin her journey?

Let's break the process down.

HOW TO FIND COMPETITION-FREE CONTENT

To find her competition-free content niche, she can start with this three-part framework: look, research, and strategize. It's the simple trifecta anyone can do, regardless of budget or time constraints. As you follow along, you can download the Competition-Free Content Worksheet for free at https://www.coschedule.com/10x-toolbox

Look

The first step is to observe her competitors by surveying the landscape and dissecting what kinds of content they're creating.

Are they running ads like crazy on TV, radio, billboards, and other traditional channels? Are they working digital angles like Facebook ads, giveaway contests, video, or email marketing? Do they have engaged audiences on blogs or social channels like Pinterest, Instagram, or Twitter? This step is about taking a critical look at the market and diagnosing strategies and tactics like a scientist.

She should ask, What content resonates most, and least, with her ideal customers? This is where she can start to find the cracks and avenues into creating competition-free content.

Research

After tracking her competitive landscape, it's time to head to Google for some simple research. Here, she's looking beyond channels and into content. She'll search for terms related to her products and look at the top ten search results. She's looking for two main things:

1.   What is consistent about their content?
2.   What stands out most prominently?

_____

1. HOW LONG IS MY COMPETITOR'S CONTENT?

2. HOW MANY IMAGES DO THEY USE?

3. DO THEY USE STRONG CALLS TO ACTION?

4. HOW STRONG ARE THEIR CUSTOMER TESTIMONIALS?

5. ARE THEIR PRODUCT SALES ATTRACTING LOTS OF ATTENTION LOCALLY, REGIONALLY, AND NATIONALLY?

She wants to answer questions like, How long is my competitor's content? How many images do they use? Do they use strong calls to action? How strong are their customer testimonials? Are their product sales attracting lots of attention locally, regionally, and nationally?

By asking questions like these, she can analyze the content landscape. In fact, she can even create a spreadsheet to keep track of these data points for a high-level view of what everyone else is creating. And this type of research will make finding her competition-free content niche far easier than simple guesswork.

Strategize

Now that she's researched the content and methods her competition is using, she can create her competition-free content strategy (aka "the fun part"). However, coming up with competition-free content isn't simply about creating content that's different—it's about creating content that's different and that her team can execute well. The path to finding that niche is asking and answering these questions.

- *What is she and her team really good at?*
  Understanding what she and her team can do better than anyone else is important at this stage. She's looking for something that's both different and that she can execute well.

- *What are her competitors doing that's similar?*
  Next, what patterns is the industry falling into that are like her team's strengths? These are opportunities to disrupt them and stand out. They are also guardrails to avoid red-ocean competition.

- *What's in it for her customers?*
  This question, above the others, should be her primary guide. Ultimately, the tactics she uses won't matter to her

customers. They don't care if they find valuable content from her or from somewhere else. They care about the message and how it directly benefits them.

This is often called a "What's in it for me?" (WIIFM) statement. Here, she needs a compelling answer she can communicate clearly. Additionally, notice I said "customers" and not simply "audience." It's vital that she keep her paying and most profitable customers in mind. Her competition-free content is not simply meant to build a following. Its sole purpose is to drive growth and yield positive financial results.

To attract more of her brand's ideal customers, she must focus on creating and communicating value tailored to them.

- *Are there people in her customer base or audience her content underserves?*
  Next, there may be customer and audience segments key to growth she isn't serving well. Here, she's dissecting two segments: who is already walking into her stores, and who is following her brand online. If there are critical buyers, or potential buyers, her content is neglecting, this is a huge opportunity to course correct.

- *What has she and her team created already that she's most proud of?*
  Finally, are there things she's proud of because they've worked well and she can create them at an elite level? These are things she knows she and her team can consistently execute well.

These three stages are the quickest path to locating her competition-free content niche. And they are yours, as well. Their power is the singular clarity they bring to both your strengths and the competition you face.

Now, you may be thinking, "Hypothetical situations are great . . . But are there real-world results this process has achieved?"

Great question.

WHAT HAPPENED WHEN WE FOUND OUR COMPETITION-FREE CONTENT NICHE

We followed this process at CoSchedule, and found our primary way of generating enough demand to achieve growth. And I'm not just talking about keeping the lights on and the bills paid. I mean genuine bottom-line growth directly attributable to going all in on competition-free content.

When we began surveying our market competitors, we found lots of companies blogging, just like we were. However, we immediately found a chink in their armor: their blog posts were following current industry best practices. They were working the same methods, mediums, and angles as everyone else.

Their posts were between 500 and 1,000 words long and included an image. Most of the time, this image was a generic stock photo. Sometimes companies didn't even realize they were using the exact photos as their competitors. Talk about a bloody ocean.

As we dug into their content and deconstructed it, we found another opportunity. Nearly all the blog posts and articles we found (even in major publications) were filled with the same tired advice. They neither told nor showed readers how to put the tactics into action. Instead, they threw out phrases like:

Make sure you work from a marketing plan approved by all project stakeholders. This will remove roadblocks for you down the road, thus increasing profitability and decreasing scope creep.

You know, the stuff you read that leaves you saying, "Gee, thanks for the same 'expert advice' everyone else is peddling."

To us, it was apparent that our competition-free content niche would be:

Actionable and unique

First, content that isn't actionable is seldom beneficial. This is the stuff that tells what to do without ever showing how to do it. We knew actionable, how-to content would outshine anyone peddling fluffy advice. We also heavily invested in keyword and audience research to discover what unique questions our potential customer base was looking to solve.

This made it easy to identify topics we knew would:
1. Have a high volume of search traffic,
2. Be unsolved by our competitors,
3. And ensure we'd stand out because we'd become the one-stop-shop for marketers with problems we were perfectly suited to solve (and, incidentally, so was our product!).

3-5x longer than average

Second, our content was easily three to five times longer than our competition's. Understand, though, that length isn't a magical formula for content success. Instead, longer content is nearly always requisite for actionability. You can easily dispense marketing advice in 500 words. Rarely can you provide advice *and* demonstrate, step-by-step, how to implement it within that constraint. Length was never our only goal; it was a byproduct of content that solved problems for our customers while generating demand for our product.

Packed with free content upgrades

Another element attendant to actionability was free content upgrades. We created these for every piece of content we published. They ranged from Excel-based worksheets to free software tools. And they always served the reader and facilitated implementation. This proved to be an incredible one-two punch, especially for building our email list. (More on exactly how to do that later.)

Include 5-6x more images

Finally, we knew stock images added zero value. How does some guy in a gray suit scribbling nonsense on a whiteboard help a reader? It doesn't. So, we hired a designer to completely own our visual content for blog posts. This meant we had custom infographics, charts, pull quotes, and more. And the best part was, we made them all insanely shareable. (In fact, one of our infographics was pinned on Pinterest over 100,000 times in just a few months.)

As a result, our content instantly took on a different flavor. Also important is we found that our team was really good at written content. This meant we could hang in the competition-free space we'd identified, and move quickly. We weren't taking months to publish. Over the long haul, we've worked our asses off to do this better, and faster, than anyone else. However, we weren't so hot at creating video content at that stage. It was a weakness, so we avoided it and invested in what we were best at.

The immediate impact was that our traffic and subscriber base doubled in short order. And it has continued to grow four years in.

This content strategy is still the driving source fueling our growth.

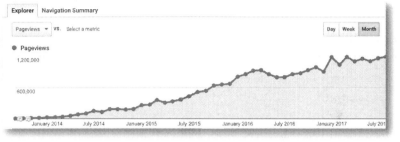

Data from CoSchedule Google Analytics

To date, here is the evolution of our numbers:

Our competition-free content is the linchpin for growth by generating consistent demand. It's hard work, but it's the *right* work.

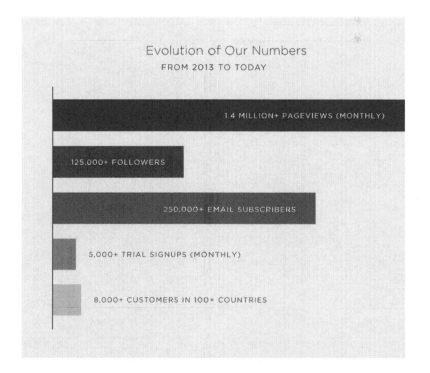

YOUR RESULTS

As marketers, we're competing for attention, eyeballs, visits, leads, subscribers . . . and the list goes on. So, our content has to earn the right to our audience's time. But this is extraordinarily hard if we're creating the same fluff as everyone else. Just like we work to differentiate the way we position our products and services, we need to differentiate our content and marketing methods.

In this chapter, we looked at three real-world examples of sailing from a red to a blue ocean: Peirce College, GrooveHQ, and us at CoSchedule. Each one showcases the value of finding a niche no one else can cover or serve. Peirce pivoted to underserved student demographics. GrooveHQ became wildly transparent and chronicled their numbers, successes, and failures. And we doubled down on helping marketers solve their problems with our content *and* our software.

Your results can look just like ours. Not because you will mimic the content in these examples. But because you can follow the process to uncover your competition-free content niche.

Your 10x Toolbox
Put this chapter into action with your 10x Toolbox by visiting https://coschedule.com/10x-toolbox

Worksheet: Competition-Free Content Niche
This worksheet will help you identify and outline your own competition-free content niche.

CHAPTER FOUR

FINDING YOUR CONTENT CORE

Google these three words: "lots of traffic." Don't press enter. Let Google guess what you're searching for. Here were my results:

Google

lots of traffic

lots of traffic
lots of traffic **no sales**
lots of traffic **in spanish**
lots of traffic **but no sales**
lots of traffic **in french**
lots of traffic **to akamai**
lots of traffic **lights london**
lots of traffic **lights**
lots of traffic **jam**
lots of traffic **from russia**

Google Search   I'm Feeling Lucky

Report inappropriate predictions

Incognito search suggestions from October 23, 2017

There's a problem content marketers face, and Google guessed it within the first two autocomplete suggestions. Many struggle to convert traffic into paying customers. And whether it's thousands, or hundreds, of visitors, unconverted traffic is a signal something isn't working. In this chapter, we're going to solve this problem with a simple framework called the "content core."

To begin, understand that finding content your audience is interested in isn't good enough to get results. That's too damn easy. For instance, CoSchedule's head of demand generation loves Metallica, beer, and marketing—so he'd show up to read about those every day. But is there an overlap between my product and his interests? Unless I market Metallica-themed beer, then probably not.

So, the next step in the *10x Marketing Formula* is to find your content core, which determines exactly what you should be creating for revenue growth. In my case, this means I won't be writing about beer and heavy metal anytime soon. What it will mean for you, though, is wholly dependent upon your customers and product or service.

THE CONTENT CORE

Simply put, your content core connects the dots between what your customers care about and what you have to offer them. Notice I said "what your *customers* care about," and not "what your audience cares about." There's a difference. Because if you're going to get really good at generating leads and converting traffic, you have to intimately understand the customers who are already paying you.

So, the purpose of the content core exercise is to understand the confluence between what you do and what you need to talk about. Here, you'll go beyond traffic, eyeballs, and audience building and into creating content that gains customers.

Visually, it's best represented by two overlapping circles. Sitting side-by-side, the circle on the left represents the content your audience cares about. The circle on the right represents the value you provide as a business. The place where the circles overlap is the content core, and is the bullseye of your content strategy. This is content that aligns with your audience's interests while simultaneously generating demand for your product or service.

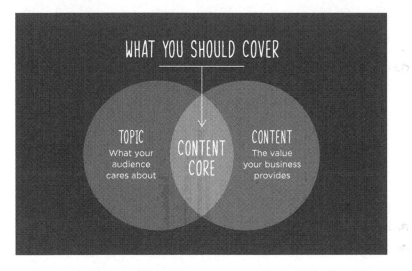

The content core helps marketers avoid two big traps:

The Traffic Trap
This trap is creating content your audience cares about, but fails to convert traffic into customers. The danger is that web traffic becomes a false signal. Increasing traffic looks like a positive sign—but revenue doesn't increase proportionally.

The Promotional Trap
This trap is creating a constant barrage of promotional content that fails to connect with your audience's needs, pains, and interests. The danger with this "me-centric" content is that it adds little, if any, value to an audience. This will fail to generate traffic, and no traffic means no conversions.

Finding your content core is like applying guardrails. It helps you avoid either extreme that hamstrings growth. I loop both traps into something called "parallel content." It's parallel because that's exactly what results you'll achieve: parallel to last year's (even if they do bring traffic).

THE CONTENT CORE AT WORK

Recently, I spoke at a marketing conference about this topic. After my talk, a marketer came up and asked me some follow-up questions. His company was religiously creating blog content that solved their customers' problems. However, their revenue growth was stagnant, and traffic wasn't increasing the number of purchases their customers made. So, he asked, "Is it okay to mention our products in our posts? Or will that seem too salesy?"

They were blogging about content their customers were interested in. That was great. But, because they never mentioned additional products, the only way for visitors to find out about new or related products was to randomly click on an ad for their online store. This meant their content was helpful to their audience—but not to their business. It was content that drove traffic and added tons of value (the standard recipe for successful content marketing). But it did little to increase profitable customer action.

As we talked, I suggested he could start by weaving in contextually relevant calls to action (CTAs). His company sells office supplies. So, the CTAs could be as simple as, "Many {company} customers like the {brand} stapler because it doesn't hurt their fingers to use." Even a simple CTA like that is a big step forward for his company.

The marketing industry makes a lot of noise about providing value to readers, but if it isn't balanced by your business's interests, you'll be left with no results. While this marketer's CTA-less content built trust and traffic, it was actually doing his company a disservice.

The content core is key here. He had half the equation dialed in because he knew exactly what his audience was interested in. But because he was missing the other half that drives demand, his marketing efforts cost the company more money than they generated. But by weaving some CTAs into this already useful content, that content became a lot more helpful for the reader who'd just found a better stapler! And that's the double value of the content core. It helps the customer while helping the business.

Fortunately, the solution was simple and quick to implement. And better yet, it left tons of room for content hacking experiments. We'll dig deeper into writing killer CTAs and conversion psychology in Chapter Fourteen. But before we do, it's paramount you find exactly what your content core looks like. Create the right content, and you'll build an audience primed to convert.

PARALLEL CONTENT VS. CONTENT CORE

The perfect place to start is by diagnosing what kind of content you're creating right now. The stuff that converts will use angles that intersect with customer and business interests. However, most marketers settle for what we call parallel content topics.

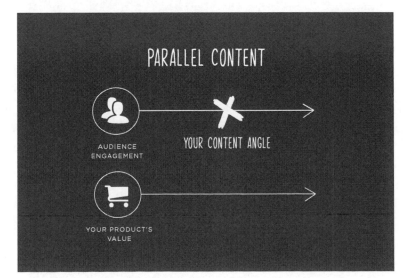

Parallel content looks good on the surface. It's stuff that's related to your core business and that your audience is interested in. But it converts poorly because it lacks strong, clear CTAs to become a paying customer. It runs parallel to your core business, but doesn't intersect with opportunities to increase revenue.

Compare this to content core topics that fulfill the main criteria. These are topics your audience is interested in that also intersect with your core business. Here, you're identifying the perfect angles, or points of intersection, between the two.

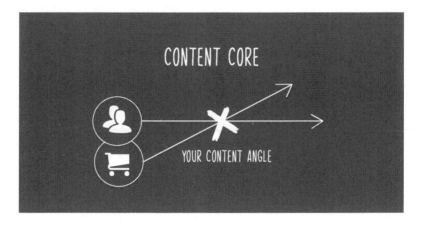

To illustrate, imagine you run an ecommerce gardening tools business. Obviously, your audience will be interested in all things gardening. With this in mind, you start creating content to help your growing audience solve their gardening problems. You write blog posts, design infographics, and create videos around key topics like soil health, planters, and keeping pesky rabbits at bay. Traffic is on the rise, so you decide to go all in on a new guide: "The Ultimate Guide to Common Garden Weeds."

This topic makes sense, right? After all, you sell gardening tools, and weeds are public enemy number one. You know this is a topic your audience cares about and involves a serious problem they're looking to solve.

Checkmate.

So, you sink hours into researching, writing, and designing the definitive online guide to weed identification. You publish and promote this premium piece of content. And, on the surface, things seem to be going great. However, even though you've got a steadily increasing stream of backlinks, social media engagement, and traffic, sales remain stagnant.

The reason? You have a parallel content problem.

"If you teach people to be successful without you, they'll be dying to be successful with you."

While your ultimate guide adds major value, the content doesn't directly intersect with your products. You're helping your audience while starving your business.

Instead, the content core approach would look something like this: "The Ultimate Guide to Killing the 12 Most Common Garden Weeds." Throughout the guide, you can show your audience *how* to kill pesky weeds like crabgrass and dandelions. Now, a light bulb may have just flicked on in your brain, but be careful not to get ahead of yourself. The obvious thing to do is to repeatedly show them how to kill these weeds with your products.

Instead, ensure your content answers this question *without* promoting your products: *If my readers do exactly what I show them in this piece of content, will they gain the same or a similar benefit to buying my products?*

The goal is that your content provides real value without the need to buy your products. But, as you weave CTAs to buy throughout your content, you can position them as the proverbial easy-button. The content shows them how to get the promised results all on their own. But your products are also there to make their lives *so much easier*.

Many marketers are hesitant to give away so much value. After all, you're providing them a path to get results without you. This seems counterproductive to the entire premise of the content core. But here's the truth: if you teach people to be successful *without* you, they'll be dying to be successful *with* you.

HOW TO FIND YOUR CONTENT CORE

Through this approach, you're helping your audience while actually training them to become customers. You can teach them to think exactly like you, and therefore use the same toolsets to solve real problems. The important element is finding the angle that intersects the needs of both your audience and your business.

To find your content core, create the right content, use the right angles, and employ strong CTAs.

CREATING THE RIGHT CONTENT

At CoSchedule, we recently launched a feature called *Marketing Projects*. It helps teams manage marketing campaigns. It's a perfect way to drive leads and conversions for our product. However, we use the content core to create valuable content around the core topic.

To do this, we used some good old-fashioned audience research to find two things:

1. A *topic* they're highly interested in
2. An *angle* that matches their needs

Now, I love tools—after all, our product is a tool. But when it comes to research, I never get too fancy. What I want, and what you should want, too, is to talk directly to your customers. And I think some of the best ways to do this are Google, Facebook, and LinkedIn user groups; email surveys; and simply picking up the phone and making some calls.

What you're looking for are conversations and subtopics around the main topic you'll be covering. In our case, we used Google to research similar content, plus we talked with our customers about their struggles and problems around our new feature. With both tactics, our primary goal was to hear how they described their problems.

First, we found popular blog posts and articles on marketing-project–related topics. Then, we scrolled down to the comments section for each one. Here, we were able to read verbatim questions and comments from people in our target audience. This helped us pick up on the exact phrases they use that were related to our feature, while at the same time helping us more deeply understand their problems and gaps for which there wasn't a current solution.

Second, we talked with our customers. Loaded with the conversational ammo from our initial research, we dug even further into the struggles our current customers faced. We learned they were looking for four primary things:

1. They needed ways to "organize everything in one place."
2. They wanted a "marketing schedule template."
3. They needed help with "marketing campaign planning."
4. They had gaps in "marketing project management."

From this stage, we were able to perfectly tailor our feature launch to these problems. And we did so with content that fit perfectly into our content core. Not only did we know our audience was interested in the topic; we knew exactly *how* they explained their needs. And because it was a brand new CoSchedule feature, the angles we chose for our content intersected directly with our business interests.

For example, one of our most successful blog posts in this feature launch was entitled "The Complete 16-Step Marketing Project Management Process That Will Get You Organized." Notice how the title is divided into two parts: subject and angle. The subject is {Marketing Project Management Process}, and the angle is that it will {Get You Organized}.

The promise baked into the headline gives the reader the exact benefit as the feature itself. It's also an extremely useful post, clocking in at over 2,500 words, plus free templates to manage and organize marketing projects. And because that value is matched exactly with our feature's value, it converts traffic very well.

Finally, we included a single, clear, and compelling CTA. Here is the in-line body copy and companion graphic:

If you're ready to manage the execution and monitoring phases better than ever, try CoSchedule! It's your marketing project management software designed to get you organized.

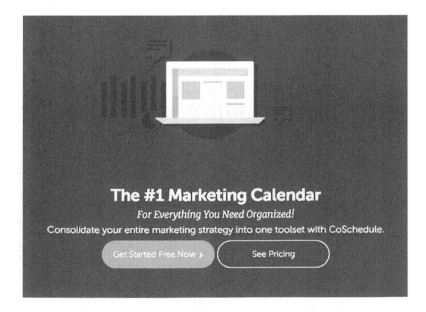

Remember my conversation with the ecommerce office supply marketer? He was worried that CTAs would be off-putting and alienate his audience. However, with content core topics, we have found the exact opposite to be true—and so will you.

The article solved the problem they had, and so did the product. In this case, our CTA was actually helpful. So, we really did them a favor. You're welcome, internet.

FIVE QUESTIONS FOR EFFECTIVE CUSTOMER RESEARCH

The content core certainly isn't rocket science, but it's highly effective. This is because it helps you avoid sinking time into those pesky parallel topics. For example, if we had written an article chronicling "The 10 Most Interesting Marketing Trends of 2017," we would've gotten some traffic—maybe even more than our actual piece did! Our audience would certainly be interested. However, we would have received no leads because that content would be outside of our core. Sure, our audience cares about marketing trends—but our product can't help them with that.

So, using the content core for every single piece you publish will make your life tremendously easier. This is because guessing what will convert visitors into customers is really hard. You can start with simple customer interviews.*

To find the words your customers say as they dream up the perfect solution to their problems, ask the following five questions:

1. What prompted you to start looking for a solution like {your product}?
2. Why did you choose {your product}?
3. What is the most significant difference {your product} is making in your business today?

* To download the free Content Core Customer Interviews worksheet, visit https://coschedule.com/10x-toolbox

AUDIENCE VERBIAGE

_____

1. WHAT PROMPTED YOU TO START LOOKING FOR A
   SOLUTION LIKE {YOUR PRODUCT}?

2. WHY DID YOU CHOOSE {YOUR PRODUCT}?

3. WHAT IS THE MOST SIGNIFICANT DIFFERENCE
   {YOUR PRODUCT} IS MAKING IN YOUR BUSINESS TODAY?

4. HOW WOULD YOU BRIEFLY DESCRIBE {YOUR PRODUCT}
   TO SOMEONE ELSE?

5. WHAT IS THE SINGLE GREATEST BENEFIT {YOUR
   PRODUCT} PROVIDES?

4. How would you briefly describe {your product} to someone else?
5. What is the single greatest benefit {your product} provides?

You can conduct interviews over video chat, on a phone call, via email, or even through a survey. Regardless of the platform you use, the answers to these five questions will give you laser-like focus on revenue-generating content. Then, have every single person on your marketing team watch, listen to, or read the answers—including new hires during onboarding. You want your entire marketing team to be equipped with the most effective phrases to fuel their copy, content, and CTAs.

It's also key to understand that these aren't your typical content marketing questions. Usually, marketers ask questions like "What publications do you regularly read?" Or, "What kind of content do you consume?" And they ask so they can create more stuff in those same veins. The logic is that if they create similar stuff, they'll grab attention. By now, though, you can probably see this strategy for the red ocean it is.

Instead, with these questions we're going much further. We aren't simply trying to understand our audience; we're trying to understand our audience's customers. There's a big difference here.

Customers don't buy because of content; they buy because a given product or service solves a problem. And if you can solve problems that help them win more clients, you're in business. You'll also find that understanding those problems and how they talk about them will provide a treasure trove of ideas for content core topics.

Lastly, if it's tough for you to talk directly with customers, a secondary approach is interviewing your sales team or account managers. The point is to get as close as possible to your customers' problems and the language they use to describe them.

PUTTING YOUR CONTENT CORE TO WORK

Here's my challenge to you: Don't publish another piece of content without ensuring it fits within your content core. If it doesn't connect the dots between what your customers care about and what you have to offer them, don't publish it. Parallel topics and subjects that fall outside of your content core will fail to generate revenue. But the stuff that sits in the sweet spot will prove valuable for both your audience and your company.

So, before you move on, find your content core. It's critical to the rest of the *10x Marketing Formula*. You simply won't get 10x results without it.

Your 10x Toolbox
Put this chapter into action with your 10x Toolbox by visiting https://coschedule.com/10x-toolbox

Worksheet: Content Core Customer Interviews
This worksheet includes five content core questions to ask in target customer interviews.

Worksheet: Finding Your Content Core
This worksheet will help you connect your customers' needs with your business value.

PHASE TWO: EXECUTE

In Phase Two, you will execute the highest-growth projects of your career. This phase of the formula helps you: brainstorm 10x projects to achieve tenfold results, map them out onto your 10x calendar, create lean workflows that skyrocket efficiency, create the best content in your niche, and build an agile 10x team.

CHAPTER FIVE

10X PROJECTS

Have you ever made a tpyo?

I have—and there's a select group of people who love letting me know when it happens. If you create content, you've probably had similar experiences. Whether it was a spelling error or grammar faux pas, the grammar police love showing up in force to correct you. They pop up in blog comments, on Twitter, and anywhere else content can be found.

The reason I start this chapter on 10x projects with something as trivial as typos is because it perfectly illustrates what kind of mindset 10x marketers need to assume—and to avoid.

@garrett_moon disagree w/ fact that u don't correct misspellings/ grammar. It takes 2 seconds & will make you look much smarter! #INBOUND17

11:09 AM - 27 Sep 2017 from Boston, MA

2 Likes

Actual tweet from a card-carrying member of the grammar police.

Here's what I mean. Recently, I spoke at INBOUND conference and mentioned how I don't make our team revisit blog posts to correct typos. Not one bit. And that ruffled some literary feathers. Afterward, I received this lovely tweet from an attendee.

First, I do love it when people disagree with, push back against, and talk openly about my content. That's a major point of any good content— it provokes both controversy and conversation and allows us all chances to learn. So, I'm not using this tweet as an example to bash someone who disagrees with me. Instead, I believe this marketer is focusing on the wrong things.

I responded:

My response to the grammar police.

It may be counterintuitive, but I think typos and grammar mistakes are actually chances to humanize your brand. It shows there are real people behind your screens, keyboards, and products. We make mistakes. But guess what? It's okay. Because the incorrect usage of "their" or "you're" doesn't make our content unclear.

It's not an atom bomb on your brand value—it's just a damn typo!

"I think typos and grammar mistakes are actually chances to humanize your brand."

The attendee still disagreed with me. But that's okay, because typos or not, our content is still extremely valuable to our customers and company. A spelling error here or there has never dampened our results. What's really going on when people freak out over details like this is ego-driven posturing. What would be even worse is if I let myself have a stomach ache every time one of my presentation decks had a misspelling. It's going to happen—but it doesn't matter, because a few errant words don't detract from the value the content provides.

I'm not the only CoScheduler who experiences the heckling of the grammar police. Our blog posts are routinely 3,000-plus words long. And we publish at least twice per week. That means we're pumping out north of 24,000 words each month in blog posts alone. We're gonna screw some words up. And, according to a reader, Nathan, our head of demand generation, made a "desparate" mistake. This kind reader pointed it out in an email:

Our "desparate" struggle is real.

Fortunately for us, there is data that sheds light on this judgmental breed of literary luminaries.

WHAT WILL YOUR CONTRIBUTION TO THE WORLD BE?

In a recent study entitled "If You're House Is Still Available, Send Me an Email," researchers found that people who comment negatively on typos tend to be—well—jerks.* Sorry grammar police, but that's science talking, not me. The researchers grabbed a wide swath of participants to evaluate people based on manipulated ads for a housemate. Each participant then gave feedback about the person who wrote the ad. They answered questions about how good a roommate they thought this person would be and whether or not they'd be friends with them.

Unsurprisingly, the people who judged the "ad writer" negatively based upon typos were far less agreeable when measured against these major personality traits: extraversion, agreeability, conscientiousness, neuroticism, and openness.

So, what does this teach us as marketers?

First, let's ask ourselves a simple question: "What will my contribution to the world be?" What kind of value do you hope your work will add to people? If you're a content marketer, you'll publish millions of words, thousands of minutes of video and audio content, and scores of graphics. Not only that, but you'll interact with thousands of people across the world.

So, what kind of mark do you hope to leave? I suggest that if you want to add real value to your customers and your company, a grammar-police mentality will haunt and inhibit you from doing so to your fullest ability.

"What kind of mark do you hope to leave?"

Next, we learn the importance of focus. Your priorities receive your effort and energy. When you focus only on the most important things, 10x results can happen. Alternatively, when you assume a nitpicky mindset, one that sweats the small stuff, 10 percent results will be the norm.

* https://doi.org/10.1371/journal.pone.0149885

THE MILLION-DOLLAR GAP BETWEEN 10X AND 10 PERCENT

So, what is the difference between 10x and 10 percent projects in the wild? A 10x project multiplies your results tenfold. A 10 percent project improves your results by a measly 10 percent. (Think fixing typos, on this one.)

A visual way to understand 10x projects is as those that can positively impact a huge number of people in your audience and produce incredible revenue returns for your business. If plotted on an X–Y chart, a 10x project will always fall high on the upper-right quadrant.

Ten percent projects, on the other hand, provide just a little bit of value to only a few people. Looking at things in this way provides a framework for understanding and predicting impact. And therefore, it's perfectly suited to help you prioritize which projects to take on, and which ones to pass up.

At CoSchedule, you'll hear this mantra daily: "Think 10x. Forget 10 percent." That means prioritizing the work you do to reach your marketing goals ten times faster. Don't do the trivial minutiae that sucks productivity away and fails to drive growth. You see, the goal of 10x projects is to drive positive outcomes, not perfection. Our goal isn't flawless work; it's effective work with huge results.

If we spent time going back into every blog post to correct spelling and grammatical errors, we'd be far less effective than we are. Why? Because it's a 10 percent improvement that distracts from 10x projects. I can tell you from experience that the grammar police will let you know when they find these mistakes. They're being helpful so you can stop your 10x project to:

1. Login to WordPress
2. Search for that blog post
3. Hunt for the specific paragraph and sentence
4. Change a couple characters
5. Hit update
6. View your blog post
7. Scroll to the specific paragraph and sentence

8. Reread everything so it sounds and looks great

9. Then you can get back to the real work that actually adds measurable, 10x impact to your goal.

Do you see the real cost of focusing on piddly 10 percent stuff?

THE COST OF LOSING FOCUS

Research from the University of London found IQ drops fifteen points when multitasking.* Even worse, another study shows that task switching can cost up to 40 percent of someone's productive time.† According to the researchers, the evidence suggests that there are two processes involved in task switching that explain this. The first is a stage called "goal shifting," and takes place when we make a decision to move from one task to the next. The second is a stage called "rule activation," where our minds wrap around the particular set of parameters for a new task.

These stages are awesome at helping us move between tasks. However, the productivity costs become enormous when we're bouncing from task-to-task. This means chasing down 10 percent tasks is incredibly expensive.

Now, let's spend the rest of our time in this chapter looking at an example of a 10x project, and then working through the steps so you can ideate high-impact projects of your own.

BUILDING A 10X TOOL

One of my favorite 10x projects we've undertaken at CoSchedule is our Headline Analyzer. It launched in November 2014. We realized that in our tool we had north of 1,000,000 headlines with social share data for each. Since we've always been serious about our headlines as a content hack, we analyzed them to improve our own. Through intensive research,

---

* https://techcrunch.com/2010/08/04/schmidt-data/
† http://www.apa.org/research/action/multitask.aspx

we boiled down the best, most clickable, and most shareable headlines into a formula that our team started using.

Next, because we're software dweebs, we built an algorithm that could score the quality of any headline we typed into it. It predicted the likelihood for everything from potential clicks to social shares. We simply automated the manual process we'd been following. Then, we went a step further.

We also love providing value to our audience, so we launched a 10x project to make our algorithm available to the masses for free. The Headline Analyzer was born. And immediately, email addresses poured into our coffers. Literally.

CoSchedule's free Headline Analyzer tool

When marketers hear this story, we get the question, "Why wouldn't you charge for that tool and let it become a direct revenue source?" Honestly, it's free because . . . Why the heck not?!

It's shocking that such a valuable and actionable tool is free to use. It epitomizes the spirit of content marketing. Give free advice, information, and resources so your audience can become wildly successful. Our customers and audience are helpful to us, so we gave it away to them. We exist to make marketers' lives easier. So, we give "results" back to the community as much as we're able to. In fact, it was so well received that we integrated it into the CoSchedule platform itself.

As I write this, this free tool has helped 1,841,218 marketers analyze over 11,000,000 headlines. And it's been a huge win for CoSchedule, as well, resulting in 55,040 email subscribers. It's also generated huge results for us, with zero ongoing maintenance required. Creating the Headline Analyzer fit squarely into our content core and was 10x in every respect—both in results for our audience and customers, and for our company.

As a similar example, check out the free version of the Moz Keyword Explorer tool (https://moz.com/explorer). It allows users to do in-depth keyword research for free up to twenty times per month.

Free Moz Keyword Explorer tool

You can also find a litany of freemium software operating on the same principle.

The process for you to create similar tools is straightforward. Do the research, crunch the data, turn it into content, and get results. Like the Headline Analyzer, sometimes you just need to "productize" a system or process you are already using! However, getting over the hump of finding the right ideas and angles that will fit your content core can be daunting. So, let's work through how to conceive and prioritize your own 10x projects.

THE PROCESS FOR GENERATING 10X IDEAS (QUICKLY)

For some people, the idea of 10x projects feels a bit out of reach, if not altogether unattainable. You may be thinking, "It's a great framework in theory, but how in the world am I supposed to become a 10x idea factory?" Even more, it's unlikely that you have the luxury of waiting for the marketing muse to inspire such a brilliant idea. Instead, you might owe your boss results by the end of this week. So, you don't have time to twiddle your thumbs and wait for a zap of creative lightning.

But, what if I told you that all you needed was one hour? In just sixty minutes, you can go from no project and content ideas to fifty-plus. I'll walk you through the exact three-step process we use as a team at CoSchedule. And if you follow it, your results will be as advertised.

The 10x ideas process will help you achieve three things:*

1. It forces you to consider what your customers want from you.
2. It cuts through the ambiguity of which projects should take priority.
3. It galvanizes consensus within your team to chase results, treating projects as a means to the goal of all marketing activity.

STEP ONE: 10X BRAINSTORM

The process begins before the team ever meets. I ask everyone to spend ten to twenty minutes brainstorming as many ideas as they can that will answer this question: "What can we do to grow our {metric} tenfold over the next {timeline}?"

Sending a guiding question keeps everyone focused and ensures ideas are aimed at solving a specific problem. Also, notice how the question is structured. When boiled down, there are four components: idea, metric, goal, and timeline.

Idea: How are we going to achieve growth?
Metric: What specific number correlates with revenue growth?
Goal: We are going to multiply growth of this metric by a factor of ten.
Timeline: What is the specific duration in which we'll accomplish this?

---

* To download the free 10x Project Ideas and Prioritization Template, visit https://coschedule.com/10x-toolbox

1. IDEA: HOW ARE WE GOING TO ACHIEVE GROWTH?

2. METRIC: WHAT SPECIFIC NUMBER CORRELATES WITH REVENUE GROWTH?

3. GOAL: WE ARE GOING TO MULTIPLY GROWTH OF THIS METRIC BY A FACTOR OF TEN.

4. TIMELINE: WHAT IS THE SPECIFIC DURATION IN WHICH WE'LL ACCOMPLISH THIS?

Here's an example:

We will launch an {email subject analyzer tool} to increase {email signups} by a factor of {ten} within {four weeks} from start date.

Idea: Create an email subject analyzer tool
Metric: Email signups
Goal: 10x growth!
Timeline: Four weeks

STEP TWO: 10X SCORING

Now it's time for the big meeting. Everyone has their ideas ready to share. And usually, they'll have a lot of them. To kick it off, give your team a bunch of sticky notes and pens. Then ask them to boil down their ideas into three words or less, writing each concise idea on a single sticky note. Next, stick them up on a board, a wall, or somewhere else in plain view. Here's what our team's actual board looked like at this stage:

One, Two, or Three?

Now it's time to score them. To do this, you'll score the ideas by answering two questions. The first question is: "How long will this idea take?" You'll mark the score on the corner of the corresponding sticky note. Here's the scoring breakdown in three levels:

Level One: The idea will take one week or less to execute.
Level Two: The idea will take two weeks to execute.
Level Three: The idea will take three weeks or more to execute.

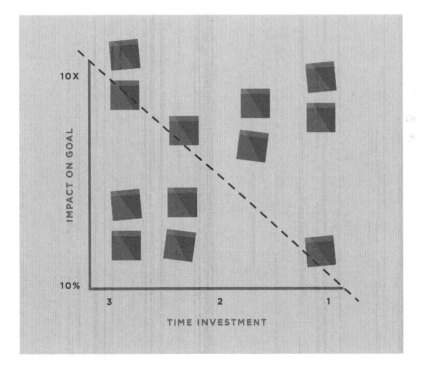

10x Or 10 Percent?

The second question is: "Is this idea 10x or 10 percent?" This measures impact, determining whether or not it can genuinely multiply your goal metric tenfold. Designate each idea by marking it either

"10x" or "10%" as well. Here are four additional questions to help you evaluate these ideas:

What's in it for them?

How will this opportunity benefit your audience? If they won't receive value, then there is no value for you, either.

Can you execute this well?

Do you have the resources and ability to execute this opportunity at the level that you require of yourself? Or will you need to recruit outside help or incur substantial cost? Skew toward ideas that leverage your team's strengths.

What can you ship right now?

Is there a smaller version of the opportunity that you can ship quickly to gather feedback and refine your idea?

Is this competition-free content?

Does this give you a blue ocean, or leave you swimming in red water?

If you have a whiteboard, you can sketch out a grid that looks like the one on the previous page and plot your ideas accordingly:

STEP THREE: FIND YOUR 10X IDEAS!

At this point, you're looking at a ton of categorized ideas. For our team, we usually leave a brainstorming session with about thirty to fifty ideas. Ready for the best part of this system? Your ideas are now prioritized like magic. Projects that are both 10x and quick to execute are by default at the top of your list. Treat everything high and to the right like it's gilded with gold.

Done. Prioritized.

DOING THE RIGHT WORK

So, it shouldn't come as a shock that our team's practice of this process never resulted in a full onslaught to correct typos. Instead, it's continually put our high-impact opportunities into sharp focus.

At this point, you too have put your ideas through serious rigor. And if you've been honest in your assessment, the projects with the highest, fastest, and most likely revenue impact will have risen to the top. This final step simply mandates the discipline to follow the process and relentlessly execute the right projects. This means it's time for the final stage of Phase One, mapping out your project into executable steps and timelines.

It's time for the ultimate marketing tool, the 10x calendar.

Your 10x Toolbox
Put this chapter into action with your 10x Toolbox by visiting https://coschedule.com/10x-toolbox

Template: 10x Project Ideas and Prioritization
This is a template for you and your team to brainstorm, score, and prioritize your 10x ideas.

CHAPTER SIX

10X CALENDAR

Every January, gym traffic skyrockets by as much as 40 percent.* Thousands of people who've made resolutions to lose that extra twenty pounds flood in. The sound of treadmills whining, weights clanging, and heavy breathing reaches a fever pitch. Then, two weeks later, it's back to normal. And gyms are left with the consistent athletes who pound it out three to five times per week. Everyone knows it happens. Well-meaning resolution makers fall off quickly. But meaning well doesn't produce the results so many are after.

In content marketing, a similar phenomenon occurs.

Marketers decide to finally get organized. They decide this is going to be the quarter they publish consistently. It's all mapped out on their editorial calendar. Twice per week on the blog. One message per day on Facebook, twelve tweets, and a few LinkedIn messages. Everything is plotted two weeks ahead. And, at first, it feels awesome. Pressing publish, send, and post promises some real results.

Then, a fire starts. Something happens and they're pulled away. Our once faithful content marketers start to slip. Deadlines are missed.

---

* https://www.washingtonpost.com/news/wonk/wp/2016/01/05/
what-your-new-gym-doesnt-want-you-to-know/

"THE REAL PROBLEM IS THAT MARKETING AND EDITORIAL CALENDARS GET TREATED LIKE GYM MEMBERSHIPS."

— GARRETT MOON

At first, it's only an Instagram post or two. No worries; you can catch up on those over lunch. However, the overwhelming tide of meetings, correspondence, reporting, and more pulls these marketers back adrift at sea. And before they know it, it's a return to square one. What began with such high hopes has ended with a thud.

The real problem is that marketing and editorial calendars get treated like gym memberships. Great intentions melt into the fray of constant demands and busywork. What these marketers are really missing out on, though, is the number-one productivity tool available to them: the 10x calendar.

A 10x calendar refuses to be treated like a gym membership. It's an unavoidable, productivity-enhancing machine that pushes marketers to publish better, faster, and more effectively. In this chapter, we're going to walk through the distinctive characteristics of a 10x calendar, what results you can expect when using one, and how to create one of your own.

WHAT IS A 10X CALENDAR?

To begin, let's define what you'll be building. A 10x calendar is a bad-ass editorial calendar fueled by 10x projects, absent of 10 percent work, and the master plan for all marketing activity. We'll quickly highlight each element.

Bad-Ass Editorial Calendar Fueled by 10x Projects

Editorial calendars have been used for decades by publishers. Traditionally, they've served a dual purpose. First, publications would make portions of their content available months ahead of time to attract advertisers. Second, they kept massive amounts of content and dozens of writers, editors, reporters, designers, printers, et al. on track to hit deadlines.

For our use, "deadlines" is the operative word. A 10x editorial calendar isn't filled with wishes or maybes; it's filled with hard deadlines. Projects and content ship when the calendar says they'll ship.

No questions. No exceptions. And each item on the calendar has a person responsible for completing it.

Next, these deadlines are mixed with the rocket fuel for growth: 10x projects. Your 10x editorial calendar, then, is your roadmap to creating and launching only the most high-impact, high-growth stuff your team is capable of producing. And the timelines are not leisurely strolls through the park. They're sprints across the content hacker's shortcuts. (More on this later.)

Absent of 10 Percent Work

Because the 10x calendar contains only 10x projects and content, it will be absent of 10 percent work. At this stage, you and your team have put in the work of generating, scoring, and prioritizing your 10x ideas. And because your prioritized 10x projects are what you'll be mapping onto your calendar, there is simply no room for the inconsequential stuff.

Even better, it will give you permission to say no to 10 percent stuff. In turn, busywork and low-yield activities simply won't make the cut—so, they won't show up on your calendar. This unleashes you and your team to focus relentlessly on growth-producing tasks. This is why 10x growth can (and will) be accomplished quickly.

Master Plan for All Marketing Activity

A 10x calendar is also central command for all of your marketing activities. It's the master plan that shows, at a glance, everything that's being created, posted, and published. In effect, it's your documented strategy laid out in a bird's-eye view.

It also removes the guesswork completely from the process. Everyone on your team will focus on what's important without even needing to think about it. And this will ensure your marketing activities are 10x across the board.

IS YOUR EDITORIAL CALENDAR 10X?

Now, what if you already have an editorial calendar? Maybe you don't suffer from an inconsistent publishing schedule and keep your content organized neatly into grids, rows, and columns. If this is the case, well done. But, let's put your calendar to the test and see if it's really driving the biggest results you're capable of producing.

Look at the last thirty days of content you've published and projects you've shipped. Scroll through your blog roll. Visit your Facebook page and Twitter feed. Take another look at your content upgrades, whitepapers, and email copy. After reviewing the work you've produced over the past month, can you honestly say it's the best work your team is capable of creating?

Were your pieces of content and shipped projects:

- Within your competition-free content niche?
- Aligned with your content core?
- Focused on 10x growth over 10 percent improvement?
- Successful at driving revenue or growing other key growth metrics?

If not, there's good news and bad news. The bad news is that you left revenue on the table by not creating the best, most tightly focused work you are capable of. But the good news is twice as awesome. One, you now have data to analyze. And two, this is the last thirty-day stretch where you'll ever ship less than the best you're capable of producing.

THE 90 PERCENT GOOD RULE

Notice I didn't say *perfect* work. I said *the best you're capable of producing*. There's something I call the "90 percent good" rule, and it'll help keep things in context. The reason the calendar works is because you're removing all the 10 percent work that's diluting your results. Creating 10x stuff isn't easy, but it's possible when you get your projects and content to 90 percent good.

Here's what I mean. You can get something to a nine out of ten really fast. But the last 10 percent—the distance between great and near-perfect—is where the real time, energy, and morale is sunk. What you'll find is that the last 10 percent takes as much time as the first 90 percent of the project. By removing the "perfection phase" of your process, you'll find your 10x opportunity.

"This is the last thirty-day stretch where you'll ever ship less than the best you're capable of producing."

I'm not simply coaching you to lower your standards, either. Actually, just the opposite is true. I'm calling you to raise them. When we built the Headline Analyzer (the 10x project I talked about in Chapter Five), we could have spent a year or more analyzing headlines. Instead of using a data set of one million, we could've studied two million. We could have gone deeper down the rabbit hole and added a dozen more metrics and insights.

But what would all of that time and effort have really produced for our company and for our customers? Essentially nothing. Why? Because the Headline Analyzer has the essential elements of the greatest headlines in history covered. It works quickly and as advertised. It also provides the right value to the right people using the right amount of our time and effort. This is the 90 percent good rule at work—and this is where your 10x opportunities lie. If we had delayed shipping for a larger sample size, we would have unnecessarily delayed the value we'd generated. Or, even worse, we may have never shipped at all! This is the peril of shooting for perfection.

Seth Godin describes it like this in his book *Poke the Box*:

Starting means you're going to finish. If it doesn't ship, you've failed . . . To merely start without finishing is just boasting, or stalling, or a waste of time. I have no patience at all for people who believe they are doing their best work but are hiding it from the market. If you don't ship, you actually haven't started anything at all. At some point, your work has to intersect with the market. At some point, you need feedback as to whether or not it worked. Otherwise, it's merely a hobby.

You can have the best ideas in the world—but if you haven't shipped, you haven't done anything.

In addition to this, give yourself permission to completely remove 10 percent activities. Perhaps it's an extra layer of approvals that don't need to be there? Maybe you shorten the writing time by 10 to 20 percent? Or perhaps you should strategically add some automation for social or email promotion to reduce the time it takes?

"You can have the best ideas in the world—but if you haven't shipped, you haven't done anything."

The key is to find the extra 10 percent of busywork that is preventing you from moving faster. If the *10x Marketing Formula* were only about one thing, it would be about learning to move faster. You will never reach perfection, so don't bother. Cut back 10 percent and hit publish.

Besides keeping useless projects off your calendar in the first place, this is the best way to de-10 percent your calendar.

SEPARATING STRATEGY AND EXECUTION

So, the next evolution of your team's ability to ship 10x projects quickly is realizing it's also forcing you to separate strategy from execution. What I often hear from marketers is they're so busy trying to keep all of their plates spinning that they don't have time for strategy. No matter how much they get done in a day, their task list somehow ends up longer. So, they get stuck in a cycle of shipping *anything* rather than *the right thing*.

I get it. It's tough to press pause when your boss is breathing down your neck. But that's exactly the problem the 10x calendar solves. It emphasizes both strategy and execution, and puts each in its rightful place. How? Because in just a couple of hours, you and your team have ideated 10x ideas, scored them, and then prioritized what to work on.

That's strategic work at its finest. After all, what is strategy if not prioritizing the best path to results? Now, you take these strategically prioritized projects and map them out onto your calendar. You set a date for when your project or content will ship, and then reverse engineer the work involved from there. In this way, you visually document what needs to happen, when it needs to happen, and who's responsible to make it happen.

(That sounds an awful lot like a documented strategy to me.)

Now, your 10x calendar guides your actions toward accomplishing your goals. And because you've done the strategic work, you can fully trust your calendar. This means it puts you full-on into execution mode. You can blindly follow it because you know you've eliminated the 10 percent crap from your to-do list. You'll know exactly what to do next and have confidence it'll be high impact.

"They get stuck in a cycle of shipping anything rather than the right thing."

Content creators are practitioners who usually jump into the execution phase too soon. But if you follow the formula and let strategy lead what makes the cut on your calendar, you'll have removed myriad roadblocks. The 10x calendar ensures you'll never stare at the dreaded blinking cursor again. Effective execution is dependent upon strategy. But strategizing doesn't need to take weeks or even full days. This means any marketer, no matter how busy, can put strategy and execution to work as a powerful one–two punch.

MAPPING OUT YOUR 10X PROJECTS

When you map out a project on your calendar, you're creating a marketing project timeline. This is simply a roadmap for all of the content within a single project, or campaign, over a specific period of time. The purpose of a marketing project timeline is to understand when to start working on a specific project so you can realistically set and achieve your deadlines.

This process also helps give you an overview of the work your entire marketing team will be putting in. This way, you can understand when people can execute specific phases of content development.

For efficient project mapping, we've developed a simple framework. It's about breaking down your project into phases of execution with detailed workflows. We'll take a deep dive into workflows in the next chapter. So, let's start by looking at how to take this phasic approach.

At a high level, the majority of content marketing projects will consist of the following phases: write, design, build, and promote. By breaking your projects up like this, you can map out when individual pieces of the project need to be completed. And the best part is that this maps out nicely onto a 10x calendar.

PLAN EACH PIECE OF CONTENT IN PHASES:

WRITE
DESIGN
BUILD
PROMOTE

Write

The first phase is all about creating the individual pieces of content that will make up your larger project. This means copy for landing pages, CTAs, blog posts, social media messages, email campaigns, and any other content required.

Design

The second phase is where visuals are created. This means everything from post headers to infographics to the user interface of a tool. Whatever you're creating, this is the phase where you brand it and design for maximum shareability.

Here's what CoSchedule's 10x calendar looks like for the week.

Build

The third phase involves writing the necessary code—or using software tools to build project components. This could mean coding pages yourself, building them with a subscription software service, or engineering a new software tool itself (if that's your project). Essentially, any component that needs to be built to present your designed content happens within this phase.

Promote

The fourth phase is as important as all of the others combined—which is why there are two chapters solely dedicated to it ahead. This phase is where you promote the heck out of the 10x project or content you've built. The 10x calendar is no place for an, "If you build it, they will come" mindset. Here, you promote, promote, promote.

For example, let's imagine the 10x project you're mapping out is an educational course. In this case, your team will need to create content similar to the following so the project successfully influences our marketing goals:

Launch brief and talking points: A short document to explain the goal, target audience, what the project is, and how you'll market the project. Keep this short. Anything more than a few bullet points, a KPI, a goal, and a timeline, and you've put yourself into the 10 percent category of no return.

Brand brief: Since you're creating multiple pieces, your designers may need a way to make sure the visual identity of the campaign is consistent.

Signup landing page: This is the page where you'll direct all promotional traffic.

Lesson pages: These are the actual course materials, and there will likely be multiple pages to create.

Lesson videos: Some courses may include visual content on every lesson page.

Lesson quizzes: True courses teach, so you may want to quiz or test your students on every lesson page.

Workshops: Most courses have some live action training that would include speaking points and a deck, like a webinar.
Certificates: You may consider creating certificates for the students

who pass all quizzes.

Facebook group: This provides a way for students to collaborate and build community around your brand.

Emails: You will promote the course to your email list. This will likely be more than one email to plan, write, and schedule.

Social media campaign: You will share the course with all of your social media followers.

Facebook ads: This is a way to reach a larger audience than those who already follow you.

Here's our calendar containing the above elements for a recent course launch. From email sequences to Facebook engagement to webinars, every piece is planned and grouped as a single marketing project.

In this example, you see how a large project breaks down into many pieces of content. You will do the same thing for your highest priority project. And when you organize each element into the four phases of execution, you can move quickly and in optimal coordination as a team.

DISCIPLINE, PERSEVERANCE, AND THINKING LIKE A STARTUP

After mapping out your project, it's time to execute. While this isn't easy work, it will be clear. You will know exactly what needs to be done, by whom, and by when. Ultimately, the point here is focus and discipline.

You've planned your work. Now, it's time to work your plan.

If you've made it this far in the *10x Marketing Formula*, you should understand that everything you do is colored by the startup mentality. And thinking like a startup is essential for this stage, as well.

Here's the reality. You can't quit when you're a startup—quitting is a bullshit option that's completely off the table. Perseverance through failure and hard work is key. It's also the right thing to do.

"You've planned your work. Now, it's time to work your plan."

Think about it like this. Startups raise money by casting a grand vision of what they will become and accomplish. And when they get the money, they have to do it. They're forced to flip the switch from planning and selling the vision to executing and getting results. Startups fail when they're adept at telling the big story to get investors' checks, but suck at actual growth. Simply put, it's not okay to accept someone's money and then fail to deliver.

That's obvious in the results-or-die! world of startups. But is it any less true for marketing teams, managers, employees, and their respective organizations? You've taken the paychecks. You've consumed the resources. You've enjoyed the benefits. They have invested in you to get results. They haven't poured money into you so that you can scheme up great ideas—they're counting on you to do the work!

Fortunately, a 10x Calendar is a tool for those serious about growth. And this next story will help prove that to you.

"THERE WAS NO WAY FOR ME TO FEEL LIKE I WAS ACTUALLY ON TOP OF THINGS; EVEN WHEN I WAS PUBLISHING ON TIME, I FELT LIKE I WAS ALWAYS BEHIND."

—PAT FLYNN,
SMART PASSIVE INCOME

10X MARKETING INTERVIEW:
PAT FLYNN AND THE $300,000 LAUNCH

Pat Flynn is the founder of Smart Passive Income and author of best-selling books like *Will it Fly?* and *Let Go*. He and his team are content marketing extraordinaires. So, I interviewed Pat to learn how he's gone from the blinking blog cursor to a well-oiled machine built on strategy.*

Pat's work helps thousands of business owners break free of paycheck-to-paycheck living. He and his SPI team publish actionable and ultra-transparent content on everything from building email lists to podcasting to his own monthly income reports. Just like he's helped people escape the paycheck-to-paycheck grind, his approach to creating and publishing content has helped his team transcend living blog post to blog post. Pat explains:

> *When I first started out, because I was doing it all on my own, I was creating content on the go. So, I'd publish a blog post, which I always hated, because the moment I hit publish, I knew that I would have to figure out what I was going to do for next week's post. I was so frustrated because I always felt behind. There was no way for me to feel like I was actually on top of things; even when I was publishing on time, I felt like I was always behind.*

For Pat, this all changed when he built a team to help him keep pace with, and even increase, his prolific output. Each new team member owned a part of the process that used to be Pat's. This meant the content scramble of publishing random things just to put something out was over. They transitioned to a system where every piece had a purpose as part of an integrated whole.

Pat says, "This helped me grow my email list, which helped my bottom line. And has helped me with productivity and efficiency. It helped spread the message . . . I only wish I had started sooner."

---

* You can listen to the full interview for free by visiting https://coschedule.com/10x-toolbox

Central to their team's productivity and profitability on the back of their great content is their editorial calendar. It has become a 10x workhorse for them by keeping everyone focused on the same goals and tasks. It's a visual roadmap outlining exactly when 10x projects will ship, and what needs to do between ideation and launch to make them happen. Here's what their results look like in action.

THE $300,000 "POWER-UP PODCASTING" LAUNCH

Pat has become well-known as an authority in the podcasting space. And with over 33 million downloads, he should be! In June 2017, Pat and his team launched their first public course, called Power-Up Podcasting. It teaches people everything they need to know to launch and market a podcast. Ahead of the launch, they put their editorial calendar to work.

You see, the SPI team plans content two quarters ahead of time. So when Q1 rolls around, they're already looking at content that will drop in Q3. Because the team is so organized with how their content will work together to accomplish their business goals, they planned a content sequence that focused on podcasting the month ahead of the course launch. They continually offer ways for Pat's audience to go deeper into the content core topics with content upgrades and deeper-level learning, like his PDF file, "The Podcast Cheat Sheet."

In Pat's words, "Each of those pieces of content showed people how to get started by giving them a good introduction to why podcasting was really important, and showed them how to actually go through the motions of getting one up and running. This allowed us to address every single objection that a person might have related to podcasting that would stop them from wanting to get started."

In turn, the entire month of content planned out on their calendar became a promotional accelerant for the new product launch. Because of the momentum of his podcasting content, the Power-Up Podcasting course became the next logical investment for tens of thousands of people. And when launch day came, Pat's team crushed it with over $300,000 in sales.

On the heels of this launch, it also opened up Pat's offer of a live, two-day workshop in San Diego, California, that even more were quick to jump on. And, as Pat says, "Podcasting was on everybody's mind because we planned ahead. We utilized the editorial calendar, and we hit a home run."

HOW CAN A 10X CALENDAR HELP GET 10X RESULTS?

For the SPI team, it's clear that their output of focused, intentional content has been the most important factor fueling growth. As an authority, Pat crushed it with podcasting because it was core to his competition-free content niche. He could do what few others can with the subject matter— and he'd built a massive audience beating down the door to buy his new course. Again, this is the lure of content marketing.

Stories like this are inspiring. It's easy to be buoyed by the idea that you can follow in Pat's footsteps and achieve 10x growth with your content. While this can happen, the question is, how can a 10x calendar help you achieve similar results?

WHY EVERY MANAGER NEEDS A 10X CALENDAR

The SPI team uses their 10x calendar to manage everything from content themes, to strategy, to pieces of content, to launch sequences, to their individual tasks. So, what does the calendar do for Pat as the manager of this marketing team?

"More than anything," Pat says, "it gives me comfort to know everything is happening. And it also is motivational, because I know that my team's working hard on these things and I see them being checked off as they go.

It makes me want to be sure I check off my stuff so I can uphold my responsibilities for the team, too. Because on our team, it's not just me telling everybody what to do. I have certain things that need to get done that my team relies on. For example, if I don't record that podcast episode when it's supposed to be recorded, then my team is held back a day, right?"

The 10x calendar gives managers a bird's-eye view of where every project is at. Are you ahead, behind, or right on track? Where this breaks away from simple project management is that progress lives in the same place as your content strategy itself. The 10x calendar is the ultimate version of truth. And in turn, it allows for peace of mind because you have a handle on precisely where every project is at.

It also sparks motivation by detailing real-time progress. With every task, the needle moves forward. But perhaps the most powerful benefit of all is the accountability it affords, for both a team to their manager, and a manager to his or her team. Just like Pat says, if someone fails to hit a deadline, everyone is impacted. This is especially important when you're working at the aggressive pace of a 10x marketer.

FAIL FAST

Just like Pat and the SPI team, when it comes to executing on your 10x projects, you must demand results of both yourself and your team. Anything less is not okay. And to produce results, you must keep pace with your calendar. But before you develop an ulcer from worrying, remember the rule of 90 percent good.

You're going to fail. A lot of the stuff you thought would work is going to flop. However, because you're moving quickly and pursuing results instead of perfection, you can learn and pivot. We embrace the motto "Fail fast."

Honestly, we've failed a lot more often than we've won. But that has made the wins all the sweeter. Startups are prepared for failure, and the best ones embrace it as part of their process. Marketing teams must assume the same mentality.

There's a quote from Leonard Rubino that encapsulates this perfectly: "Show me a person who doesn't make mistakes and I'll show you a person who doesn't do anything."

Too often, we let our fear of failure keep us from shipping something. We allow ourselves to push back deadlines and tinker with something longer than necessary. At CoSchedule, we're not immune from this fear, either.

Recently, we shipped the largest update to the product in our company's history. It was a complete rebuild, redesign, and reworking of our pricing, billing system, and many other integrated elements. It was a massive undertaking months in the making. And in CoSchedule time, a timeline of months is like years at most other places.

Every single product and engineering team had major roles to play and hard deadlines to meet. But do you know what happened when the time came to ship the project? Every team, without exception, asked for extensions. And I told everyone the same thing: "No."

"To put your 10x calendar to work, you need to trust your strategy and commit to your deadlines."

We shipped on time, even amidst worry. What happened? We lost no customers. We met an incredibly ambitious goal as a team. And we gained weeks of better pricing for our customers and thousands in revenue for our company.

This shows us something incredibly useful. Our teams didn't actually need more time—they needed to ship. Everything was 90 percent good, but they were thrashing as teams usually do when they get to the end. It was clawing and scratching to achieve the last 10 percent. But, because we had a KPI (ship on time), a goal (new billing system), and a definitive timeline, we had no excuses. And it worked. Sure, there were some bugs we had to fix the next week, but nothing major. In retrospect, considering it was the biggest change we'd ever made since launching CoSchedule itself, the issues were relative non-events.

To put your 10x calendar to work, you need to trust your strategy and commit to your deadlines. It's not a magic bullet. Just like a gym membership alone, it doesn't do the work. That's up to you. But it does ensure you're doing the right work in the right amount of time. Your 10x calendar will become your number-one productivity tool when you follow the framework laid out in this chapter. And when fear of failure crops up, kick it to the curb and ship anyway.

To those who persevere go the results.

Your 10x Toolbox
Put this chapter into action with your 10x Toolbox by visiting https://coschedule.com/10x-toolbox

Template: 10x Calendar
This is a simple editorial calendar template for you to map out your 10x projects.

10x Marketing Interview: Pat Flynn and the $300,000 Launch
Pat Flynn and I talk about how he and his team at Smart Passive Income used their 10x calendar to power an online course launch that resulted in $300,000 of revenue. You will have access to the full audio interview plus transcript.

CHAPTER SEVEN

10X WORKFLOWS

I'll never forget the night of November 2, 2016—and neither will my kids. As a lifelong Chicago Cubs fan, I won't forget it, because that was the night they won their first World Series championship in over a century. And my three kids won't forget it because I let them stay up to watch the entire game (on a school night, no less). The Cubs won 8–7 over the Cleveland Indians, and did so in epic fashion. They clinched the game in the tenth inning after a rain delay and an Indians rally. So, they may have also seen me get more than a little excited.

Of course, team manager Joe Maddon is the hero who led the Cubs storming out of their 108-year drought to win the World Series in 2016. And even outside of my undying love for the Cubs, his coaching philosophy is genius in its simplicity. He explains that you win games "through the relentless execution of fundamentals and technique."[*]

In Major League Baseball, there are 162 regular season games. To win the World Series means your team will play nearly 200 games. That's thousands of swings, throws, slides, catches, and (hopefully) runs scored.

[*] http://www.chicagotribune.com/sports/baseball/cubs/ct-joe-maddon-stresses-repetition-20150526-story.html

And to Coach Maddon, that's thousands of opportunities to beat your opponent, one inning at a time.

MONEYBALL MARKETING

Ultimately, home runs and grand slams don't win championships. Flashy plays might make highlight reels, but it's the consistent execution of fundamentals that brings home the Commissioner's Trophy. So, it's no wonder that Game 7 was won on a string of two-base hits and a double, not a high-stakes homer. The 2011 film, *Moneyball*, is a great example of this.

The movie tells the true story of the 1990s Oakland Athletics, a small-market team with a garbage stadium. They had no money, dismal attendance, no star players, and slim prospects of winning anytime soon.

Facing this reality, the Oakland A's front office realized there was only one way to fill the stadium: by winning games. But how would they win against big-time teams like the New York Yankees and their nine-figure budgets? The team's managers began to look past the prime-time sluggers and dug into the stats. And simple as it sounds, they realized to win games, you need to score runs. But to score runs, you need to get on base. The more players that got on base, the more points they'd rack up.

"10x ideas are only as good as your ability to relentlessly execute them."

So, they started buying players with the highest on-base percentages. In a sport that valued the home run above anything else, they were undervalued, which meant the A's could scoop them up with the few nickels they had in the bank. As they did, something strange happened . . . The Oakland Athletics started to win. And while their base hits didn't make any SportsCenter highlight reels—they did lead them to set the record for the fifth-longest winning streak in MLB history.

The authors of *The 4 Disciplines Of Execution* describe the team's success like this:

> *The Oakland management team reframed the game by acting on the lead measures that produce wins. Through hard research, sifting through endless statistics to get at the key factors that produced runs, they discovered high-leverage lead measures no one had noticed before.* [*]

The authors explain that lead measures are factors that predict success toward a goal and are influenceable along the way.[†] For the A's, they doubled-down on base hits. Coach Maddon's Cubs relentlessly focused on executing fundamentals. And for us, 10x marketers will embrace disciplined workflows that finish the right tasks, at the right time, in the right ways, and with the right amount of effort.

The reason for this is simple: *10x ideas are only as good as your ability to relentlessly execute them.*

Can your team methodically complete the tasks that need to be done—and do so on aggressive deadlines? Can you amass dozens of base hits each week? If you can, you'll win championships while your competitors are sitting in the dugout wondering how you produce so much, so fast. The secret is really no secret at all. It's by designing lean, repeatable processes called 10x marketing workflows.[‡]

DEFINE YOUR 10X WORKFLOWS

Your 10x workflows will embody three characteristics. They will: be pre-approved, be lean, and include high standards of performance. Because they're pre-approved, they will reduce rework and needless hangups getting the green light from your boss. Because they're lean, they will include only

---

[*] McChesney, Chris, Sean Covey, and Jim Huling. *The 4 Disciplines of Execution: Achieving Your Wildly Important Goals.* New York: Free Press, 2016. 57–58.
[†] *Ibid. 59*
[‡] To download the free 10x Marketing Workflows Blog Post Template, visit https://coschedule.com/10x-toolbox

the essential tasks while being clearly and efficiently organized. And lastly, because they include a high standard of performance, quality won't suffer even though you're able to execute quickly.

When you create your workflows according to the following steps, you will be able to showcase a smartly organized process that will streamline productivity and get consistent results. You'll decrease the friction added by post-work approval processes because you will also limit the number of people involved. The fewer people weighing in on every detail, the faster work ships.

Just like the Oakland A's, your workflows will produce base hit after base hit. Your score will rise steadily inning after inning. Through the relentless execution of the fundamentals, what used to take you seven weeks—or even seven months—can now take just seven days.

STEP ONE: GET YOUR 10X WORKFLOWS PRE-APPROVED

To start, imagine this scenario Nathan Ellering, CoSchedule's head of demand generation, found himself in at a former corporate job. He was the manager of their in-house marketing team and invested heavily in content—or, at least he tried to. One of Nathan's main channels was the company blog, which ran on a daily publishing schedule.

This can be a grueling frequency for any marketer to keep up. However, difficulty was compounded by a messy workflow that looked like this:

1. Get post idea from a subject matter expert (SME)
2. Assign post to one of the writers
3. Receive draft from writer
4. Submit draft to SME for review
5. Address SME's notes and revise
6. Re-submit to SME for approval
7. Receive approval from SME

_____

1. GET POST IDEA FROM A SUBJECT MATTER EXPERT (SME)

2. ASSIGN POST TO ONE OF THE WRITERS

3. RECEIVE DRAFT FROM WRITER

4. SUBMIT DRAFT TO SME FOR REVIEW

5. ADDRESS SME'S NOTES AND REVISE

6. RE-SUBMIT TO SME FOR APPROVAL

7. RECEIVE APPROVAL FROM SME

8. SUBMIT SME-APPROVED DRAFT TO THE VICE PRESIDENT OF MARKETING FOR HIS REVIEW

9. RECEIVE APPROVAL (OR REVISIONS) FROM VP

10. IF REVISIONS, EDIT DRAFT AGAIN AND RE-SUBMIT TO VP

11. IF NO REVISIONS, SUBMIT TO DESIGN

12. PUBLISH POST

8. Submit SME-approved draft to the vice president of marketing for his review
9. Receive approval (or revisions) from VP
10. If revisions, edit draft again and re-submit to VP
11. If no revisions, submit to design
12. Publish post

That's twelve steps involving five people, four levels of bureaucracy, and three layers of approval for each blog post. This meant approvals accounted for 58.3 percent of the total process. That's a lot of approving going on for one blog post.

This anecdote is a prime example of a broken, 10 percent workflow. Instead of being created with a bias toward shipping, testing, and getting results, it was bloated with unnecessary approvals solely in place as a check-your-ass measure. This bureaucratic process existed because one time, someone did something wrong—and this cascaded into wrapping an entire process around failure avoidance. Unnecessary approvals are a poison pill to culture, and become huge obstacles to getting the marketing results you were hired to achieve.

If approval-laden processes like the one above sound familiar to you, good news is coming your way: 10x workflows solve this problem immediately. Nathan worked to restructure and fix this process in the same way Step One works. The key to streamlining is to reframe expectations. Instead of completing work and then submitting it for approval when completed, you will organize and gain approval on your workflows. Here's the process:

1. Create the 10x workflow.
2. Approve the 10x workflow.
3. Work the 10x workflow.

You will approve the workflow rather than making approval part of the workflow. When approval is part of the process, it becomes the enemy of shipping work quickly. Once you pass things up the ladder, approval will take forever. And you'll be buried in small, 10 percent tweaks because everyone who has a hand in the pie-making process wants to ensure their thumbprints are visible. After all, who wants to submit something to their boss—or their boss's boss—without looking like they've done some work?

"You will approve the workflow rather than making approval part of the workflow."

If you get your workflows pre-approved, you'll ship faster. In turn, you'll get to 10x results in a fraction of the time. To create your 10x workflows, understand that the simplest approach is the best place to start. Your goal will be to pare down each workflow into its essential components. This process will do exactly that if you follow it closely.

STEP TWO: MAKE YOUR 10X WORKFLOWS AS LEAN AS POSSIBLE

Recall the four phases of execution from last chapter: write, design, build, and promote. Now, you're going to deconstruct each phase into clear tasks you can delegate to your team. Use the following framework to define a workflow for a single piece of content. You'll repeat the process for each content type you've chosen to execute within your projects.

Write Down Every Task That Needs to Be Done

Map the flow chart of the complete content creation process without omitting a single task. At this point, you're looking to understand everything you'd typically do to publish a specific piece of content.

Former Intel CEO and chairman Andrew S. Grove writes in his book High Output Management that in order to boost efficiencies in your workflow, you need to understand your existing process:

You first need to create a flowchart of the production process as it exists. Every single step must be shown on it; no step should be omitted in order to pretty things up on paper.

So, write everything down without exception.

For example, let's say my team needs to create a workflow for the landing page planned as part of the educational course. They'll need to do everything from building the page to writing the "What's In It For Me?" points so the reader knows exactly what they'll get and why they should care. So, this workflow might look something like this to begin with:

Write down *every* step in your workflow in chronological order.

- [ ] Confirm it's a 10x idea
- [ ] Approve idea
- [ ] Find keywords
- [ ] Define angle
- [ ] Write WIIFM and outline
- [ ] Write 20-30 headlines
- [ ] Peer review outline
- [ ] Write landing page
- [ ] Proof read landing page
- [ ] Optimize for search engines
- [ ] Approve landing page writing
- [ ] Write social messages
- [ ] Write Facebook ads
- [ ] Write blog post
- [ ] Design landing page wireframe
- [ ] Design landing page header graphic
- [ ] Design landing page body content graphics
- [ ] Design social media graphics
- [ ] Design Facebook ads
- [ ] Design blog post header graphic
- [ ] Design blog post body graphics
- [ ] Approve landing page wireframe
- [ ] Approve landing page header graphic
- [ ] Approve landing page body content graphics
- [ ] Approve social media graphics
- [ ] Approve Facebook ads
- [ ] Approve blog post header graphic
- [ ] Approve blog post body graphics
- [ ] Code landing page
- [ ] Insert graphics into landing page
- [ ] Insert graphics into social helpers
- [ ] Schedule social template
- [ ] Schedule landing page to publish
- [ ] Email audience

Big, little, and everything in between, write down every task in your process as it exists today.

Remove Unnecessary Tasks from Your List

Grove continues in *High Output Management*:

Second, count the number of steps in the flow chart so that you know how many you started with. Third, set a rough target for reduction of the number of steps. In the first round of simplification, our experience shows that you can reasonably expect a 30 to 50 percent reduction.

To implement the actual simplification, you must question why each step is performed. Typically, you will find that many steps exist in your workflow for no good reason. Often they are there by tradition or because formal procedure ordains it, and nothing practical requires their inclusion.

To summarize, you will reduce the number of tasks in your current process that:

1. *Are actually part of other workflows.* These are tasks that likely complement different content, and therefore don't need to be managed as part of the workflow you're creating at this moment.

2. *Are no longer necessary.* For example, sometimes tasks exist in new workflows to serve as reminders, but after time, your team learns the process so well that these reminders aren't needed.

3. *Exist because of unnecessary approval processes or office bureaucracy.* Create the workflow, approve the workflow, work the workflow. Eliminate lengthy back-and-forth approvals by planning your work, then working your plan.

For our landing page example, we set a task reduction target of 20 tasks (and actually found 21 opportunities to remove):

Remove unnecessary steps from your workflow.
- [ ] Confirm it's a 10x idea
- [ ] Approve idea
- [ ] Find keywords
- [ ] Define angle
- [ ] Write WIIFM and outline
- [ ] Write 20-30 headlines
- [ ] Peer review outline
- [ ] Write landing page
- [ ] Proof read landing page
- [ ] Optimize for search engines
- [ ] Approve landing page writing
- [ ] Write social messages
- [ ] Write Facebook ads
- [ ] Write blog post
- [ ] Design landing page wireframe
- [ ] Design landing page header graphic
- [ ] Design landing page body content graphics
- [ ] Design social media graphics
- [ ] Design Facebook ads
- [ ] Design blog post header graphic
- [ ] Design blog post body graphics
- [ ] Approve landing page wireframe
- [ ] Approve landing page header graphic
- [ ] Approve landing page body content graphics
- [ ] Approve social media graphics
- [ ] Approve Facebook ads
- [ ] Approve blog post header graphic
- [ ] Approve blog post body graphics
- [ ] Code landing page
- [ ] Insert graphics into landing page
- [ ] Insert graphics into social helpers
- [ ] Schedule social template
- [ ] Schedule landing page to publish
- [ ] Email audience

In this example, we whittled out 62 percent of our workload by strategically removing tasks that:

1. Are part of other workflows,
2. Don't need to be completed, or
3. Exist for unnecessary approval processes.

For your workflows, target a specific number of tasks to remove from your process, then review your existing workflow and identify those productivity improvement opportunities.

Combine Similar Tasks

There are probably opportunities to batch tasks that happen in conjunction with each other. This exercise will increase your team members' productivity by helping them knock out all of the similar tasks in one fell swoop.

To continue the landing page example, this is what the final consolidated workflow looks like:

Consolidate your tasks.
- [ ] Find keywords
- [ ] Define angle
- [ ] Write WIIFM and outline
- [ ] Write 20-30 headlines + body + proof read
- [ ] Optimize for search engines
- [ ] Design landing page wireframe + graphics
- [ ] Code landing page + insert content
- [ ] Schedule landing page to publish

We consolidated eight tasks into three, bringing the total down from 43 to eight:

- *3 into 1: Write headlines + body + proofread*
- *3 into 1: Design landing page wireframe + graphics*
- *2 into 1: Code landing page + insert content*

Here, you will wield the power of batching similar tasks together. In turn, this increases team member productivity by paring down the workload and enhancing focus. However, not only will your team be more productive, they'll be able to move faster than ever. Speed is the result of productivity, and that is what we are after.

As 10x marketers, we are looking to do more with less. If every blog post we publish helps us grow our email list, why not try to find a way to publish twice as much? Or at a minimum, keep the same publishing schedule and ship additional 10x projects? Content hacking, 90 percent good, and the 10x calendar are each dependent on you not only getting things done, but doing them so fast your competitors freak.

As you increase your output, 10x workflows will also serve to reduce switching costs. This matters because not only does frequent task switching crunch productivity by 40 percent, but it also increases errors.* Efficiency is both performing work quickly and doing work well the first time. Thus, you avoid rework.

According to a 2005 study in the construction industry, rework can add between 7.25 and 12 percent to the direct cost of an entire project.† Even if you don't have high overhead costs, your team's time is still worth a great deal—not to mention the project deadlines put at risk. In all, lean workflows will compound their value each time they're performed.

In addition, ensure your tasks are written with a definition of what "done" looks like. This final point of clarity removes ambiguity, reduces back-and-forth, and lets your team know exactly when they're finished. For example, rather than "Write headline and post," the task is labeled, "Write 20–30 headlines + body + proofread." Now the person executing the task understands exactly what the finished product of the task will look like.

---

* https://www.psychologytoday.com/blog/brain-wise/201209/the-true-cost-multi-tasking
† http://xlcatlin.com/-/media/fff/pdfs/const_whitepaper_cost-of-rework_xl_june2013.pdf

Assign Responsibility For Each Task

Now, you already know at a high level which team members need to be involved in specific phases of content development. At this point, you're looking for the names of those who will execute specific tasks.

In general, it's best practice to assign one task to a single team member. The moment you assign a single task to more than one person is the moment each of those people think someone else is completing the work. Accountability works best when targeted at a specific team member.

This is who will complete the work for CoSchedule's landing page example:

Choose who will complete each specific task within your workflow.
- [ ] Find keywords (Ben Sailer, blog manager)
- [ ] Define angle (Emma Tupa, conversion copywriter)
- [ ] Write WIIFM and outline (Emma Tupa, conversion copywriter)
- [ ] Write 20-30 headlines + body + proof read (Emma Tupa, conversion copywriter)
- [ ] Optimize for search engines (Ben Sailer, blog manager)
- [ ] Design landing page wireframe + graphics (Megan Otto, web development designer)
- [ ] Code landing page + insert content (Megan Otto, web development designer)
- [ ] Schedule landing page to publish (Megan Otto, web development designer)

Choose who will complete each task within your workflow.

Determine When Each Task Should Be Done

Generally speaking, most marketers run their content through the process, and once it is done, schedule it for publish. The problem is this leaves a lot of room for thrashing during that all-too-common 10 percent push. Instead, adopting the content hacker mindset means picking a drop-dead publish date and working backward. Then, execute against that timeline and repeat for every post going forward.

This will mean a transition to thinking about task due dates in terms of *number of days before publish*. Begin by defining the due date for the last task in your workflow. This way, you know exactly when the entire piece of content will be 100 percent complete.

From there, work backward up the list, assigning due dates to the second-to-last task, third-to-last, and so forth. When you're done, you'll know exactly when the first task on your list needs to be complete. Armed with this knowledge, you can start working through the piece with an aggressive timeline to complete the work by your drop-dead publish date (forcing the 90 percent good rule into action).

This is what the exercise looks like when applied to CoSchedule's landing page example:

Determine how many days before publish each task must be completed.
- Find keywords (Ben Sailer, blog manager)
  - 18 days before publish
- Define angle (Emma Tupa, conversion copywriter)
  - 17 days before publish
- Write WIIFM and outline (Emma Tupa, conversion copywriter)
  - 17 days before publish
- Write 20-30 headlines + body + proof read (Emma Tupa, conversion copywriter)
  - 15 days before publish
- Optimize for search engines (Ben Sailer, blog manager)
  - 14 days before publish
- Design landing page wireframe + graphics (Megan Otto, web development designer)
  - 7 days before publish
- Code landing page + insert content (Megan Otto, web development designer)
  - 2 days before publish
- Schedule landing page to publish (Megan Otto, web development designer)
  - 1 day before publish

For each task for which you create a 10x workflow, you'll notice an immediate bump in efficiency. And the fun part is, this is possible because you're eliminating redundancies and streamlining necessities. Now, who doesn't love doing less work and getting better results?

The goal here is for your team to produce more than ever before. This will happen because of the sweet synergy that happens when 10x workflows are combined with a 10x calendar. Your team will publish more focused content on a regular basis, giving you measurable results.

Estimate How Long Each Task Should Take

Next, we have a small, yet important step. Take a moment to set a limit on how long each task should take. When you do this, your team will understand the level of effort and time they should invest into each task. And, you're able to understand how long the entire workflow should take to accomplish.

> Determine how long each task should take.
> ☐ Find keywords (Ben Sailer, blog manager) [30 minutes]
>   • 18 days before publish
> ☐ Define angle (Emma Tupa, Conversion copywriter) [15 minutes]
>   • 17 days before publish
> ☐ Write WIIFM and outline (Emma Tupa, Conversion copywriter) [60 minutes]
>   • 17 days before publish

These time limits remind me of a phrase used in agile software development regarding scope. Frequently, we will say a portion of a feature is "out of scope" when we are discussing a new development project. This means that before we start building anything, we make a decision about how much time we are willing to dedicate to the feature. The length of the timeline is based on the value the feature will provide the business.

So, if a feature will be only mildly useful to our customers, we may only budget one week for development. This means that our engineers will need to properly scope that feature to fit the timeline. Of course, we will forgo many "nice to have" elements by default, but the reality is that those things were unlikely to result in more value to the business, as we'd already measured the value in terms of one week.

The point is that time limits prevent thrashing, encourage shipping, and enforce the 90 percent good mentality. When you decide 10 percent projects don't matter, you need tight timelines to keep both yourself and your team in check. With this process, your team will immediately know when they are out of scope.

STEP THREE: BAKE A STANDARD OF PERFORMANCE DIRECTLY INTO YOUR 10X WORKFLOWS

Finally, your workflows will be complete with a standard of performance to guide your team. A standard of performance is exactly what it sounds like. It's the quality and expected outcome of each workflow. This matters because it's a key facet of getting your workflow pre-approved.

The goal is for workflows to produce agreed-upon results. At CoSchedule, the standard of performance for each piece of content we publish is as follows:

1. *Content Core:* The topic must be aligned with our content core.
2. *Keyword Driven:* The content must be keyword driven for maximum traffic and long-term search performance.
3. *Well Researched:* Our content is thoroughly researched so it contains zero fluff and provides facts rather than opinions.
4. *Comprehensive and actionable:* The content will cover absolutely everything pertinent for our audience to know: what to do, how to do it, and how to get the results we promise.
5. *Content upgrade:* Every piece of content will have a custom content upgrade that will help our audience do what we're teaching them to do that they can access in exchange for their email address.
6. *Single, Clear CTA:* Finally, every piece of content includes a single, clear, and compelling call-to-action—the content has a job to do, and the CTA is how we close the deal.

Marketers create content to produce results. Content is never the end goal; growth is. When you create your standard of performance, every person involved will understand the *results* your content (or any workflow you create) is executed to achieve.

In the next chapter, we're going to go deeper into our standards of performance for content. But it's paramount that whatever work you and your team are doing, you understand the results you're supposed to achieve.

WHY ARE WORKFLOWS 10X?

The *10x Marketing Formula* is about moving fast and lean like a startup. So, you may be asking yourself, "Why is defining workflows according to this process *10x* work, rather than *10 percent*?" This is a fair question. Especially since we've dispatched with over-documented marketing plans.

The core of 10x marketing doesn't equal haphazard and disorganized activity. Sometimes, this is the perception of the startup culture ethos. However, the *10x Marketing Formula* is firmly rooted in this premise: people work faster, better, and more consistently by creating repeatable processes that consistently produce big results on a dime. This is all about focus and discipline.

In many ways, it's similar to the 10x ideas brainstorming process. There is a time for strategy, and a time for creation. There is also a time to develop process strategy—affectionately dubbed 10x workflows. And by compartmentalizing these processes, you can create an efficient, 10x producing machine.

Just like Coach Maddon and his Cubs, and Billy Beane and his Oakland A's. The relentless execution of the fundamentals, getting base hit after base hit, wins ball games. And more importantly, it wins championships, too. So, when you approach crafting your 10x workflows, just envision the Cubs' epic Game 7 World Series win. It was a 10x moment, and the same moments are waiting for you.

Your 10x Toolbox

Put this chapter into action with your 10x Toolbox by visiting https://coschedule.com/10x-toolbox

Sample: 10x Blog Post Workflow
This is a sample of our 10x Blog Post Workflow. Combine the process laid out in this chapter with the real-world example of what it looks like.

CHAPTER EIGHT

10X CONTENT

In 1920, an American psychologist named Edward Thorndike published a study describing the way commanding military officers rated their soldiers. In his research, the officers were asked to rate their subordinates on four traits without having spoken to them.* The traits were: intelligence, physique, leadership, and character. What he reported was surprising.

He found the taller, more attractive soldiers were rated as more intelligent and better soldiers than those who were shorter, and less attractive. From this and other evidence he concluded that people generalize based upon one positive trait, especially related to their first impression. In this case, the tall and handsome soldiers made a positive first impression based upon their appearance. The commanding officers then extrapolated from that first impression, extending a favorable view of the soldier across the other traits: intelligence, physique, leadership, and character.

He described this as the "halo effect."

Twenty-five years later, in 1946, psychologist Solomon Asch observed a similar phenomenon. Asch found that people's first impressions were

---

* https://www.britannica.com/topic/halo-effect

given more weight and power than subsequent impressions. In his study, "When positive traits were presented first, the participants rated the person more favourably; when the order was changed to introduce the negative traits first, the same person was rated less favourably."*

THE HALO EFFECT IN PRACTICE

The impact of the halo effect extends well beyond military and scientific studies. Two consultants, Melvin Scorcher and James Brant, wrote in *Harvard Business Review* in 2002:†

> *In our experience, CEOs, presidents, executive VPs and other top-level people often fall into the trap of making decisions about candidates based on lopsided or distorted information ... Frequently they fall prey to the halo effect: overvaluing certain attributes while undervaluing others.*

And if we travel further downstream, we see the halo effect manifest itself in marketing, as well. For example, car companies will "roll out what they call a halo vehicle, a particular model with special features that helps to sell all the other models in the range."‡ For Audi, this was the $180,000 R8 V-10 Spyder, described as a convertible that "can scrape 90 mph in second gear."§

This psychological principle is hardwired in humans, no matter the context. So, when it comes to content marketing, your first impression matters. But not in the way we often think. As a 10x marketer, your first impression isn't simply about spelling-error free content or other superficialities—it's about creating the best damn content on the internet.

* *Ibid.*

† Scorcher, M. and Brant, J., "Are You Picking the Right Leaders?", Harvard Business Review, February 2002

‡ http://www.economist.com/node/14299211

§ http://www.popularmechanics.com/cars/a8075/what-good-is-a-halo-car-anyway-12206624/

To capitalize on the halo effect, you *need* to create content so good it makes everyone else look like they didn't even try. But I'm not simply giving you a tip about "quality content" like you've heard so many times before. What I'm really talking about is writing, recording, and designing something so good it's the only resource someone needs to read, watch, or look at for a given topic. They don't need to hop around, bouncing from one site to the next. Instead, they found you and now they're set.

At CoSchedule, we treat every piece of content like it's our homepage. In our minds, we have 800 homepages that *must* add more value than any other content on a given topic. Both search engine and social media traffic have a lot to do with this.

Marketers love to think of their websites in linear terms, as if their audience's journey starts on the homepage and then continues, following their intended progression. This isn't true. The reality is that search and social will likely generate the bulk of the traffic to your site. And that means the first (and maybe last) interaction many will have with your brand will happen on your blog.

For proof, consider our year-to-date traffic breakdown, from January 1, 2017, through November 30, 2017:

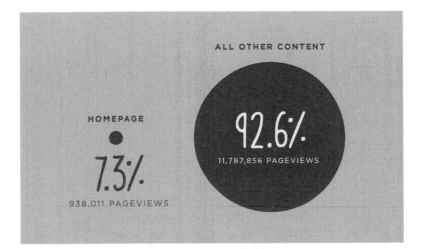

ALL OTHER CONTENT

92.6%
11,787,856 PAGEVIEWS

HOMEPAGE

7.3%
938,011 PAGEVIEWS

While we certainly have pages on our website, like our pricing and signup pages, the lion's share of the traffic is generated by our blog content. Have you ever run the numbers on your site? If not, I suggest you do. Because if your numbers follow ours (which I would wager they do) you'd better make a damn good impression with your content. And quickly!

When our content proves ten times more valuable than anyone else's, our audience will automatically grant the rest of our company— including our product—that same level of awesome. This is so important because users don't follow the prescribed funnel from homepage to blog content. Search and social media will generally send traffic straight to individual pieces of content rather than your homepage. That means, the first (and maybe last) interaction many people will have with your brand happens on your blog. So, you'd better make a damn good impression— and quick!

So far in this book, we've stressed the importance of moving fast. Now, we'll add to the formula a system of ensuring you *always* produce insanely high-quality work. We'll pop the content creation process under the microscope from three different angles to map out how to create the best stuff there is while maintaining an aggressive shipping schedule. To do this, we'll break down how you can use 10x content to leverage the halo effect, build trust and influence with your audience by adding obscene amounts of value, and create content that produces results.

CREATING YOUR 10X CONTENT SCORECARD

To start, 10x content is stuff so vastly superior to everything else on a given topic it renders any other pieces irrelevant. To continue our metaphor, it's ten times better than anything currently produced on the topic. And because you're creating stuff squarely within your content core, it will produce results proportional to its quality.

Last chapter, we briefly touched upon the quality we expect from our content at CoSchedule. However, we're certainly not alone in having high standards of performance. Author, blogger, and speaker Jeff Goins consistently produces some of the best stuff on the net about how to write professionally, blog better, and grow your audience. And content marketing is the key aspect of his overall marketing strategy. One of the big moments for his content marketing evolution was developing a content scorecard.*

The content scorecard is a tool Jeff and his team actually developed by accident. But, it still proved transformational for Jeff's blog, Goins, Writer. The story goes that while Jeff was writing a book, he was also trying to build his team and business. As part of this process, that emerging team took a critical look at their content. Some pieces performed exceptionally, achieving a 150 percent bump over their average daily traffic and trending toward double, or even triple, the comments.

As they evaluated the pieces, one of his team members identified four threads woven through each of the majorly successful content pieces. This led them to identify four questions against which they evaluated their content before it was published. These questions are:

1. Do you open with a promise?
2. Do you close with delivering upon that promise?
3. Are you following an internal style guide?
4. Is there so much value people would pay for it?

The scorecard itself is really simple. You get a point for each question. And if you get all four points, you get a perfect score. The idea is to nail a 4.0 GPA. They were not aiming for perfect content, either. But if a piece of content satisfied all four, it was ready to publish. If it didn't, they wouldn't ship it.

The divide in content that hit each mark versus the pieces that even hit three out of four was profound. If a piece hit three of the marks, it would receive about a 30 percent read-through rate. However, if a piece was a four out of four, it would be read at 80 percent or above.

* You can listen to the full interview for free by visiting https://coschedule.com/10x-toolbox

I love this evaluation method because it's so dang simple. It's four questions (easy to remember) and a totally simple scoring method. No one could screw this up! Frameworks like this may sound overly simplistic, but the problem is that most of us read stuff like this and move on. You can't do that today; not if you want 10x results.

"If you simply become one of the few that write it down, you can stand out from the crowd."

We all say we aim to produce high-quality content, yet few of us actually write down what that means. If you simply become one of the few that write it down, you can stand out from the crowd. You need a way to execute higher quality, competition-free content, without having to go past the 90 percent good mark. All of this works together and is an absolute must.

ANALYZING CONTENT

Like Jeff, we analyzed our content to trace the patterns of which content drove results and which didn't. To do this, we looked at the last fifty blog posts we'd published. At the time, unique pageviews was the 10x metric we were optimizing for. So, out of those fifty posts, we read the top ten with the highest unique pageviews, and then read the bottom ten with the lowest unique pageviews.

As we did, it became quickly evident what qualities were reflected in these top performers. Because we compared them to each other, we found the qualities present in the best performers. And notably, those same qualities were either absent or underdeveloped in the ones that performed poorly. So, we planned posts based on these ideas, and they performed better than ever.

By developing our standards of performance based on data, rather than gut feelings, we consistently created high-performing content. This happened because we did the analysis and disciplined ourselves to stick to the standards. We decided we shouldn't publish something unless it was the best content in its category on the whole damn internet.

HOW TO CREATE THE BEST CONTENT ON ANY TOPIC ON THE INTERNET

So, how do we evaluate this? And more importantly, how can you do the same? The beauty is that it simply comes down to a disciplined process—as we outlined in Chapter Seven, 10x Workflows. But here are the five pillars for a quick refresher on how we create 10x Content.

HOW TO CREATE THE BEST CONTENT
ON ANY TOPIC ON THE INTERNET

☐ FIND THE KEYWORDS

☐ READ TOP 10 PAGES THAT RANK

☐ NOTE COMMONALITIES

☐ NOTE WHAT THEY'RE MISSING

☐ DRAFT COMPREHENSIVE OUTLINE

Find the Keywords

Every piece of content we create is driven by strategic keyword research. This is because we want to optimize our content so our audience can find each piece when they need it most. However, our team goes further down the rabbit hole of search engine optimization (SEO). We begin with a content core topic, then use tools like Moz (http://moz.com) and Ahrefs (http://ahrefs.com) to find a primary keyword, or longtail phrase, for it. We then outline three to five semantically related terms, which are simply terms closely related to your main keyword for which your content can also rank. Think of them as secondary keywords or phrases people may also search for when looking for content like the piece you're publishing.

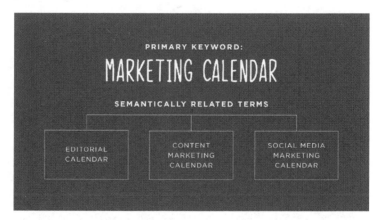

You can find related terms with the keyword research tools I listed above. There is also an ever-evolving host of other tools to do the job. The bottom line is that your content can rank for way more than one keyword or phrase. And that's where semantically related terms come in. They amplify your content in search results for the long haul.

Read Top 10 Pages That Rank

Next, we search Google using our exact primary keyword. Then, we read, watch, or listen to every single piece ranking on page one. This means we study the top ten performing pieces.

Note Commonalities

As we study these pieces, we note the commonalities they share. This means we look at things like:

- Content length
- Content structure
- Custom graphics and visuals
- Social media engagement by platform
- Content upgrades
- Actionability and comprehensiveness
- Tone of voice
- Number of comments
- Unique angles covered
- Point of view and controversy
- Data and research used

Note What They're Missing

This careful survey then allows us to note what the top-ranking pieces are missing. This is a vital step so we can create competition-free content. We don't want to waste time talking about the same angles in the same ways as everyone else. That's a red ocean; we want to swim in the blue ocean. With this step, here are a handful of things we can define:

Seek out a unique angle no one has talked about.
This is a perfect place to not only find competition-free content, but also to assert a contrary perspective. Controversy is attractive and interesting. So, if we disagree with someone, we'll say so, and then prove precisely why our experience and data support our point of view.

Find ways to be more actionable.
This often means going beyond tips and into the territory of showing people exactly how to do what we're talking about. When you do similar research, you'll often find thin content that tells people what to do, but not how to do it. This is a fantastic way to set your content apart.

Identify gaps in visuals and graphics.

With even a quick pass, you can see how graphically intense your competition is. Are they just using the low-hanging fruit of a stock photo as a header graphic? Or have they invested in custom design, infographics, videos, GIFs, or other visual content? This helps our content creators and designers determine how to go beyond the top-ranking pieces.

Draft a comprehensive outline.

Last, we take all of the research we've gathered and focus it into a comprehensive outline. This outline defines five things:

1. The opening hook, along with two or three complementary CoSchedule pieces we're going to link to.
2. The content upgrade that will increase value, add actionability, and therefore be worthy of an email or trial signup.
3. The body content with subheads that include the main keyword and related terms, as well as custom images to be designed.
4. The supporting data and research we will use to prove our assertions.
5. The next step, or action, we will call our audience to take.

In all, this process ensures we create the best damn content on the internet every single time. It takes work—but it's worth it. Here's the deal. If it feels easy, it's not competition-free content. Why? Because it's been done before. These five pillars of content creation ensure we nail our content core and create competition-free content.

"ALL OF A SUDDEN YOU HAVE THE CONTENT THAT EVERYONE WANTS TO TALK ABOUT (AND LINK TO)."

—BRIAN DEAN,
BACKLINKO

10X MARKETING INTERVIEW:
BRIAN DEAN AND THE SKYSCRAPER TECHNIQUE

As you can see, research plays a huge role in our content process. In fact, it's crucial to shipping 10x content every single week. But, you probably still have some questions. For instance, where should your ideas come from? If you've never had content produce big results for you, how do you figure out what has the greatest likelihood of short-circuiting the growth loop?

Whether you've experienced content marketing success or not, here's a simple, three-step hack that will work. It works so well, in fact, it's part of our own workflow. It's called the "Skyscraper Technique," and was developed by Brian Dean of Backlinko.* Brian is a noted SEO authority and has used the technique to more than double his website traffic in less than two weeks after first putting it together.

I interviewed Brian about the technique and how it applies to creating content. He named it the Skyscraper Technique because creating 10x the value of the competition is fundamentally what it's about.† He describes it this way:

"Have you ever walked by a really tall building and said to yourself, 'Wow, that's amazing! I wonder how big the 8th tallest building in the world is.' Of course not. It's human nature to be attracted to the best. And what you're doing here is finding the tallest "skyscraper" in your space . . . and slapping 20 stories to the top of it. All of a sudden YOU have the content that everyone wants to talk about (and link to)."

It's a technique that will help you blow everything else on a given topic out of the water. And the best part is, it's dead simple. To do this, you follow three steps:

1. Find a keyword for which you want to rank on the first page of Google.

* https://backlinko.com/skyscraper-technique
† You can listen to the full interview for free by visiting https://coschedule.com/10x-toolbox

2. Analyze what content currently ranks in the top 10 positions on Google.

3. Create content that's 10x better than what's already on the first page.

Let's look at each step to put it to work in your 10x content.

STEP ONE: KEYWORD RESEARCH

In Step One, you're really doing search engine optimization (SEO) work. You're finding the content core, competition-free topics you want to own in search. And even though the SEO landscape shifts continuously, the Skyscraper Technique focuses on this changeless factor: search will always begin with a keyword. Whether it's someone typing a phrase into a browser or using a voice search on their phone, this will necessarily hold true.

The goal of SEO research is obviously to find keywords your target customer is searching for. Overall, as Brian explains, keyword research that uncovers the intent behind people's searches is 75 percent of the game. To begin, brainstorm topics your target customer would search for when looking for information. Your keywords, or phrases, will fall into one of two categories: commercial keywords and informational keywords.

Commercial Keywords

Commercial keywords are the things your potential customers are searching for with credit card in hand. They're looking for a solution, and it's time to buy. For your company, these keywords will be closely tied to whatever you sell. However, they are often limited and highly competitive.

Informational Keywords

Second, there is a broader set of keywords called informational keywords. Researching these keywords is more nuanced. You must ask,

"What are my customers searching for when they're not shopping for my product or service?" Then, list out all of the different topics they are searching for.

You can do this through customer conversations or even research on sites like Quora and Reddit. These keywords should be related to what you sell, but they don't have to be exact. For instance, if you were selling weight loss plans, your customer base is likely looking for things like workout routines and exercise equipment, as well. A perfect way to think about these things is as content core topics.

There are plenty of keyword research tools available to you, as well. There are too many to list or name here. But remember, if you can put a tool to work for you to save time *and* get better results, do it. A little research into the right SEO tools for you can go a long way.

STEP TWO: ANALYZE WHAT'S RANKING NOW

After your research, it's time to analyze your competition. Simply read, watch, or consume every single piece of content that's currently ranking on the first page of Google for your chosen keyword. One of the mistakes Brian said he made early on was assuming if he created enough content, someday he would get more traffic from Google than everyone else—sort of like whoever has the biggest pile of content wins the game. However, he quickly realized that path was futile. After all, every piece of content is in competition with hundreds of articles —including the ten top dogs on page one. It's a red ocean out there! So, if you create something that's even the tenth best on the internet, you're still not going to appear on page one of Google! It's not a volume game; it's a value game.

STEP THREE: 10X THE COMPETITION IN THE FACE

Last, it's time to create content that's ten times better than the landscape you've just surveyed. One of the first articles Brian created using the

Skyscraper Technique was about the roughly 200 ranking factors Google's algorithm used to rank web pages at the time. He knew the keyword phrase "Google ranking algorithm" was one he needed to own to become a leader in the SEO field.

So, he analyzed and read every top-ranking article for the keyword. And what he realized was that none of the articles had all of the ranking factors in one place. They may have had 50 percent of them—but not all. It was time to create his own piece of 10x content that added 20 levels plus a penthouse suite on top of the content skyscraper.

"It's not a volume game; it's a value game."

Brian created his content to be a one-stop shop for the topic. He made it as comprehensive as possible by curating every single published ranking factor. His resulting article provides an incredible experience for visitors. Because now, instead of having to track down the factors and cobble them all together themselves, they had it all right there in Brian's article.

There are endless ways to create content that's 10x better than the competition's. In this case, it was sheer comprehensiveness. Brian relates that he's also had success in 10x-ing design with detailed graphics, data-rich charts, infographics, companion videos, and real-life case studies. This is a great opportunity to put a content scorecard to work, as well. Because, as Brian noted, "A common misstep is to overrate your own content, and underrate what's already on the first page." In the same way parents generally think their kids are the smartest and prettiest, our own content appears leagues better if we wear rose-colored glasses rather than look reality in the face.

Additionally, even if your content is better, it's truly a matter of degrees. Think about your content like a product. If you launch a new and improved product, but it's only 5 percent better than current solutions, it won't be enough to galvanize people into switching teams and buying from you. Your content is the same way. You must create something that is 10 times better—the 10x principle at work. You must blow the existing content out of the water with comprehensiveness, actionability, design, and value.

THE ANATOMY OF 10X CONTENT

The reason we're putting such an emphasis on how to create 10x content is because everything you create has a job to do. It must have utility for your company and your audience. Over the years, we've had a variety of ultra-successful content pieces. We've also published a bunch of duds. To bring creating 10x content in for a landing, I'll drill further into our content standards of performance.

The most successful content we've published has exemplified eight unique characteristics that now guide all of our content production:

Topic

The topic is always aligned with our content core. It needs to be well chosen to help both our intended audience and our company. This means it directly intersects with the value our product adds *and* with our audience's needs. No parallel topics allowed.

Keyword

Next, this is where the Skyscraper Technique shines. It makes sense to help our audience find our content when they need it most, even if it's long after we've published it, right? And this is another place the Skyscraper Technique shines. Search engine optimization helps us make the most of our investment into content creation for the long haul. It also connects what we want to say to the words our audience uses to describe their challenges. This helps us create content optimized for search engines, consumption, and application.

Research

Data, examples, and experience fuel 10x content. And each helps us make sure the angle we target is backed up with facts while proving our advice will produce big results after practical application. One of our most successful articles ever is entitled "What 20 Studies Say About The Best Times To Post On Social Media." It clocks in at roughly 5,500 words, contains dozens of custom images and infographics, and goes über deep into the science behind social media posting. And just like the title suggests, it presents findings from twenty different studies to prove what we're talking about.

Actionability

In our content, we never simply sprinkle a few bites of free advice people will struggle to put to work for them. Instead, we publish work that includes research-fueled advice coupled with actionable, step-by-step guidance, deep attention to detail, and a path to execution. The audience should be able to do exactly what we're talking about if they follow the process we provide.

Content upgrade

Closely related to actionability is our use of content upgrades. They help people put our teaching to work. But they also exist to attract potential customers to use CoSchedule as their marketing calendar. So, we optimize everything to convert traffic into email subscribers who will continue to get this awesome, actionable content from us while also giving us the opportunity to share more information about the tool we offer that helps organize the chaos of content marketing.

Single CTA

To the end of content serving a business use, everything we do includes a single, clear call to action. We aren't trying to get our audience to do three or four different things on a page. We want them to do one thing, and we make that one action abundantly clear.

VISUAL BREAKS

1. SHORT PARAGRAPHS THAT ARE RARELY MORE THAN THREE SENTENCES

2. CALLOUTS FOR QUOTES AND TAKEAWAY STATEMENTS

3. LOTS OF BULLETED AND NUMBERED LISTS

4. CLICK-TO-TWEET PLUGIN SO OUR AUDIENCE CAN SHARE IMPACT STATEMENTS WITH A SIMPLE CLICK

5. SUBHEADS TO GUIDE THE READER THROUGH THE CONTENT

Whether it's to sign up for our email list or trial our product, every piece of content has a clear next step for our audience to take.

We'll devote an entire chapter to CTAs and conversion psychology. But it's important to mention here, because revenue-generating action is the purpose of 10x content.

Graphics

Design has been a mainstay of our making our content competition-free from the beginning. We invest heavily in custom graphics in all our content, from blog posts to podcasts to webinars. As an example, we design between five and seven custom graphics for each piece. And, we design custom images for every social network, as well. High-caliber design immediately sets your content apart while also providing an opportunity to be useful to your audience. Visuals help reinforce and illustrate key concepts in our content.

Structure

The web is different from printed media. Blogs aren't books, and microsites aren't magazines. So, you need to write differently for the web compared to other media. Our content uses a structure that employs frequent visual breaks:

- We use short paragraphs that are rarely more than three sentences long.
- We use callouts for quotes and takeaway statements.
- We use lots of bulleted and numbered lists.
- We use the Click-to-Tweet plugin so our audience can share impact statements with a simple click or tap.*
- And finally, we organize our content well with subheads to guide the reader through the content.

---

* You can find the Click To Tweet WordPress plugin free by visiting https://wordpress.org/plugins/click-to-tweet-by-todaymade/

Structure, though seemingly simplistic, is a vital part of the user experience. This is especially true for people reading our content on mobile devices. These best practices ensure a seamless experience on any screen.

HOW TO USE A CONTENT SCORECARD

Let's look at an example of our content scorecard in action. We'll apply it to one of our most popular posts of 2017, written by Nathan Ellering, "How To Promote Your Blog With 107 Content Promotion Tactics." The piece is exactly what it sounds like, an explanation of 107 ways to promote blog content to gain more traffic. Now, let's examine the piece against our content scorecard.

This blog post met every benchmark of our content scorecard. So, how did it perform? In its first thirty days alone, it generated 23,358 pageviews and 21 trial signups. In the following six months, it scored nearly 150,000 pageviews, and is ranked solidly in the number one position on Google for its keyword. In fact, it's even captured the coveted "Featured Snippet," which Google explains this way:

> *When a user asks a question in Google Search, we might show a search result in a special featured snippet block at the top of the search results page. This featured snippet block includes a summary of the answer, extracted from a webpage, plus a link to the page, the page title and URL.*

---

* According to Ahrefs: "Traffic potential shows how much organic search traffic you can possibly get if you rank #1 for the Parent Topic keyword. We estimate this traffic potential by looking at the organic search traffic of the current #1 ranking result for that Parent topic keyword."

† According to Ahrefs: "Keyword Difficulty is an estimate of how hard it would be to rank in Top 10 Google search results for a given keyword. It is measured on a non-linear scale from 1 to 100 (low difficulty to high difficulty)."

CONTENT SCORECARD

MEASURE	SCORE ✓
TOPIC *Is this content core?*	✓ Yes. CoSchedule has robust content promotion features intrinsic to our unique value proposition.
KEYWORD *Is this content optimized for a keyword we want to rank for that also has substantive traffic potential and an attainable ranking difficulty?*	✓ Yes. This piece ranks for the long-tail term "how to promote your blog" that has a global search volume of 3,000 searches per month and a 45 ranking difficulty.
RESEARCH *Is this content data rich, with all points supported by trustworthy evidence?*	✓ Yes. Every tip includes data, either original or from a trusted study, to back up its claims.
ACTIONABILITY *Is this content comprehensive enough that our audience can do what we're teaching them without going elsewhere?*	✓ Yes. Every tip explains how to put its information into action.
CONTENT UPGRADE *Does this content include a valuable content upgrade that enhances and enables actionability?*	✓ Yes. The content upgrade is a checklist for our audience to use in their own blog post promotion.

MEASURE	SCORE ✓

SINGLE CTA OR CTV?

Does this content include a focused call-to-action (CTA) or call-to-value (CTV)?

✓ Yes. This piece uses a CTV that compels readers to download the content upgrade and get more traffic to their blog via the promo tactics explained.

GRAPHICS

Have we designed 5–7 custom graphics to complement this content, enhance understanding, and increase social shareability on all networks?

✓ Yes. This post includes over twenty custom graphics, including shareable infographics optimized for social, as well as over forty additional screenshots of data and examples.

STRUCTURE

Is this content created according to the medium's best structural practices for all devices?

✓ Yes. This piece uses excellent structural hierarchy. It's easy to consume and navigate, and even includes a custom, section-by-section menu that allows readers to jump straight to the most pertinent section with just a click or tap.

FINAL SCORE   **100%**

How To Promote Your Blog With Social Media

1. Share your content in many places. ...
2. Include your blog link in your social media profiles. ...
3. Rock the power of 100 rule. ...
4. Clean up your open graph data. ...
5. Share your blog posts on social media right when you publish them. ...
6. Share your brand new posts more than once.

More items...

How To Promote Your Blog With 107 Content Promotion Tactics
https://coschedule.com/blog/how-to-promote-your-blog/

Google search for term "how to promote your blog."

CREATING YOUR OWN CONTENT SCORECARD

Both Jeff Goins's content scorecard and ours at CoSchedule have proven invaluable. By holding your content to a high standard, you can also identify likely performance gaps before you publish. So, what about your content? Do you have a content scorecard that drives what you publish?

If not, now's the time to create one. Or heck, you can even swipe Jeff's or ours!† Remember, statistically, your content is the functional homepage for your website. So, if your site is going to produce real business results, your content needs to meet the standards of performance to which you'd hold any other marketing effort. To create your own scorecard, start simply, and use this basic framework of questions:

- What is our content's goal?
- What characteristics are present in the content we've published that has accomplished this goal?
- Is the topic within our content core?

---

* We will discuss CTAs and CTVs at length in Chapter 13, "Conversion Psychology." But for context, a CTA compels your audience to take an immediate action, such as, "Sign Up Free Now—No Credit Card Required." A CTV compels your audience to enter the next stage of your marketing funnel by inviting them to value, such as, "Get More Traffic To Your Blog Posts Within 7 Days."

† Download the 10x Content Scorecard Template for free by visiting https://coschedule.com/10x-toolbox

Now, your content scorecard can certainly expand and evolve. However, make it as easy as possible to focus your work on the goal of your content. If your aim is traffic, ensure your benchmarks are fine-tuned for generating it. If it's email subscribers, you'd better have something valuable to exchange for your audience's email address. And down the line it goes.

Creating a content scorecard isn't enough, though. It also requires discipline to stick to it. Saying, "No, we won't publish this piece until it meets our criteria," is a big step. But you, and your team, must commit yourselves to the practice if it's going to work. As with every part of the *10x Marketing Formula*, the magic happens when you put it into practice. It's on you to make it happen. But when you do, you'll see results.

THIS IS YOUR SHOT

This chapter could be summarized like this: create every piece of content with the assumption that it's your only shot at publishing the best piece of content ever produced on that topic. This will mandate well-researched 10x content that performs in line with your scorecard. It means creating stuff that wows your audience, to capitalize on the halo effect, thus bestowing love on every new page visited, and even your product itself.

Every piece of content you create is your one shot to get results with your website. So, the primary question to ask when you start, and right before you publish, is this: "Will this content turn readers into customers by taking the next step in the process?"

Action is the measure of success—and creating a content scorecard is the place to begin.

Your 10x Toolbox

Put this chapter into action with your 10x Toolbox by visiting https://coschedule.com/10x-toolbox

10x Marketing Interview: Jeff Goins and the Content Scorecard
In this interview, author and speaker Jeff Goins explains how his team developed the content scorecard—a tool he says transformed their results. You will have access to the full audio interview plus transcript.

Template: 10x Content Scorecard
This template helps you score your content before it's ever published. It's a dead simple way for ensuring consistent quality and measuring potential impact before a piece is published.

10x Marketing Interview:
Brian Dean and the Skyscraper Technique
SEO expert Brian Dean and I discuss his "Skyscraper Technique." It's a brilliant method for creating the best content on a given topic. You will have access to the full audio interview plus transcript.

Checklist: The Skyscraper Technique Checklist
This is a checklist for using Brian's "Skyscraper Technique" for content research and creation.

Free Tool: Headline Analyzer
The Headline Analyzer is a free tool that will help you write headlines that drive traffic, shares, and search results. It is available absolutely free at https://coschedule.com/headline-analyzer

CHAPTER NINE

10X TEAM

Startups are a funny thing. You scheme up an idea, and then convince people to give you millions of dollars to pursue it. And all of this when everyone in the room knows the pitch is laden with assumptions and your strategy is rooted in best guesses.

This same problems exist with marketing plans. Piles of assumptions are amassed about what will work, how their audience will respond, and more. Yet, marketers tend to operate as if they've nailed it. They write and execute the marketing plan. But even if they are best in class, it's still based on a bunch of guesses.

Here's the deal: You suck at guessing. Your team sucks at guessing. I suck at guessing. We all suck at guessing. The good news is that the goal of a 10x team isn't to get better at guessing. Rather, it's to embrace the guess as just that, a guess; 10x teams know they guess, and therefore they know that they need to adapt.

In short, 10x teams embrace a process that acknowledges guessing, embraces failure, thrives on learning, and consistently pursues the best results over activity.

WHEN WORKING YOUR PLAN DOESN'T WORK

Launching rockets into space is a great analogy for 10x marketing teams. The job is tough to do. It is rocket science, after all. In 2006, Elon Musk and SpaceX launched their maiden rocket—and it failed after just thirty-three seconds in the air.* In 2016, a rocket exploded before it even left the launchpad. And from this failure alone, it's estimated the company lost $260 million—and NASA lost $115 million in cargo the rocket was scheduled to deliver.† Yet, the company keeps on launching. And NASA keeps on shipping cargo with them.

"Your team sucks at guessing. I suck at guessing. We all suck at guessing."

SpaceX embraces the potential—and the reality—of failure. They're not scared of it. They don't try to run or hide from it. Instead, they learn everything they can from it. This attitude is obvious in Musk's responses to failures:

Tweet after a failed Falcon 9 landing attempt

* https://timeline.com/spacex-musk-rocket-failures-c22975218fbe
† https://www.recode.net/2017/5/28/15695080/spacex-falcon-9-rocket-launch-successful

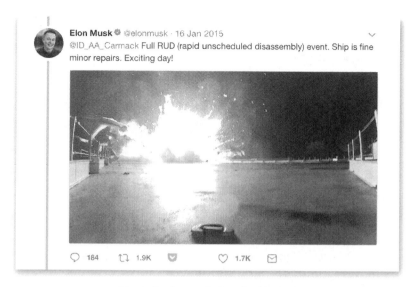

Tweet after fiery crash aboard a ship at sea

What's his definition of an exciting day? Learning something valuable. And even their video entitled "How *Not* To Land An Orbital Rocket Booster" is a montage of failed mission attempts.

How many crashes should Musk have tolerated? Where was the financial kill switch in dollars lost? The answer isn't a number—it's a mission. They were founded to "revolutionize space technology, with the ultimate goal of enabling people to live on other planets."* So, until we're walking on Mars, they're not done.

In many ways, Musk and SpaceX carry on the ethos NASA has cultivated. When the Columbia space shuttle tragically disintegrated mid-flight in February 2003, it seemed an irredeemable failure. However, NASA astronaut Dr. Charles Camarda believes the tragedy gives current and future engineers a motto to live by: "Where there is failure, there is knowledge and understanding that doesn't come with success."†

If you haven't failed, you haven't tried hard enough. This isn't some masochistic impulse. Neither is it an irresponsible sprint through a field of landmines. In reality, it's a calculated mindset adopted in preference over the standard *modus operandi.*

TWO PATHS DIVERGED IN THE MARKETPLACE

Let's illustrate the divergent mindsets of the 10x marketing team with those still hanging onto their marketing plans. Imagine a company has a new product line they're rolling out. So, the marketing team gears up to make a splash and get cash flowing around the fresh products. We'll look at two approaches taken by two different teams.

Team A: The Marketing Plan Team

Team A kicks into gear immediately. They call a meeting and get to work building out their marketing plan. The document grows steadily, section after section being written and codified. Once drafted, the plan hits the stakeholders' desks. They are greeted by the comforting Executive Summary, offering a high-level view of

---

* http://www.spacex.com/about
† https://www.nasa.gov/offices/nesc/press/070221.html

the strategy and a nicely penned mission statement tagged on for good measure.

They quickly thumb through thirty more pages, seeing section titles like "Environmental Analysis," "Competitive Forces," "Economic Forces," "Legal and Regulatory Forces," and "Marketing Implementation." It's peppered with charts, graphs, and bullet points. All the work will be done "on time and on budget."

This looks good to the stakeholders. No need to read the entire thing. After all, it's thorough and demonstrates the ability to think long term.

"Will the marketing plan work? Not sure. But we'll find out twelve months from now."

However, what goes unnoticed is that no campaigns begin, no projects ship, and no content is published for more than ninety days. Instead, extensive analysis will be performed. And at the end of this quarter-long window, reports are turned in to the managers and stakeholders. Then, ninety days after that, a customer satisfaction survey ships for all current clients—overseen by the marketing director, of course.

Thus, Team A is six months in before anything even goes out the door according to the plan that's been written over the past two weeks. The same plan drafted without something as simple as speaking to existing customers. The plan that's packed with unread words that were labored over by an already busy team.

Will the marketing plan work? Not sure. But we'll find out twelve months from now.

Team B: The 10x Marketing Team

Now, let's compare them with Team B. They, too, begin immediately. They work just as hard as Team A. They're not separated by level of effort or intelligence. Rather than a primarily planning team, they are primarily a learning team. So, they start with a question rather than a plan: "What can we do to grow our new product sales by 10x over the next ninety days?"

Then, the ideas start pouring in. They're weighed as 10x or 10 percent. They're measured in terms of time frame of execution. And at the end, the 10x projects are prioritized. Team B quickly decides to sit in on sales calls and send a qualitative survey to pick up customer language. This will help them check the assumptions they're making against reality, and will take one week, zero dollars, and limited effort.

Team B isn't concerned with pleasing the stakeholders with an elaborate plan that has a contingency for anything that might have a whiff of failure. They're concerned with learning what will work to increase sales, and what won't, as quickly as possible. Results are their North Star.

Then, they continue to build projects, ship them, measure results, and learn. All activity is mapped out and driven by their 10x calendar so they know exactly what they're creating:

- Two blog posts per week
- One Level Two project in the next month
- Two Level Three projects over the course of the next quarter

Along the way, they realize many of their educated guesses and projections were off, because they didn't know their main competitor was launching a competing product just four weeks into their plan. Fortunately, they were able to make a few small adjustments in their messaging. They were also able to see that their messaging was out of sync with the phrasing their customers were using. They adjusted accordingly.

Every week, their messaging is tighter. Traffic is increasing. And they're generating leads for the sales team to nurture. However, every week they're also shipping content and projects that absolutely biff it. Some ideas they were certain would work are blowing up in a fireball and cascading, SpaceX-style, into the ocean. Yet, they do find tests that strike a chord—they're getting traction, and following the results.

Understand, this isn't simply because they're better than Team A. It's because they're willing to risk failure by assuming a bias for activity rather than crafting an elaborate yet largely unread plan.

Now, make your prediction: Who's going to hit their goal? If your livelihood and last $100 were on the line, which team would you pick?

"They're willing to risk failure by assuming a bias for activity rather than crafting an elaborate yet largely unread plan."

Sure, Team A might make it, but you would likely starve to death long before you ever found out.

A 10X TEAM IS A LEARNING TEAM

Ready for an interesting piece of context? I didn't simply dream up Team A's plan. I copied it from a marketing plan found in the appendix of a marketing textbook.* This is the entrenched mindset. It's the way things are done. But it's not the way 10x marketers live, breathe, and work.

Again, this is why startups are such a perfect model for us. The best entrepreneurs are the ones who say, "Eff the consequences. I know this is *going to work*, because I'm going to *make it work*." And the best marketing teams must assume the same mentality. Like a scrappy startup, their job is to take the house money and get results.

Teams like SpaceX are remarkable not just for their ingenuity and brilliance. They're remarkable for their response and adaptation to

---

* https://college.cengage.com/business/pride/foundations/2e/resources/pf_found_sample_mkt_plan.pdf

failure. This trait is portable for the best marketing teams, as well, and it illustrates an important lesson.

It's not failing that's important; it's the willingness to fail so you can learn. What's crucial is overcoming the fear of failure in favor of action, of shipping, of testing. However, this doesn't mean learning teams gloss over their failures and label them as inconsequential. Failure sucks. But learning is worth more than never failing. A 10x marketing team is a learning team, not one willing to execute blindly on a plan they've guessed on. It's a team willing to fail, learn, and adapt what they're doing to get better and faster. And when you do fail, ask yourself and your team these questions:

- What happened?
- Why did this happen?
- What are we learning from this?
- How can we get this project back on track?
- How would we do it differently?

Before you breeze through these questions too quickly, it's worth noting the question that's *not* on the list: "How do we prevent this from happening in the future?" How many times have you heard that one? Probably too many to count. After failure, most teams make a beeline right for that question. They try to prevent failure rather than learn from it. But a mission of failure prevention is where bureaucracy comes from. It happens when unnecessary layers of process are dropped into place to prevent failure.

"Failure is requisite for innovation."

This isn't how 10x teams react. We learn from failure rather than try to avoid it. We embrace it as part of the brambly shortcut to growth. The truth is, failure is requisite for innovation.

CREATIVITY AND INNOVATION FROM FAILURE

What does the word innovation mean to you? Too often we think of it as some sort of magical lightning bolt that strikes randomly, delivering brilliant ideas. But, just like storks don't actually deliver babies on doorsteps, innovation doesn't mystically appear via random flashes.

So, I sigh when I hear of great companies like Apple or Pixar referred to as simply "innovative." While they certainly are, this label only tells a fraction of the story. The genius of Pixar and Apple doesn't lie in their "innovative thinking." Rather, it comes from their commitment to the actual, failure-fraught process of creativity.

"Creativity is a learned skill."

In his book *Creativity, Inc.*, Pixar co-founder Ed Catmull (with Steve Jobs and John Lasseter), outlines how the legendary animation studio has made innovation a habit. In many ways, Catmull unlocks the creative process; and it is something that we 10x teams can use to do better work. This includes our content marketing.

He explains how inspiration works. When you look at something great, like the iPhone or the first *Toy Story* movie, you can't help but feel like it was the result of some sort of divine inspiration—but it wasn't.

As Catmull describes, creativity isn't about an idea or a sudden burst of information. It is a process, and often a messy one. It is nonetheless, a process. Creativity is a learned skill. Innovation is the result of learning how to use this skill. And this is why learning teams work better than planning teams. They embrace the idea that creativity can be learned, and that innovation follows when we learn to see things differently.

CREATIVITY IS A PROCESS

Catmull is known for saying that, early in their lives, Pixar films aren't all that magical. In fact, some of them are downright terrible. In his book, Catmull describes their films as "ugly babies" in the beginning:

*"Having seen and enjoyed Pixar movies, many people assume that they popped into the world already striking, resonant, and meaningful—fully grown, if you will. In fact, getting them to that point involved months, if not years, of work. If you sat down and watched the early reels of any of our films, the ugliness would be painfully clear."**

This view is usually the exact opposite of what we expect. When we watch a Pixar movie, we see a great film with a great story. It is easy to label it as "innovative" and "creative" without realizing the painstaking process of transforming something from not so great into something truly world class.

We see the end, but we never see the beginning, or the years that it took to make one of their films. And often, we don't make room for this in our own creative process, either. We expect things to be great from the start—but that isn't how innovation works.

The iPhone is another great example. When we think about it, we imagine the sleek, polished product it is today. Normally, we don't think about the hundreds of versions that came before the one in our pockets. I'm not talking about the iPhone 1, either. I'm talking about the ugly smartphone babies that came prior to that. The versions that Apple never even showed us, like the rumored click wheel iPhone that never was.

Apple is frequently heralded as one of the most creative and innovative companies of all time, but I wonder what we would think if they had revealed some of these early versions to us. Would we respect their creative process, or would we question their label as a true innovator?

Innovation is a process, not something that wakes us up at night in a moment of inspiration. Removing this misconception from our minds can help us understand and experience true creativity. This means that in order for us to make our content and our marketing more creative, we need to continually create our "most recent worst version." By this I mean that with every iteration, our content should slowly get better. The truth

---

* Catmull, Ed. "Creativity, Inc.: Overcoming the Unseen Forces That Stand in the Way of True Inspiration" (p. 131). Random House Publishing Group. Kindle Edition.

is that it will never be our best. And it certainly won't be perfect. It will simply be our "most recent worst version."

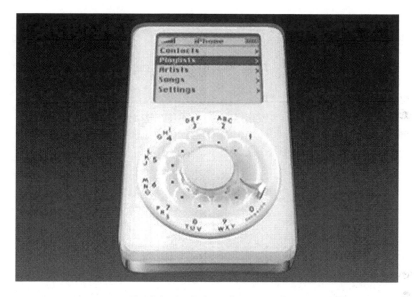

The click-wheel iPhone that never was

In the case of Pixar, that's what we see at the box office; but it may have only come after thousands of prior worst versions. The one we see is simply the most recent. It just so happens that it is usually pretty darn spectacular. Innovation is a process that is developed over time—and 10x marketing teams embrace this.

So, what sets Pixar and Apple apart from every other company is not their ideas. Their ideas are no better than anyone else's. Instead, it's the process their teams use to arrive at and execute those ideas. Just like SpaceX, they have mastered the process of iteration: improving an early idea and making it something unique, valuable, and worthwhile. They continue to evolve and adapt.

Perfection was never their end goal. And if you want to build and cultivate a 10x marketing team, it shouldn't be yours, either. Instead, you should aim for sprint-by-sprint improvement. Plus, I've got some great news for you: perfection is impossible to achieve anyway. So, you and your team can stop trying.

10X MARKETING INTERVIEW: ANDREA FRYREAR ON "WHAT IS AN AGILE MARKETING TEAM?"

To embrace this mindset, 10x teams need to act less like traditional marketers and more like agile software developers. Now, you've probably never been encouraged to behave like an engineer in order to be more creative. But Andrea Fryrear, founder of Marketing Sherpas, helps marketers across the globe do just that by applying agile methodologies in their work. In a recent interview on our podcast, she did a great job clarifying how marketers can appropriate and apply agile methods.*

To start, she dispelled a common misconception. Agile marketing is not simply doing things faster. It isn't permission to change your mind all the time and sprint without a plan. Instead, it's actually using principles and approaches originally developed for the world of software and then applying them in a marketing context. In reality, it's rigorous and requires discipline to execute.

It employs small, low-risk experiments to move fast, learn quickly, and discern what works and what doesn't. Then, you can build on things that are successful and leave things that aren't successful behind you. The elegance of such a steady cadence is that it also has a team-centric focus. After all, the people doing the work usually have the best ideas about how to make things better and communicate clearly with the audience. So, getting the boots on the ground involved sooner, rather than simply kicking projects down from the top, will result in better end products—and they'll make it happen faster, too.

* You can listen to the full interview for free by visiting https://coschedule.com/10x-toolbox

THE SCRUM APPROACH

Scrum is the most popular approach to agile. It involves time boxes, or sprints, lasting anywhere from one to four weeks. A team then commits to achieving X amount of work within their sprint time frame. Ideally, they are then left alone to execute against only that work. At the end of the sprint, they release the work, review it together, and find ways to make it better next time. So it's about a continuous cycle of releasing new work. It's not simply a focus on speed; it's a focus on steady production, shipping, and results.

What this does is shrink the feedback loop. Applied in a marketing context, it means that there are no more campaigns lasting three months where you have no idea how they're working. Rather than drawn-out campaigns that leave you blind to results for ninety days, you track results in real time with strategic tests and analysis.

This is precisely what scrum is designed to do.

WATERFALL VS. AGILE

Waterfall is an alternate method of project management that organizes projects into a sequential process. Picture a waterfall cascading over a terrace-like rock formation. It flows from high to low, one step at a time. From the outset, waterfall methodology is a fixed sequence. One step is completed at a time. For most of us, this is the normal process of project management—or at least what we think of first. We make a grand master plan and work on it task by task. Then, the project is complete once we've checked off 100 percent of the steps.

The disturbance in the waterfall, however, is that it assumes you know everything up front. Therefore, it calls for crafting beautifully precise and detailed plans that are supposed to hold true until a project or campaign is finished. If this were really how things worked, that'd be spectacular! It would work well and pay dividends along the way. However, in marketing we seldom (if ever) know everything from the outset. The landscape changes irrespective of our plans and forecasts.

Reality is no respecter of tidy spreadsheets, and circumstances often shift dramatically between project kickoff and launch.

"When you make a really big guess, and then get it wrong, it turns into a really big mess."

The agile approach differs in both mindset and method. Rather than assuming a static environment, it assumes factors will change. So, rather than planning a big project in rote sequence, agile marketers plan a bit of work, execute it in a short time frame, and evaluate the results. Then, they repeat this process continually. This allows for adaptation to the volatility and uncertainty of day-to-day marketing.

Really, the difference between these two approaches is guessing up front versus testing in real time. And as Andrea says, "When you make a really big guess, and then get it wrong, it turns into a really big mess." That sounds an awful lot like marketing plan teams to me.

FIVE WAYS AGILE MARKETING HELPS PRODUCE RESULTS

So, what will adopting agile methodologies actually look like, and where should you start? There are five main benefits you can expect:

1. *Goal Setting:* Growth from accomplishing 10x goals
2. *Daily Scrums:* Fluid communication through daily touchpoints and understanding real-time progress
3. *Continuous Shipping:* Rapid results from continuous publishing and project launching
4. *Self-Organizing Team:* Increased ownership of projects by everyone on your team
5. *Retros:* Embracing reality and learning quickly by analyzing your results consistently via a simple framework

To start, we'll dissect each of those benefits and connect them with the agile activities to put into place. The goal of this section is to help marketing teams shape a new way of working.

ONE: GOAL SETTING WITH USER STORIES

First, you will set goals at the beginning of each sprint, which is a one- or two-week work period where your team accomplishes the goals you define. However, a "goal" for an agile team isn't what you'd normally think. It's not simply, "We're going to ship X piece of software by Y date." Yes, there are deadlines. However, the process is more nuanced than mere heads-down execution. Instead, it's something called a user story.

For marketers, these work a lot like projects. However, engineering teams like to define them as stories, or as descriptors of what their work will enable users to do. To do this, they'll outline their user story by completing a statement like this:

"As a {user}, I want {a feature} so that I can {do something}."

Here's a quick example of what a user story might have looked like for one of our teams.

"As a {CoSchedule customer}, I want {a drag-and-drop function} so that I can {easily reschedule content publish dates visually}."

Okay, so what the heck does this have to do with your marketing team? Let's make the connection. Agile software teams are working in those one- or two-week sprints. As marketers, we can think of those as our campaigns. Campaigns run for a defined amount of time and have a specific goal in mind.

Next, let's apply the user story concept. For agile software teams, those user stories guide their tasks. Each task is another baby step toward helping their users accomplish things using their software. For 10x marketers, this is the goal of our marketing projects. This means our projects are meant to add business value by helping your audience do something they want to do.

In this case, your marketing projects are a combination of content core plus the actionability of what you produce. Here's an example:

"As a {CoSchedule audience member}, I want to {learn to manage my marketing projects} so that I can {ship more projects in less time}."

The mindset shift here is a focus away from what work you're doing to complete tasks, and *toward* what you're getting done for your audience. This allows your entire team to focus wholesale on adding tremendous value with 10x projects. And when those projects are content core in nature, you will achieve business growth *while simultaneously* being incredibly helpful to your audience.

Next, by working on aggressive timelines, you will also work within forced constraints. This means you have to keep the project's scope in check and embrace 90 percent good. There are a zillion ways to solve the "CoSchedule audience member's" user story I described. Some of them are very hard and complex, and would take a long time to create—like an online course on marketing project management, for example. However, some of them are shortcuts—much like our content hacks from Chapter

Two. They are the dirt paths rather than the tidy sidewalks. And because the team has given themselves a tight deadline, they're forced to look for the dirt paths.

Goal setting in this way helps teams focus on getting results, and not simply creating content, running campaigns, or shipping projects. Your marketing team is filled with people who love to write, craft perfect social messages, and design stunning infographics. Just like software engineers, there is a risk of "overbuilding" your marketing. As a matter of course, constraints are the only thing that prevents teams of people doing what they're great at from overbuilding.

> **Take action**
> Map out your next campaign in your first one- or two-week sprint. Set a high-level goal, then help your team develop a series of user stories to describe what you're going to help your audience do.

TWO: DAILY SCRUMS AND COMMUNICATION

The next principle marketers can learn from is the daily rhythm of scrums and communication agile teams use. Remember, they're working in sprints, short periods of work where they're biting off small bits of their projects at a time. Essential to staying connected and rowing in the same direction is their daily habit of standups. These are meetings first thing every morning where the team gets together for about fifteen minutes. The sprint goal is stated, and then everyone answers three questions:

1. What did you work on yesterday?
2. What are you working on today?
3. What roadblocks are in the way of getting your work done?

This is perfect for any team—not simply software teams. It works because it allows everyone to communicate what they're doing, to say it aloud. The process of talking it through is powerful and makes the work real.

It's also wildly efficient. In just two sentences, "What did you work on yesterday?" and "What are you working on today?", the entire team knows if everyone's working on the right things to achieve their goal.

Here's the truth: a practitioner left to his or her own devices will always wander. It's not because they're dumb, lazy, or bad. It's because they're really great at making things and they enjoy the process. These two questions allow the team to rein them back in if, and when, they've lost the plot. Essentially, it keeps everyone connected to the sprint goal.

Next, these meetings allow for rapid change when necessary. These three questions are designed to push roadblocks and issues to the forefront. And this is one of the biggest requirements for 10x teams. If they do nothing else, they should start doing daily scrums around these three questions. They work like magic.

Like anything we do in rhythm, they can sometimes feel routine and boring. But the reality is that they spark the right conversations that lead to positive changes and adjustments. For example, someone may describe a roadblock by saying, "This is taking way longer than I expected."

Now, rather than allowing them to spin their wheels on that for two weeks with no results, the team can come up with an alternative solution immediately. For example, another team member might pipe up and say, "What if we try using this online tool to do something similar?" This minor transaction could save days worth of wasted effort. And it happens all the time.

Thus, roadblocks are addressed and cleared. And even if the roadblock is a larger issue that requires time to deal with outside of the meeting itself, it will still be dealt with in real time, rather than after the sprint is over and the work is unfinished.

Take Action

Each day, gather your team for fifteen minutes to answer the three questions:
1. What did you work on yesterday?
2. What are you working on today?
3. What roadblocks are in the way of getting your work done?

With these answers, you should be able to evaluate:
- Is everyone on your team working on the right things to accomplish your goal this sprint?
- Is everyone on your team keeping the pace required to meet your goal this sprint?
- Are there any roadblocks facing your team right now?

THREE: WORKING SOFTWARE

Third, there is a principle called "working software" that we use in every team at CoSchedule. Here's how it works. Generally, people's instinct is to build something one piece at a time, like a puzzle. The problem with this approach is that it isn't done until all the pieces are in place. That means it doesn't "work" until the very end. The principle of working software doesn't operate like this. Instead, it focuses on building things in a way so that, at the end of each phase, you have a functioning item. It's something you could ship because it actually works.

For example, imagine you are building a wooden rocking horse. The worst way to build it would be to cut out each shape independently, sand each piece independently, paint each piece independently, and then try to glue them all together at the end. You'd end up with one ugly horse.

In contrast to this, working software says: "Hey, let's make sure this is a functioning horse all along the way. This way we'll make sure nothing is screwed up when we're done."

Operating with this mindset, the team will start by roughly cutting out each piece. Then, they'll push the elements together—*without glue*—and hey . . . It's a horse! It's kinda wobbly, the head is misshapen, and the dang thing has no neck—but it's still a working rocking horse. From here, the team adjusts each piece, refining the horse as they go.

In the first example, they didn't know they had an ugly horse until the end. This made adapting super hard and painful. In the second example, they learned how ugly their horse was right away, so they were able to make adjustments without ripping everything apart.

When you build in puzzle pieces, you can't see the finished product until the end. When you can't see until the project is "finished," you have lost control, or the opportunity, to change. Agile teaches us to work in layers (or iterations).

For example, you might take one blog post from a campaign to a completed rough draft state. That's one piece of "working software" (or marketing, in this case). Now, you can give it a second pass. That's another piece. Before too long, it's a 100 percent "done" blog post. And, you've refined a bunch of the campaign talking points and visuals along the way—saving you tons of time on future projects. That method sure beats writing a rough outline for all of the campaign projects at once.

Take action:

Build your campaigns and projects in working pieces, co-creating multiple facets of the required content with each new stage. Build a campaign that resembles a "working rocking horse" along the way, rather than a smorgasbord of parts to be assembled at the end.

FOUR: SELF-ORGANIZING

Fourth, 10x teams are driven by a clear KPI with a deadline, and allowed the freedom to accomplish it. The managers trust their team to self-organize, deciding for themselves who is best-suited to complete which tasks.

As programmers work, they will take ownership of different user stories. There is always at least one owner (and sometimes two.) These engineers become responsible for that story. This is the programmer's KPI: complete story XYZ by the end of this sprint. But the user story doesn't spell out exactly how to do it. Remember, user stories aren't specific tasks. Rather, they encapsulate the results we want to achieve. We want our user to be able to do XYZ by [date]. Getting that done is the programmer's KPI.

Our demand generation team at CoSchedule is a great case study for how this works in marketing. Each week, everyone on the team has a scorecard that they are in charge of. They have a clear KPI and a deadline, but each team member is in total control of how they will accomplish their KPI goal.

For example, Rachel, an inbound marketer on our team, has a KPI of accounting for 14 percent of our monthly trial signups goal. Her

	A	B	C	D	E	F	G	H
1	Rachel's Scorecard: Weekly Trials							
2		DG 6K60	RW	Month Goal	Days	Day Goal	Week Goal	Notes:
3	November	6000	14%	840	30	28	196	
4	11/3-11/9		11%	660		22.00	154	
5	11/10-11/16		16%	934		31.14	218	
6	11/17-11/23		19%	1,119		37.29	261	
7	11/24-11/30		16%	930		31.00	217	Thanksgiving weekend: 11/23-11/26
8	Totals:		15%	911		30.36	850	
9	December	6000	14%	840	31	27	190	
10	12/1-12/7		18%	1,089		35.14	246	
11	12/8-12/14		12%	709		22.86	160	
12	12/15-12/21		11%	647		21.57	151	holiday shenanigans
13	12/22-12/28		9%	544		18.14	127	holiday shenanigans

scorecard breaks down exactly how many signups she's responsible for by month, week, and day.

Rachel's scorecard

Our blog manager, Ben, has a KPI of organic traffic with a goal of roughly one hundred thousand users each week. Breonna, a content writer, is focused on email signups driven from each piece published.

In this way, every team (and team member) knows if they're performing well or not. The point in both cases is that the team owns both the KPI and the results. They also own the path to the results, and therefore own the solution.

Contrast this with most marketing teams, which delegate specific tasks and to-dos. This usually means that the manager owns the problem, solution, and result. The marketers on their team are just responsible for checking off tasks. This underutilizes them, and makes life way more stressful for managers. It also tends to be far less effective at generating results. People are creative. They are smart. When you give them end-to-end ownership, you give them room to thrive. It may sound cool and trendy to use agile for marketing, but that misses the point. The real point is giving your team ownership and the room to generate real results.

The assumption is that the people in the room will be able to find the best paths to hitting their goals. Why? Because they're experts! That's why they're on the team in the first place, right?

Ultimately, this is about getting your team to think about high-level goals and letting them decide how best to accomplish them. This level of ownership means they can react to project changes quickly to keep things on schedule, or get better results.

Take action

Allow your team the freedom, trust, and flexibility to find their own solutions to achieving high-level goals. Do your part by ensuring they are clearly defined and have a deadline attached.

FIVE: RETROS

Fifth, at the end of every sprint there is a team retro meeting. To begin, three questions are asked:

1. What went well?
2. What went poorly?
3. What can we improve?

The teams can reflect on the process and really dig into whether or not they achieved their user story.

First, it's a way to highlight the wins. By bringing the positive results into the foreground, they can be both celebrated and repeated. In essence, you're searching for the things you *must* keep doing.

Second, it's also an opportunity to analyze the mistakes. After all, agile teams don't ask, "Did we make any mistakes?" They assume, "We made some mistakes. Now, what were they?" In fact, retros actually assume there was failure, and are a process for learning from it.

"After all, agile teams don't ask, 'Did we make any mistakes?' They assume, 'We made some mistakes. Now, what were they?'"

Third, your team can take the time to learn from the inevitable, "Oh shit!" moments. And again, you're not asking, "How can we prevent such an error from occurring in the future?" You're asking, "How did we respond to our failures?" Always evaluate your response to fires, not the fact that you started one in the first place. Fires will happen. You can't control that. What you can control is how your team reacts to them.

Take action

Gather your team for a thirty-minute retro meeting where you analyze the week according to the questions:

1. What went well?
2. What went poorly?
3. What can we improve?

With these answers, you should be able to evaluate your wins and how you responded to the failures that took place. Retros are a masterclass in learning.

RESULTS > ERROR PREVENTION

The 10x team understands this premise: error prevention is extremely costly. Rather than trying to prevent errors, 10x teams focus on making them so rapidly that they are barely noticed. Failures are a catalyst for speed and learning. That's why Elon Musk doesn't sweat a rocket falling into the ocean. He doesn't see the broken rocket; he sees the shortcut they just made. He sees the corner cut on the sidewalk heading toward a "perfect" rocket—their next best version.

He might say: "Yeah, our rocket got pretty wet. But think of all the data we collected about how NOT TO DO IT! Wow, we are going to be super good at this next time."

The teams that achieve 10x results are the ones that prioritize learning over perfection. They embrace the reality that innovation will entail failure; that creativity requires risk. However, they're not blindly sprinting along, just hoping to get lucky. Instead, they're extremely focused, disciplined, and tactical in the methodologies they work by.

They set goals, have fluid rhythms of communication, create projects in pillars, organize themselves around the work to be done, and then retro each week, ready to learn from their failures. Oh, yeah, and they don't rely on old-school marketing guesses (plans). However, just because 10x teams ditch marketing plans doesn't mean they aren't strategic.

Instead, they work from a strategy and theory of *how* things work and *why*. And the difference is that they see their work as theory driven rather than marketing plan driven. This means they'll rely on testing, learning, and iteration to hone in and get results. The 10x team treats the office like a lab where they conduct science experiments to test, and adjust, their theories.

Pattern your team after a 10x team to achieve 10x results.

Your 10x Toolbox
Put this chapter into action with your 10x Toolbox by visiting https://coschedule.com/10x-toolbox

10x Marketing Interview:
Andrea Fryrear on "What is an agile marketing team?"
In this interview, founder of Marketing Sherpas Andrea Fryrear dives deep into how marketing teams can appropriate and apply agile methods. You will have access to the full audio interview plus transcript.

PHASE THREE: PUBLISH

In Phase Three, you will adopt the
minimum viable marketing process to
test your assumptions, de-risk projects,
and ship projects quickly. You will also
learn to how to use intelligent social
automation for 10x social promotion, as
well as build and monetize an email list.

CHAPTER TEN

MINIMUM VIABLE MARKETING

In 1981, American Airlines was in dire financial straits. They were low on cash and high on expenses. To pull themselves from the money pit, they cooked up what seemed like a clever home run of a marketing campaign. To get millions dripping into their coffers, they offered unlimited first-class travel for life for $250,000.*

To most of us, a quarter-million bucks sounds steep (and it's roughly $600,000 in today's dollars). However, to the consumers who spend as much time in the air as they do on the ground, this was an incredibly good deal. A Los Angeles Times interview recounts one of the frequent flyers who took advantage of this deal:†

> *'We thought originally it would be something that firms would buy for top employees,' said Bob Crandall, American's chairman and chief executive from 1985 to 1998. 'It soon became apparent that the public was smarter than we were.'*

---

* https://www.economist.com/blogs/gulliver/2012/05/lifetime-airline-passes
† http://articles.latimes.com/2012/may/05/business/la-fi-0506-golden-ticket-20120506

The unlimited passes were bought mostly by wealthy individuals, including baseball Hall of Famer Willie Mays, America's Cup skipper Dennis Conner, and computer magnate Michael Dell.

Mike Joyce of Chicago bought his in 1994 after winning a $4.25-million settlement after a car accident.

In one twenty-five-day span this year, Joyce flew round trip to London sixteen times, flights that would retail for more than $125,000. He didn't pay a dime.

'I love Rome, I love Sydney, I love Athens,' Joyce said by phone from the Admirals Club at John F. Kennedy International Airport in New York. 'I love Vegas and Frisco.'

American Airlines soon went upside down on this big bet—and they still kept it going for nearly ten years!

Oops.

This historic marketing blunder is a good lesson for us 10x marketers. Because this story is far from an isolated incident. Here's how it goes. A giant X-factor company puts loads of money into a big campaign. Problem is, this campaign does more harm than good. And whether money is lost from lack of sales, or poorly projected financial impact, the big bet goes belly up.

MINIMUM VIABLE MARKETING

We've now arrived at the third phase in the 10x Marketing Formula: *publish*. And we begin with this cautionary tale because it illustrates exactly what I'm going to show you how to avoid.

Minimum viable marketing (MVM) is a process of testing your assumptions about the results a project or idea will generate. In turn, you decrease your risk of making a big investment on a lame horse. This way, you can figure out what works, and what doesn't, before you dump hundreds, thousands, or even millions, into marketing campaigns or projects destined for failure. Validation is the name of the game.

"MVM is a process of testing your assumptions about the results a project or idea will generate."

The MVM concept stems from the minimum viable product (MVP) methodology, which was popularized in the world of startups by Eric Ries in a book called *The Lean Startup*. At their essence, MVPs are a way of quickly validating business ideas by producing the minimum number of features to satisfy early customer or audience needs. The MVP process decreases risk by testing assumptions against reality.

Ideas for startups and marketing projects alike are loaded with assumptions. And assumptions, of course, are anything accepted as true without proof. We all carry them around, but unless they're recognized and then put to the test, they threaten to derail seemingly stellar ideas. In marketing, they sound a lot like this:

- "We assume this project will grow a certain KPI by X percent . . ."
- "We assume this campaign will generate X number of email subscribers in Y amount of time . . ."
- "We assume this idea will increase qualified leads . . ."

However, the problem surfaces when you've invested resources in a marketing project, but your KPI growth remains stagnant. Or you go all in on a campaign to explode your email list, but the number of subscribers barely budges. Or how about this: Maybe executing your idea increases leads—but not among your target customers!

If your assumptions are wrong from the start, your ideas are doomed to failure. And the problem is that most marketing is built heavily on assumptions like the ones I listed above. Admit it. Guilty, right? You're not alone—but the good news is, it's not your fault! In practice, most marketers lack solid methods for proving those assumptions. We don't teach doing so in "Marketing 101," and, as an industry, we trust in many of our assumptions as gospel.

This is why we need MVM.

While there's no guaranteed way to eliminate the risk of faulty assumptions altogether, you can certainly stack the odds in your favor. Startups are a great model for us to learn to do this. Why? Because for them, marketing (and everything else) is a results-or-die! endeavor. Thus, minimizing the risk of off-base assumptions can be the difference between runaway success and lights out.

WHY MINIMIZING RISK MATTERS

Speaking of lights out, the riskiest thing a startup can do is "go dark"— meaning they're in the workshop with the doors locked, the windows closed, and the blinds drawn, building their product. They're hard at work, but they're spending months building something they *think* is going to resonate with their target customers. But what if their assumptions are wrong? What if their product falls flat? In truth, this is actually what most marketing teams do. We come up with an idea for a project or a campaign. We assume our plan is good, because we're professionals, after all. And we carry on. We go dark until launch day. Then when the campaign goes live, we are disappointed by the results.

In contrast, we know many of the world's best startups are really good at one thing: *testing their assumptions*. Instead of going dark, these companies keep their eyes open and look for feedback by consistently releasing MVPs that test the key assumptions they're making about their product or its audience. They test these assumptions by asking questions like:

- Does our target customer need [the product]?
- Does [the product] actually solve their problem?
- Is our target customer actually who we think it is?

All of these are valid questions that good startups ask, and then answer, by deploying key MVPs. They realize the endeavor they're undertaking is fraught with both assumptions and risks. They need a way to reduce it. After all, life is results or die! for them. So, why shouldn't we as marketers take the same attitude?

For American Airlines, they could have used the MVM process to test their costly gamble. Instead of a lifetime offering, they could have simply sold a limited number. First, sell one hundred, then test! They would have quickly learned that their assumptions as to who would buy these high-priced tickets were way off base. Sure, they would've taken a brief hit in the wallet. But wouldn't losing revenue for a month have been better than losing it for a decade?

Marketers need a process for testing assumptions and avoiding risk. Most marketing is full of risk. Your job is on the line. You need a way to avoid the rough water. First let's look at how startups do this, then apply it to a few marketing projects.

THE MINIMUM VIABLE CALENDAR

I first learned about the MVP concept in software before bringing it to our marketing team. In 2013, when we began exploring what CoSchedule could look like, we immediately realized how much risk was involved in building a product. In fact, we'd recently shut down a similar social media tool that had eaten up hundreds of hours of development time with little economic success. However, with that product we hadn't used the MVP approach, and we thought it was worth a shot.

The main concept of our software was to visually organize every piece of marketing content, from blog posts to social media messages, on a drag-and-drop calendar. To do this, we could have gone dark and spent months building the final product. Instead, we built a lean version that performed the core function in roughly 10 percent of the time it would've taken to code the entire product.

So, how did we do it? Instead of building our own calendar, we used one of the most popular calendar platforms ever built: Google Calendar.

This simple tool translated blog posts and social messages to a common ICS file, which was readable by Google Calendar and many other calendar applications. So, as you added new blog posts and social messages using CoSchedule, they were automatically added to your custom Google Calendar.

Of course, this wasn't the final product by any stretch of the imagination, but it was a nice to way to get a feel for what we were building. And, it was definitely a feature that would end up in the final product. We still have a Google Calendar integration to this day. And for us, it was experiments like this, combined with user feedback, that helped us shape the future iterations of CoSchedule.

Our Google Calendar "hack" was a cheap and easy way to build our first editorial calendar to prove that it was something our users wanted before investing the time to build the real thing. And it also started a conversation between us and our "customers." Through weekly calls with our beta customers using Google Hangouts, we were able to understand what they wanted and needed in a real marketing calendar. Their direct feedback and questions were invaluable alongside our MVP.

We were able to validate they wanted the tool we were building at each stage, and the conversations also gave us a full picture of how they would actually use it. This translated into actually building a final product that mirrored real customer needs.

So, that's a great example of an MVP gone right. Now, what does MVM look like in the wild?

MINIMUM VIABLE MARKETING IN THE WILD

For a long time, launching a marketing course was in our 10x projects backlog. We believed marketing courses would drive lots of email subscribers—and more importantly, lots of trial signups. However, building an online course that doesn't suck is a significant investment. For example, today, our free Social Media Strategy Course has:

- A dedicated landing page to enroll
- An email sequence to help students understand how to use the course
- Ads to promote the course
- A social media campaign to promote the course
- A beautifully-designed course interface
- Six lessons and over 15,000 words of content
- 155 minutes of video content
- More than 10 downloadable resources
- Six quizzes
- Custom infographics
- Step-by-step image walkthroughs for key concepts and actions
- And even an entire certification track once completed

A Level 3 project, to be sure. However, starting there would have taken hundreds of hours of cumulative team time before we'd ever had something to ship. So, rather than build it and hope they'd come, we launched test projects to de-risk the course and validate the material.

Building it outright would have been the equivalent of going dark as a startup. And the most obvious risk is that we'd build it, but no one would care. But, other issues bubble to the surface once we start to ask *why* they wouldn't come. Maybe they wouldn't come because they didn't identify with the core problem that our course aimed to solve. So, the assumption to test is: "Our audience has [the problem the course solves] and will enroll in a comprehensive course that helps them solve it." This means our validation test simply needs to focus on answering this question: "Does our audience *actually* have this problem?"

Yet another assumption was that we'd be able to collect a sufficient number of leads to make it a worthwhile business investment. We assumed, "This course will drive enough leads to generate revenue growth." However, to test this meant digging deeper into what those results would need to look like by asking, "How much will the course cost to build [number of team hours]? How many leads will we need to "pay for it" [dollarizing our time]? Can we drive these leads through this course?"

One last assumption was that our users would be willing to exchange an email address for the content. Our hunch told us they would, but nonetheless it would be prudent to check. From here, we asked ourselves, "What can we launch within a week that will test our assumptions?"

Here are a few ideas we came up with:

Coming Soon

The first idea was to launch a "Coming Soon" landing page for the course and share it to our audience. Depending on the number of signups, we could choose to complete, scale back, or abandon the project.

Comments

In addition to the "Coming Soon" page, we would add a section for comments and ask our audience what they were most excited to learn in the course. This would give us feedback on how well our plans aligned with their needs. Bonus: they may even give us some fresh topic ideas.

Blog Post Series

Another test was even simpler than the first two. We would simply release each course lesson as a blog post to measure individual response to those topics. We could then test our current audience's response, whether our targeted keywords drove traffic via search, and the alignment between the actual content and their needs. Naturally, this would take longer than a week, but since these blog posts filled valuable sections of our editorial content, they were very low risk while also adding value beyond the project itself.

With this test, we could also measure email response along the way to the included cookies,* helping to prove or disprove our assumption about readers' willingness to provide an email address in exchange for the content.

In the end, we chose the blog post route. And within a few weeks, we were confident in our proof to move the project forward—but we still didn't commit fully. Rather than pre-creating, planning, and producing a large volume of video content as originally outlined, we opted to do live, ad-hoc training options instead. While these were "less good" than sharply produced video content, they allowed us to learn a lot about the medium of video, and interaction with the audience, before committing. Now, we have fully recorded and produced videos available on the course. But these were a later improvement.

MVM is about understanding the inherent assumptions and risks that any large project includes, and then finding ways to test them. Plus,

---

* Note: A cookie is a piece of data sent from a website to a user's browser while they're surfing the site. The user's computer stores the cookie and allows the site to track their activity and remember the actions they've taken. Imagine visiting a website and signing up for an email list. In this case, the website owners could use a cookie to remember that you're already a subscriber, and stop showing you popups to "Enter your email address for a free download!"

building and releasing projects in small batches allows you to pull back anytime with less consequence. At the same time, your team can move faster, which increases the pace of learning—which is the true value of MVM. It's a process designed for learning as quickly as possible, which is the definition of "failing fast."

BUILD, MEASURE, LEARN

So, test your assumptions by building in stages to learn as quickly as possible. This method of MVM capitalizes on what startups call a "lean feedback loop." As you saw in both our editorial calendar and marketing course examples, lean loops help you quickly create what paying customers actually want. (A novel concept, right?) And it accomplishes this in three steps:

1. *Build:* It starts with an idea. Our goal, then, is to create a basic project that allows a user to test our idea.
2. *Measure:* We then measure their feedback, particularly in comparison to specific assumptions we have made about their need for the product.
3. *Learn:* Based on user feedback, and the metrics of our specific measurements, we should be able to determine if our original idea (and assumption/s) was accurate or not.

In sum, the "learn" portion of the loop is really the most important step. It represents the conclusion of the loop, and should result in actionable change to the direction of the project or campaign. If you aren't learning, you aren't doing it right. Our marketing courses project was our first iteration of the feedback loop. We built it piece by piece, listened to the feedback, and immediately made exciting changes to the project for the road ahead.

We tested four assumptions that we felt we were making about our audience:

1. That marketers view CoSchedule as an authority, and will therefore enroll in a marketing strategy course taught by us.
2. That our audience actually wanted to consume our content in this more intensive format.
3. That we had the right content, and that this content added value.
4. That the time spent creating the content would result in a large enough number of leads to pay for itself.

Overall, the results spoke for themselves. At the time of this writing, 8,655 marketers have taken our Marketing Strategy Course in less than eleven months. And because of this course's success and resonance, we used the same process and created a Social Media Strategy Course. It has become even more popular, with an enrollment of 6,561 marketers in about five months.

So, how can you use lean loops in your marketing to build, measure, and learn?

HOW TO APPLY LEAN LOOPS TO YOUR MARKETING

Let's take three common marketing projects and analyze the main assumption, or guess, that's driving the work. Then, we'll outline a way to quickly test that assumption before going full-tilt. We'll look at launching a new marketing channel, a rebranding project, and crafting fresh positioning.

Launching a Podcast

Imagine an ecommerce marketing team wants to include new content types in the mix this year. Their blog gets nice traffic, their email list is growing steadily, and their social following is strong. Their content gets results, and they believe a podcast is another great way to add more value to their audience. Plus, they all listen to podcasts published by other respected marketers. They say, "Honestly, it's surprising we don't have one already."

So, how should the team know whether or not to launch?

What major assumption has been made?
Though there are many, a core assumption is that because their audience reads their blog, has subscribed to their email list, and follows them on social, they'll also consume audio content from them. But, simply because their audience consumes one type of content from them does not mean they'll be just as enthusiastic to gobble up another.

How can they validate this assumption?
To quickly test their potential podcast's viability, they can release key blog posts as mp3 pilot episodes. And production time can stay super lean by recording the sample episode on a smartphone in a quiet corner of the office.

With this simple test, they can validate whether or not their audience is interested in a podcast from their team.

Lean Loop:
- Build: Smartphone recording of pilot podcast episode shared as a key blog post.
- Measure: Measure traffic, number of listens or downloads, and listen to comments.
- Learn: Will a podcast be a viable marketing channel between us and our target audience at this stage?
- Timeline: One week.

Target Customer
Every marketing team worth their salt fixates on their target customer. Just as we talked about in Chapter Four, Finding Your Content Core, they need to deliver major value to their target customer via content that intersects with the company's business value. So, imagine a

maturing marketing team that bases decisions upon their idea of who their target customer is. They have solid hunches about who they are, so they tailor everything to suit this envisioned persona.

While the team may be right in some areas, which of their assumptions should be stacked against reality?

What major assumptions are being made?
Here are some common assumptions marketers make about their target customer.

"We assume our target customers . . .

> . . . are a healthy mix of male and female.
> . . . are in their twenties, thirties, forties, fifties, etc.
> . . . are mainly focused on narrow aspects of their job.
> . . . care deeply about the core of your value proposition that drives messaging.
> . . . work in small, medium, or large companies."

How can they validate these assumptions?
The team can quickly set up target customer interviews. This can happen over the phone, Skype, or even Google Hangouts. Actual customer conversations will attune them to the precise language customers use, the problems they face, what they care about, and more common threads.

In addition to this, the team can leverage social media as a qualitative research tool by putting in some elbow grease. To further validate their assumptions about their target customers, they can grab their company's customer list and take to the web for some old-fashioned internet stalking.

Lean Loop:
- Build: Write out all assumptions about target customer.
- Measure: Write interview questions (or data points to gather) to test these assumptions. In addition, get customer list, create spreadsheet for tracking, and research on social networks.
- Learn: Are their assumptions true or false? And what new trends have emerged?
- Timeline: One or two weeks—depending on volume of customer research.

Messaging for a Rebranding Campaign

A company is rebranding and wants to tell the world about it. Their branding campaign starts in a room with whiteboards on every wall. With the creative juices flowing, the marketing team and key leaders brainstorm everything from the new look to fresh messaging. Over the coming days and weeks, their designers, copywriters, media buyers, and sales team are set to adopt the new brand. This means new ads, a website refresh, and sales decks that reflect everything that's changed. It's all expertly coordinated, so everyone launches with the new brand on day one.

As mentioned in the example above, positioning statements (or value propositions) are driven by who your target customer is, what their primary pains and desires are, and how your product or service can make it a reality. This is core to branding.

So, what central assumption about the new brand messaging is the team making that should be tested?

What major assumption has been made?
The marketing team is assuming that, because the brand messaging resonates with their team internally, it will resonate with their target audience in the way they intend it to.

How can they validate this major assumption?

The marketing team rewrites the positioning statements on their sales decks, asking the sales team to use it on all sales calls for one week. In addition, the team can ask their salespeople to ask this question: "How would you describe [our product] to a friend?" Or they can ask probing questions near the end of the call to analyze how the new positioning statements resonated and how closely the language matched with their customers'.

As they do, they can record all of their calls for the week, allowing the marketing team to listen to and observe their customers in real life.

Before a big investment is made in the campaign, the most important facet of the rebrand can be tested: the positioning and messaging. If the messaging is off, design will miss . . . sales material will miss . . . copy will miss . . . and on down the line.

Lean Loop:
- Build: Start with core positioning statements, value propositions, and key messaging.
- Measure: Present the messaging to sales and target customers on calls for one week to gauge resonance. Record all calls for the marketing team to review.
- Learn: If the messaging is clear and relevant, continue to the next stages. But repeat this process of testing each major element before investing further.
- Timeline: One week.

By quickly using build–measure–learn loops to validate core assumptions, marketers can reduce the risk of poorly investing money, hours, and energy into a project that's likely to fail. Simple validation tests like these will pay dividends in the insights they yield.

"I DESCRIBE THE
MINIMUM VIABLE
PRODUCT AS THE
SMALLEST SOLUTION
YOU CAN BUILD
THAT ALSO CREATES
VALUE FOR THE
CUSTOMER."

—ASH MAURYA,
AUTHOR OF SCALING LEAN

10X MARKETING INTERVIEW:
ASH MAURYA AND LEAN PRINCIPLES APPLIED

These tests lie at the core of the MVM process. As you've seen with both our Google Calendar integration and iterative marketing courses approach, it's been a continual guide to how to best invest our marketing resources. I interviewed Ash Maurya, author of *Scaling Lean*, for even more insight into the confluence between MVPs and 10x marketing.

Ash added clarity to what an MVP is and how it should function, saying, "I describe the minimum viable product as the smallest solution you can build that also creates value for the customer."

Ash shared a perfect story illustrating how this principle of validation can work itself out for marketers.

LEAN MARKETING AT WORK

Before GPS tech was standard in most vehicles, an entrepreneur schemed a way to retrofit a GPS system into cars. His product idea was a license plate cover hardwired with GPS receiver and all necessary components. It could be easily popped off one car and onto another. It was a nifty idea.

The old way of doing business would've been building an expensive prototype, doing field testing, and trying to land big-time contracts. Instead, this guy found the dirt path. From research, he knew his best market would be mid-tier car rental companies. They wouldn't have the latest and greatest fleets yet, but would want the gadgetry to compete with the big-box names.

So, he picked up a license plate cover and wired it with dummy circuits. It was a model of what he would build if the idea was validated— but it wasn't functional yet. Then, he hit the streets with what essentially amounted to a physical wireframe of his GPS product. After a handful of meetings, he had orders in hand, and the idea was financially validated in little more than an afternoon. He built just enough of the product to share, demonstrate, and test the idea.

How many marketers do you know who have sunk massive amounts of time and money into projects, content, or campaigns that have produced little, if any, returns? I know plenty. But the MVP mentality rescues these wasted efforts. Perfection isn't the goal; validation is.

WHAT CAN YOU SHIP RIGHT NOW?

Okay, you've seen how American Airlines biffed it. You saw how we built a minimum viable calendar to test, de-risk, measure, and iterate. You've learned from Ash that you can run lean, and you've uncovered the dirt path of the content hacker. Now, here's where you need to answer a question.

What can you ship right now?

Through your 10x project development, you have a bevy of 10x ideas to choose from. Which one can you turn into an MVP and ship within the week? How can you build this 10x project with 10 percent of the work?

This will only be possible if you avoid the trap of overbuilding. And this will mean you need to love the process of getting results more than publishing something perfect. Results are greater than perfection. To do this requires that you take a project and ruthlessly break it down into one actionable facet, rather than creating it all at once. How can you get your project to 90 percent good? How can you quickly run through the loop of build > measure > learn?

The grand vision is an illusion—build small, ship often, and learn quickly.

As you do, you can incrementally test additional features or content and validate what your customers want, and don't want, along the way. You only know so much—your guesses will be wrong. The goal is to fail fast so you can learn what to cut and what to keep.

Elon Musk wants to go to Mars. Right now he's landing rockets on ships. See what we mean? He's solving problems one at a time. The grand vision is an illusion—build small, ship often, and learn quickly.

START TESTING

So, what can you ship right now to test assumptions and de-risk your projects? To move forward, you need to do five simple things.

1. Define what 90 percent good looks like.
Start with your big, Level 3 10x project. Then ask, what can we ship in a week to ensure this is a good idea? What minimum features or content are required to add 90 percent of the value to your customers or readers? (Notice I said 90 percent of the value, not 90 percent of the project. You need to find the shortcut that allows you to test your user story.)

2. Create.
What can you create to test your assumptions and de-risk the project? How can you do this with an iterative approach?

3. Measure.
What is the key metric that will help you define success and failure at each step or goal?

4. Learn.
Are you willing to listen to the data and make your decisions accordingly? Or will you try and hold on to an idea that's failing because you like it?

5. Repeat.
Decide if you should continue on to the next ship goal, or stop here. Then, do it all over again after deciding.

Follow the MVM process by applying the loop, and validate your assumptions. But realize that even when your assumptions are wrong and your genius idea is actually a dud—you've actually won because you reduced risk by not going dark.

Here's the deal. It can be hard to let go of a good idea, but sometimes you might need to. Once you have launched your test, gathered your feedback, and analyzed the data, be prepared to accept the results as they come.

For many, it's hard to let go of what we thought was a slam dunk. However, don't let this discourage you. Even if your content performed moderately well, the goal here is to understand why so that you can make it better and more effective before jumping in with both feet. And remember, when you miss the target on the first go 'round, use your reverts! When it's an appropriately sized test, no harm, no foul.

Now, follow the MVM process in your context and get results.

Your 10x Toolbox

Put this chapter into action with your 10x Toolbox by visiting https://coschedule.com/10x-toolbox

10x Marketing Interview with Ash Maurya

Listen to the interview audio, plus access the full transcript, to go deeper into minimum viable products (MVPs) and how to validate ideas.

CHAPTER ELEVEN

10X SOCIAL PROMOTION

Once upon a time, we ran a test around the perfect recipe for social promotion. We wanted to know how many times we should promote a single piece of content. Which networks work best? We dug into our own data packed with millions of messages from tens of thousands of users. We also crunched the numbers from over twenty industry-recognized studies on the best times to schedule social media messages on every network. I'm talking time of day, day of the week, every detail down to the hour.

Then, we published our findings in an article entitled "This Is The Social Media Posting Schedule That Will Boost Your Traffic By 192%." It's a great article, because we share exactly how we boosted our own traffic by, surprise, 192 percent! It gets good traffic, lots of social media love, and provides real value to our audience.

Well, recently, I met a marketer who was absolutely raving about this article. That was pretty fun to hear. In fact, he found so much value in it, he had it bookmarked and followed it religiously every time he scheduled a social media messages for his brand's many accounts.

"For every message?" I asked him.

"That's right, every message."

"Doesn't that take you a ton of time?" I asked.

"Nah, it's not that bad. Just a few hours per week."

He was an awesome guy, and we talked for a while longer. Eventually, though, I gave him some good news that I could get him the same results—perfectly scheduled messages—in 1 percent of the time with some of our automation features. Surprisingly, he pushed back. It took some time for me to convince him that he should give up the intensive manual labor of scheduling things by hand.

He kept saying, "It's only time—it doesn't cost me anything!" However, that's where he, and many other marketers I've met, are wrong.

THE "IT'S ONLY TIME" TRAP

In the realm of startups, your time is your most valuable asset. It's all you have. So, smart founders dollarize it relentlessly. For the marketer I was talking to, a few quick questions help me calculate that his time was worth about $100 per hour. In his mind, he was saving money by not dropping $60 per month on a tool. But by the end of our conversation, it was pretty apparent that while he was "saving" $60—he was actually spending $1,200 in time to accomplish the same function.

He was stuck in the "it's only time" trap. He was grossly undervaluing his time. And we constantly see this in marketing teams. Too many marketers think their time is free. But they don't realize that it's actually *more* valuable than their money. To make the transformation into a 10x marketer, this mindset shift is pivotal. This is because it's another matter of 10x versus 10 percent.

So far in this formula, you've learned to prioritize 10x ideas, projects, and activities above all else. Now, as we dive into social promotion (and email promotion in the next chapter), you need to see your time in the same light.

The purpose of promotion is to get the right people to the right place at the right time—all with the goal of triggering profitable action.

In the same breath, the mechanics of promotion is about ruthlessly outsourcing tasks that can be performed just as well, if not better, by automated processes.

My marketing friend was experiencing great engagement and referral traffic from publishing messages on the right platforms at the right times. To him, he was getting the exact results that he wanted. However, he was stuck in an unscalable pattern. He wasn't thinking like a scrappy startup that must scale everything to achieve growth.

He, like the rest of us, only has 168 hours in each week. And let's generously say he only worked 40 hours per week. That means the three "free" hours he spent each week on perfectly timing his social messages equates to 7.5 percent of his time.

Now, I'll ask you the same question I asked him: "How would it feel to put in fewer hours and get better results?"

Pretty damn good, right? And it's possible because that same time previously sunk into menial tasks is now available for 10x pursuits—the stuff you absolutely cannot delegate to another person or tool. I want you to drill the 10x framework into your mindset so that it becomes the lens through which you see every activity, investment, and commitment. Your habit should be to always ask this question: "Is this 10x, or 10 percent?"

If it's not 10x, you know what to do.

SMART-O-MATION

In this context, automation means using a tool to automatically post messages on your social networks. However, it may also be a word in the social media sphere that gets your hackles up. Trust me, I get it. I've seen the mechanical Twitter bots spewing out crap every fifteen minutes, too. Even worse, I've seen brands load up hundreds of generic messages and crank them out indiscriminately. This is the "dumb" side of using "smart" tech.

To clarify, then, I'm not a fan of that kind of "automation." And it's the opposite of what I'm advocating here. Instead, I call that kind of marketing "spam-o-mation." Spam-o-mation is used by crappy tools that simply regurgitate the same stuff over and over. There is little intelligence involved. You simply drop messages into buckets, the tool indiscriminately plucks a message out, and it shoots it off into the internet ether. Again . . . and again . . . and again. One of the most frequent offenders is a WordPress plugin called Revive Old Post. I know some think it's taboo to name names—but most of us know who I was talking about anyway.

Instead, harness the power of "smart-o-mation." Smart-o-mation is when you use tools that intelligently automate curated content at specific intervals and at optimized times. The right tools are smarter than you are. It's just the truth. Robots were made for algorithms, not humans. So, why spend time doing something a tool is better than you at?

Use intelligent automation to perfectly time your messages for all social promotion. My marketing friend labored over these tasks for hours. And the truth is, while timing matters, it's a 10 percent marketing task at best. When there are tools that will do the job ten times better than you without ever making a mistake or missing a step, stop wasting your time scheduling posts manually.

For example, at CoSchedule, we compared research from twenty studies about the optimal days and times to post messages on each major social network. We found the data-proven patterns of peak traffic and engagement times, then used that knowledge to build our Best Time Scheduling feature. So, rather than scheduling post times manually, the feature intelligently chooses the best time to post based on three criteria:

- individual social network,
- peak engagement time for that network based upon day of the week, and
- your other scheduled messages for that account.

This way, if you have multiple messages for a particular network posting on a single day (which every 10x social promoter will) the feature automatically adjusts the message so it doesn't seem spammy or post messages on top of each other.

INTELLIGENT AUTOMATION AMPLIFIES COMPETITION-FREE CONTENT

Now, I'm obviously a smart-o-mation evangelist. But when the subject of social media automation comes up, some experts aren't so enthused. This can be for good reason, too. There are real-world incidences of social automation harming brands and alienating followers. Or, in AT&T's case, even non-followers.

The tech giant hired an agency to run a giveaway campaign for them. Unfortunately, the agency wielded the power of automation in a spammy way. Every few minutes, the official @ATT account tweeted promotional messages to users indiscriminately. They spewed an overwhelming deluge of spam across Twitter, even tweeting to people who didn't follow them.[*]

Often, cases like this are used as proof-positive that automation is evil, lazy, and almost as bad as telemarketing. However, intelligent automation does not dumb down communication; it enhances it. When used strategically, it opens time to have substantive conversations with your audience and influencers in your industry. It allows you to focus on people and let the mechanical promotional process take care of itself.

More importantly, automation does not mean spamming out the same message fifty times per month (or per day!). Instead, it means removing the need to manually schedule social posts so you can focus on writing compelling content. Instead of investing your time in monotonous button clicking, you can focus on creating social messages that promote your content from different angles.

Sometimes you can grab verbatim power statements. Other times you can share graphics, images, or video content. Additionally, if you cite any sources, experts, or influencers, you can highlight their input and tag them in the post. Obviously, the angles are endless. But what you need to

---

[*] https://blog.hubspot.com/blog/tabid/6307/bid/31750/AT-T-s-Twitter-SPAM-Snafu-Highlights-Dangers-of-Automation-Outsourcing.aspx

internalize is that automation does not equal blasting the same message from a technological cannon.

Notice I am not advocating that you replace real communication and potential dialogue with a tool. Instead, I am inviting you to increasing your reach by maximizing your efforts.

PUBLISH MORE THAN ONCE

The right automation strategy shines brightest when you combine each of these principles with the right publishing frequency. Without further ado, it's time to get aggressive. This may surprise you, but under-sharing on social media is a marketing epidemic. It looks like this: You publish a fresh blog post, then share a link on Facebook, Twitter, or maybe LinkedIn. Hopefully it picks up some traction and nabs some likes, comments, and shares. But within a few hours, your post evaporates from people's feeds.* In fact, some studies indicate a tweet's shelf life is five minutes or less before it evaporates.† Now, couple that shelf life with the staggering amount of noise on social. Every single second, there are:

- 814 images published on Instagram
- 2,644,941 emails sent
- 7,844 messages tweeted

This is further compounded by the dismal reality of that post's reach. According to a report by Social@Ogilvy called "Facebook Zero: Considering Life After the Demise of Organic Reach," brands may experience as little as a 2 percent organic reach.‡ So, if you've got 10,000 followers, a cool 200 of them will see the post as they breeze through their feeds over the course of two hours.

* https://blog.hubspot.com/blog/tabid/6307/bid/24507/shelf-life-of-social-media-links-only-3-hours-data.aspx
† http://www.wiselytics.com/blog/tweet-isbillion-time-shorter-than-carbon14/
‡ https://social.ogilvy.com/facebook-zero-considering-life-after-the-demise-of-organic-reach/

In fact, from our own data, we know that 77 percent of our users share their content on social media less than three times. And 37 percent share content on social media just once after it's published.

Here's the deal. If you're sharing a piece of content just once, you're absolutely wasting your content. You're leaving tons of engagement *and* traffic on the table. We know this for a fact.

The results? Our blog posts got 31.5 times more click-throughs—that's a 3,150 percent increase in one week—because of our frequency. We more than quadrupled our traffic with essentially no more effort. And that was on Twitter alone. We share our content on multiple social media accounts, so you can imagine the advantage a comprehensive social media posting schedule provides our content.

Our first tweet attracted only two link clicks. A measly two people visited our content. So, if we'd stopped there, this channel would have been a nothing burger. Fortunately, we kept talking about it. In fact, you can see the schedule in the following graphic. We tweeted about this piece of content eight more times, attracting 63 additional click-throughs.

	TWEETS	IMPRESSIONS	LINK CLICKS	RETWEETS	FAVORITES	REPLIES	EMAIL SHARES
Day 1	1ST	544	2	1	1	0	0
	2ND	993	18	3	4	10	1
	3RD	1,190	7	4	5	3	2
Day 2	4TH	508	8	1	0	2	1
Day 3	5TH	471	6	2	3	1	1
Day 4	6TH	458	6	3	2	2	2
Day 5	7TH	508	6	1	2	0	0
Day 6	8TH	638	8	3	2	0	0
Day 7	9TH	677	4	0	0	0	0

So, the primary principle of 10x social promotion is to—well—promote! Get more aggressive with your posting schedule. Promote more often and for a longer string of days. With the dismal stats regarding organic reach and average post shelf life, it's no wonder sharing content only once or twice produces no return for most marketers.

Case in point: Our most popular post on color physiology from 2014 didn't catch full steam until about six months after it was published and we'd reshared it using smart-o-mation! It went viral from there, with over one hundred thousand likes, pins, and shares!

WHAT ABOUT A CROSS-CHANNEL POSTING SCHEDULE?

Now, what about social promotion and publishing beyond Twitter? The same principle applies. Like most brands, we at CoSchedule have accounts on multiple social networks. So, we maintain a 10x social promotion schedule for every piece of content we publish and every project we ship—and we do so on every network. Let's return to the bedrock of our 10x content strategy: our blog.

Through a combination of compelling copy, varied message types, custom graphics, and intelligent automation, we promote each blog post on a forty-day cycle across seven channels. And while we automate the messages, we custom-write multiple messages for each network.

Here is the CoSchedule 10x social promotion schedule applied to every blog post we publish.

CAMPAIGN SCHEDULE

PUBISH

FACEBOOK
CUSTOM FACEBOOK POST #1

TWITTER @COSCHEDULE
CUSTOM TWEET #2

TWITTER @COSCHEDULEBLOG
CUSTOM TWEET #3

LINKEDIN
CUSTOM LINKEDIN MESSAGE

TWITTER @COSCHEDULE
CUSTOM TWEET #2

TWITTER @COSCHEDULEBLOG
CUSTOM TWEET #3

LINKEDIN
CUSTOM LINKEDIN MESSAGE

1 DAY AFTER PUBLISH

TWITTER @COSCHEDULEBLOG
INFLUENCER TWEET #1

4 DAYS AFTER PUBLISH

TWITTER @COSCHEDULE
CUSTOM TWEET #5

5 DAYS AFTER PUBLISH

TWITTER @COSCHEDULEBLOG
CUSTOM TWEET #1

7 DAYS AFTER PUBLISH

TWITTER @COSCHEDULE
INFLUENCER TWEET #2

13 DAYS AFTER PUBLISH

PINTEREST
DESIGNED INFOGRAPHIC

TWITTER @COSCHEDULE
CUSTOM TWEET #2

20 DAYS AFTER PUBLISH

FACEBOOK
CUSTOM FACEBOOK POST #2

TWITTER @COSCHEDULE
CUSTOM TWEET #3

30 DAYS AFTER PUBLISH

LINKEDIN
CUSTOM LINKEDIN MESSAGE

TWITTER @COSCHEDULE
CUSTOM TWEET #4

35 DAYS AFTER PUBLISH

GOOGLE+
CUSTOM GOOGLE+ MESSAGE

TWITTER @COSCHEDULE
CUSTOM TWEET #5

40 DAYS AFTER PUBLISH

TWITTER @COSCHEDULEBLOG
CUSTOM TWEET #2

DIFFERENTIATING SOCIAL MEDIA MESSAGES

You may be thinking this is all a bit repetitive, but it's important to understand that we aren't just sending a post headline plus a link all the time. Notice that our schedule is filled with "custom" messages. This means we have a variety of message types and content. Each features a unique angle of the piece. Here is a short overview to a few of the message types we've found successful that are worthy for test runs in your social promotion, too.

Stats and Graphics

If the piece includes an infographic, that means there are notable, show-stopping statistics. These are fantastic hooks, because people like proof. And sharing compelling data that resonates with your target audiences—especially when visualized—is a perfect tactic to standing out, increasing engagement, and attracting clicks.

Here is the message and accompanying image:

> *"Curious how your KPIs stack up against other companies? Or maybe you want to know the top things other marketing teams do to produce successful results? Download our free State of Marketing Report here* 🔥 💯 👏 *"*

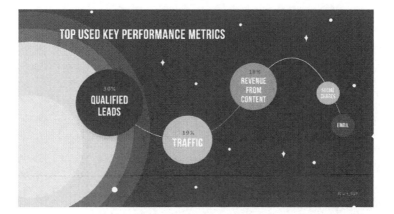

Influencer Quotes

We love quoting smart people in our content. So an easy win is to share influencer quotes from within a piece we've created. And of course, always tag the person you've quoted on social, because they'll almost always share the post with their audience.

Here's an example of a quote from Gini Dietrich, CEO of Arment Dietrich, that we shared to promote our content:

> *"Are you utilizing AI, chatbots, and/or virtual reality in your marketing? It's @ginidietrich's must do for 2018.* 👋 🎙 *"*

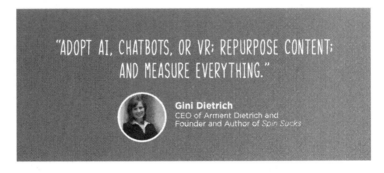

Behind the Scenes

When creating video content, behind-the-scenes images are a fun way to draw eyeballs. Who doesn't like a sneak peek at how things were made? Try promoting uncut glimpses at what it looks like behind the scenes.

Here is the message and accompanying image:

> *"Behind the scenes at a photoshoot with our founders. #bluesteel"*

Classic Copywriting Techniques

You don't have to reinvent the wheel when writing messages for social media. Instead, there are classic copywriting techniques that perennially hook people and generate action. Here is one of my favorite formulas.

PAS (Problem, Agitate, Solution)

The PAS formula is dead simple. State a problem your audience has. Rub some salt in it. Then promise a solution to the pain on the other side of your link.

For example:

> *"You're late for a meeting downtown. Now your Uber driver is on the wrong side of the street. Here's how to make sure this never happens again." [Link to content]*

> *"Spreadsheets kinda suck. But your team needs to collaborate on your editorial calendar... So you're stuck, right? Not anymore. Welcome to the easy button for content marketing." [Link to content]*

"You love spending Monday mornings frantically scheduling social media messages, right?! Just kidding. Do this instead and never stress out about social media again." [Link to content]

There are a million variations. The important part is finding the best angles to hook people into your content. Pull every lever you can to promote your content on social. And that means both differentiated message types *and* ongoing promotion.

HOW WE USE SMART-O-MATION

As I shared, we have a set forty-day promotional cycle. However, once that's through, we further harness the power of smart-o-mation by using an intelligent automation feature we built called ReQueue. Unlike other social automation tools, ReQueue interacts with the rest of our social schedule. It takes into account everything we have on our calendar, promotes our best content at the most optimal times, and recalibrates its schedule when other campaigns are going out at the same time! Like I said, it's smart-o-mation.

Just like New York City, social promotion never sleeps. It's an active process. Your content should never sit dormant. It should show up again and again in your social channels.

Think about it from this perspective. Our total social channels grow by about 5 percent each month. As I write this, we have a social following north of one hundred thousand fans and followers. This means we have five thousand fresh people every month who have never seen our content before. So, how are they supposed to know about the awesome blog post we published three months ago if we don't keep talking about it? The same goes with every other piece of content. You've made the investment to create it (hopefully according to your 10x content scorecard!). Your social media followers have each voted that yes, they do in fact want to hear from you. So create awesome stuff, then never shut up about it.

So, what does your social promotion schedule look like? If social has failed to drive traffic, you may be in for some great news. It might simply be because you're underpromoting your content. Or you've been spewing out the same messages over and over without differentiation. Our precise posting schedule is not the holy grail—the thinking that has produced it is. When you compare your schedule to ours, are you banging the drum as much as you should be? And are you pulling every promo lever at your disposal?

MASTERING MECHANICS

Undoubtedly, the most prevalent mistake in social media is anemic promotion. So to make an immediate impact, ensure you're sharing—a lot. However, there are certainly other elements at play in the social promo cocktail. For every network, there are ideal character counts, message types, emojis, and a bunch of other stuff that play best.

"So create awesome stuff, then never shut up about it."

We analyzed 6,399,322 messages sent through CoSchedule, ran the numbers, and reverse-engineered the anatomy of the top-performing messages. The insights were intriguing. We learned things like:

- Hashtags on Facebook matter as much as regularly updating your company's MySpace page
- Twitter loves messages using two emojis at a time
- LinkedIn is as boring as we all thought, so forget about the fun stuff and cut to the chase

Our research got even more granular. Because not only did we learn exactly what message type to use for optimal performance on each network, but we crunched the numbers and discovered ideal character counts, as well.

However, let's pause for a moment. This chapter is called "10x Social Promotion," so here's an appropriate question: "Is twiddling your thumbs counting characters, tallying emojis, and collating hashtags 10x work, or 10 percent stuff?"

We realized, rather quickly, it was 10 percent work. Is it important? Yes. Anything that can give you an edge to be seen, heard, and engaged with is worth considering. But the level of effort required was too staggering. After all, think about how much effort would be required to write forty-one days worth of optimized social messages for each network.

So, rather than steal from 10x work, we built a tool to analyze and optimize our social messages for every network. This tool, called the Social Message Optimizer, does the 10 percent work for us. And, we give it away for free at https://coschedule.com/social-message-optimizer

Just type in your message, give it a score, and optimize accordingly.

For 10x social promotion, then, the question should constantly be: "How can we automate 10 percent work so we can focus on 10x?" You will continually find busywork that will eat up your already limited time and energy. Therefore, your task becomes finding intelligent forms of automation, regardless of the context.

10X MARKETING INTERVIEW: VISUAL STORYTELLING WITH JOHN T. MEYER

Here's the deal. No matter how good your copy is, or how optimized your mechanics are, you're still at risk of getting your message lost in the riptide of content in social feeds. A prime way to stand out is by designing irresistible visual content. And not simply stand out, but get results.

To do this the 10x way, I interviewed John Meyer, CEO and co-founder of Lemonly.* Lemonly is a world-renowned visual marketing company that has worked with brands like Netflix, Marriott, Major League Baseball, and Under Armour.

The human eye processes images sixty thousand times faster than it does text.† So, if you play your visual cards right, you can garner some serious social media traction. John has been in the digital marketing game for nearly a decade.

He explains the power of visuals like this:

"As humans, we are visual creatures . . . For example, you remember people's faces, but you don't always remember their names. You go back to a high school reunion and see someone walking toward you. Then you think, "Oh crap! I remember this person's face, but not their name . . ."

Today, we have thousands of messages flying at us. The world is noisy and even a bit confusing. That's why simply adding a stock photo

---

* You can listen to the full interview for free by visiting https://coschedule.com/10x-toolbox
† https://www.fastcompany.com/3035856/why-were-more-likely-to-remember-content-with-images-and-video-infogr

"AS HUMANS, WE ARE VISUAL CREATURES ... FOR EXAMPLE, YOU REMEMBER PEOPLE'S FACES, BUT YOU DON'T ALWAYS REMEMBER THEIR NAMES."

—JOHN T. MEYER,
CO-FOUNDER OF LEMONLY

falls short. Instead, John advocates something beyond graphic design. He calls for visual storytelling. Visual storytelling has two functions:

1. It makes confusing things easier to understand
2. It makes boring things more entertaining

GET YOUR STORY STRAIGHT

To begin, you need to get your story right. Although there are endless angles to any piece, you can start with this simple structure:

1. What's the business goal of the piece?
Just like any piece of 10x content, the goal isn't to create pretty visuals. You produce content to produce results—no exceptions here.

2. What three points best convey the information that will accomplish this goal?
Set a hook to reel in the viewer. This can be a flashy visual, show-stopping stat, or the most intriguing information your content offers. Then, handpick three main ideas as functional body content—whether text, visuals, or a combination.

3. What singular call to action are you building toward?
Your content's job is to guide your audience to take the next step. This can be to sign up, click through to more content, or anything in between. In short, this is where the business purpose will start being achieved.

The beauty of this simple structure is that it will work for everything from infographics to microsite content. But visuals have a purpose beyond single-use social media messages, as well.

10X RESULTS WITH VISUAL CONTENT

If you're creating more complex infographics, ebooks, or the like, repurpose the main content into microcontent. Microcontent is a 10x strategy of breaking up a larger piece of visual content, like an ebook or infographic, into bite-size chunks. Each smaller piece then acts as a hook to bring your audience back to the main body of the content itself. Then, rather than just one infographic, you have ten pieces of microcontent with CTAs that drive viewers back to the entire piece.

This strategy worked brilliantly for Lemonly client Demandbase. With offices in San Francisco, Seattle, Manhattan, and London, Demandbase is an account-based marketing vendor with global reach. Lemonly created an ebook for the company. And while it was well done, that's nothing new. What generated 10x returns, though, was their method of repurposing the ebook sections into an infographic and microcontent. They broke out key visuals from the ebook and designed the infographic in strategic sections so it could be divided easily into smaller pieces. Just like a wheel with many spokes leading back to the hub, each spoke of microcontent drove viewers back to the ebook. This resulted in a 960 percent return on investment directly attributed to the project.

It's easy to think of an infographic as the content itself. But Lemonly used it as a part of a larger narrative that's continued in the ebook. Each segment of the story was told in parts, creating a curiosity gap that drove clicks, downloads, and then conversions.

Visuals can be put to work in non-suit-and-tie fashion as well. In 2012, Lemonly designed a "pop culture Halloween costumes" infographic. And what was supposed to be some simple, fun social media candy went viral. In total, the piece attracted more than 1.5 million views and appeared on major media outlets across the web. What really matters, though, are the sixty qualified leads the piece drove.

HALLOWEEN COSTUMES
Pop Culture Favorites

2011
Charlie Sheen
Angry Birds
Katy Perry
Royal Couple

2010
Lady Gaga
Mad Hatter
Snooki
Avatar Characters
Harry Potter

2009
Twilight Characters
Michael Jackson
Alan from *The Hangover*
Wolverine

2008
Batman
Joker
Hannah Montana
Politicians

10 PERCENT RESULTS FROM VISUAL CONTENT

While visual storytelling can drive big results, it can also fall flat at the finish line. John recalls a project where his team worked hard to nail the visuals, as they always do. However, when it came time for the infographics and content to be distributed, the client pumped them out through a PR channel that squished and distorted them. This poor delivery left the visuals blurry and illegible.

John describes it like this: "Failing on delivery is like training for a marathon, only to run with bad shoes." To avoid 10 percent returns, ask a simple question: "Where will this live?" Infographics were originally designed to fit the average blog width of nearly a decade ago. As anyone with an internet connection knows, things change. And fast.

YOU HAVE EVERYTHING TO GAIN

One of the ways CoSchedule embraced visuals was to create five to seven visuals in each post we publish. Essentially, we create a series of microcontent that can then fill our social feeds. This is a great two-for-one strategy (more engaging posts and awesome social content), but also a great way to add variety to our smart-o-mation system. Sure, we promote the same piece of content a lot, and for a long time, but the variety in visuals ensures that it doesn't look like we are doing reruns all the time.

At the beginning of the chapter, I introduced you to a marketer who wasted hours and thousands of dollars on 10 percent work. I illustrated the harm of underpromotion. And, I hope, I made a strong case for harnessing the power of smart-o-mation. Now, it's up to you to put these facets of the *10x Marketing Formula* into practice. When you do, you will truly amplify the incredible amounts of hard work, money, and time you've invested into your content. And by utilizing principles like visual storytelling and microcontent, you can see long-tail returns.

By adopting this mindset and approach to social media promotion, you have everything to gain. Simply put, don't put in the tremendous work of creating 10x content only to stumble at the end with 10 percent promotion.

Your 10x Toolbox

Put this chapter into action with your 10x Toolbox by visiting https://coschedule.com/10x-toolbox

Photoshop CC Action:
Social Media Image Photoshop CC Action
This Photoshop CC action will automatically size graphics for social networks Facebook, Twitter, Google+, and LinkedIn.

Infographic: Best Times to Post Infographic
This infographic is a quick reference guide to the optimal times to post on every social network. (Tip: You can automate this process with CoSchedule's Best Time Scheduling feature.)

Google Analytics Custom Report:
Best Times to Post on Social Media
This custom Google Analytics report will show you the best times to post to your social accounts based on traffic for each network.

Free Tool: Social Message Optimizer
The Social Message Message Optimizer is a free tool that uses a powerful algorithm to help you optimize your social messages for every social network. It is available absolutely free at https://coschedule.com/social-message-optimizer

10x Marketing Interview: John T. Meyer on Visual Storytelling
Co-founder of Lemonly, John T. Meyer, and I discuss how his company used visual storytelling and microcontent for a 960 percent return on investment. You will have access to the full audio interview plus transcript.

CHAPTER TWELVE

10X EMAIL PROMOTION

Marketing experts are often split on the importance of email marketing. In fact, some industry publications will publish articles that explicitly disagree. Some articles pronounce email as a necessity.* And others predict it will die a quick death, becoming obsolete within a few years.†

So, what's a marketer to do?

In this chapter, I'll side with the email-loving crowd. I'm going to show you how building a healthy email list is one of the most effective, and lucrative, marketing weapons you can wield. And we're going to outline plenty of ways to build a powerful list and monetize it. We'll also discover why email is a critical partner to social media marketing. To start, let's take a brief tour of the history of public relations and how it's influenced the social media platforms on which so many marketers rely.

---

* https://www.inc.com/peter-roesler/top-5-reasons-why-email-marketing-is-still-works.html
* https://www.inc.com/john-brandon/why-email-will-be-obsolete-by-2020.html

SOCIAL MEDIA AND THE FATHER OF PR

On March 9, 1995, a man named Edward Bernays passed away. However, his legacy still ripples through the world of marketing. In fact, his obituary dubbed him the "father of public relations."* His theories and practices stemmed largely from the work of his uncle, Sigmund Freud. Bernays combined social psychology with political astuteness and a savvy injection of marketing spin to run campaigns that went beyond merely selling products or promoting causes.

Bernays understood that the nervous system of PR success wasn't only ad spots and poignant copy. He pioneered the idea of creating the right societal conditions so that a product or idea would sell itself. His landmark book *Propaganda* begins this way:†

> *The conscious and intelligent manipulation of the organized habits and opinions of the masses is an important element in democratic society. Those who manipulate this unseen mechanism of society constitute an invisible government which is the true ruling power of our country.*
>
> *We are governed, our minds are molded, our tastes formed, our ideas suggested, largely by men we have never heard of.*

His way of social engineering became the foundation of how we run marketing and PR campaigns to this day.

One of Bernays's most notable campaigns was for the American Tobacco Company, which owned the Lucky Strike cigarettes brand. His objective was simple: sell more cigarettes to women. He knocked this out of the park—but not by promoting a pack of smokes outright. Instead, he intensified cultural pressure around women being thin. And wouldn't you know it, a great solution to a few extra pounds was to opt for a few quick drags of Lucky Strikes rather than eating some chocolate.

This matters for us today because as Roger McNamee, an early investor in Facebook, says, "Big Blue" is using the same tactics as Bernays.‡

* http://www.nytimes.com/books/98/08/16/specials/bernays-obit.html

† Bernays, Edward L. Propaganda. Brooklyn, NY: Ig Publ., 2005. 37.

‡ http://www.telegraph.co.uk/news/2017/11/10/facebook-uses-techniques-edward-bernays-joseph-goebbels-former/

"I smoke a Lucky instead of eating sweets."
Grace M. Hay Drummond Hay
Lady Grace Drummond Hay,
"The fact that we were not permitted to smoke from the time the Graf Zeppelin left Friedrichshafen until we landed at Lakehurst only increased my appetite for a Lucky Strike. Oh, how good that first one tasted! I'm really keen for Lucky Strike—the toasted flavor is delightful. I smoke a Lucky instead of eating sweets—that's what many men have been doing for years. I think it high time we women smoked Luckies and kept our figures trim."
LADY GRACE DRUMMOND HAY
The modern common sense way—reach for a Lucky instead of a fattening sweet. Thousands are doing it—men keep healthy and fit, women retain a trim figure.
Lucky Strike, the finest tobaccos, skillfully blended, then toasted to develop a flavor which is a delightful alternative for that craving for fattening sweets.
Toasting frees Lucky Strike from impurities. 20,679 physicians recognize this when they say Luckies are less irritating than other cigarettes. That's why folks say: "It's good to smoke Luckies."
A reasonable proportion of sugar in the diet is recommended, but the authorities are overwhelming that too many fattening sweets are harmful. So, for moderation's sake we say:—
"REACH FOR A LUCKY INSTEAD OF A SWEET."
Lady Grace Drummond Hay,
LUCKY STRIKE
"IT'S TOASTED"
CIGARETTES
"It's toasted"
No Throat Irritation-No Cough.

As mentioned previously, organic reach on social media platforms is taking a nosedive every year. When viewed in light of Bernays's work, this makes total sense. Here's how it works.

You're encouraged to build a large, loyal, and engaged audience on a platform like Facebook. For a while, it's amazing. You're capturing a free marketing channel that boasts 1.37 billion daily active users—or 66 percent of its total user base.* But what's the economic undercurrent here?

As your audience grows, your reliance on the given social platform increases. Then what do the networks do? They slowly decrease organic reach, thus increasing the necessity of paying for the same level of exposure. Put another way, the marketplace conditions are being engineered so that ad space on social networks sells itself. To get the return your brand wants requires you to pony up more and more cash.

This is a brilliant business model. But it's also illustrative of why social media should not be your only way of communicating with your audience. Email allows you to build an audience that you *own*. That's good. This concept has also been described as owned versus rented property. You *own* things like your website and your email list. Nobody can throttle those down. You *rent* things like your social media profiles. The networks are in charge of both the reach and the rules.

LAUNCHING WITH A LIST

Here's a little secret: before releasing CoSchedule, we focused on building an email list for our launch. In fact, we focused on list building before we even started writing code! And while social media has been an important part of our growth, email has been truly integral. We started blogging in March 2013, about six months prior to launching CoSchedule in the wild. Our goal was to build an email list, a loyal audience, and a sounding board as we developed the product. We wanted an engaged audience who

---

* "Number of daily active Facebook users worldwide as of 3rd quarter 2017 (in millions)." Statista. 2017.

understood the value we could provide and thought about marketing the same way we did.

CoSchedule's first ever blog post

We blogged at least once per week for the entire nine months we built the product. Along the way, we built an email list that trusted us, fit us, and found enough value in us to stick around. Every time we published a new post, we emailed our entire list. They wanted to hear from us, so our email list gave us the opportunity to send them things they were interested in. And this was the result: we built an email list roughly five thousand fans strong. They were marketers who were engaged in our startup story and wanted to test out the solution to their problems we'd been building. To this day, our email list is our second-most valuable asset—just behind our customer list.

The reason it's so valuable is because it's an *owned* audience, and at the end of the day, our audience drives our revenue. Today, email is still our largest driver of customers by a factor of three. The reason we began building the list in the first place was to monetize it—which is the *only* reason anyone should build a list. Remember, startups are a results-or-die! enterprise. This means we've only invested in email because it's consistently performed as a 10x channel for us.

HOW TO MONETIZE AN EMAIL LIST

To monetize an email list requires that you reverse engineer from paying customer to email subscriber. At CoSchedule, the leading indicator, and most important metric for our marketing team to track for success, is trial signups. We know our trial signups will convert to paid customers at a certain rate. We also know that the more email subscribers we get, the more trial signups we get. And because we meticulously measure all conversions back to their source, we know exactly how many trial signups every email we send should generate.

This is important because it's debunked a marketing myth. Too many marketers are scared of their email lists. They don't want to send too many emails for fear their audience will unsubscribe. They believe that audiences are fickle and scared off easily. However, our experience shows that your audience will tolerate daily emails from you if they're the right fit. And because you're a 10x marketer creating competition-free content smack dab in the center of your content core, sending fewer emails is simply poor advice.

Here's how we've come to see it. To keep the math simple, let's say we've discovered each email will generate ten trial signups so long as we don't send more than one email per day. Because we've measured extensively, we also know that there's no major uptick in per-email trial signups by sending fewer emails than one per day. So, for us to send any fewer emails would be a huge waste of this major asset.

Now, the reason so many marketers are scared of sending too many emails is because they worry about their unsubscribe rates. But here's a newsflash: unsubscribe rates don't matter; revenue matters! Also, our data showed that the increase in unsubscribes due to a greater frequency of daily emails was virtually non-existent. Your email sending frequency should be directly linked to what generates the most revenue. So, when it comes to our email list, we've learned to value new subscribers above all else. The more new subscribers we have, the more new customers we have. We believe you'll find this holds true for you, as well.

The real trick is how to build an email list filled with the right audience. And that's exactly what this stage in the *10x Marketing Formula* is all about.

FROM 0 TO 250,000 SUBSCRIBERS

In the past four years, we've worked hard to figure out what works and what doesn't in email list building. Through copious testing, plenty of failure, and eventual hockey-stick growth, we've learned exactly what's worked for us. The following strategies have helped us go from zero subscribers to more than 250,000 since our first blog post in March of 2013. Today, we routinely grow by 4,000-plus subscribers each week.

We've generated these results because, one, every email is extremely relevant to the problems our audience is trying to solve. And two, each email is directly connected to the value CoSchedule itself provides. This means we can quickly grow a list filled with exactly the right people. It grows fast because the content is so damn good—and it's monetizable because they're content consumers who will actually turn into customers.

"These strategies have helped us go from zero subscribers to more than 250,000 since our first blog post in March of 2013."

It's worked for the two reasons prior. And we've also found a few tactics that consistently amplify our results to the 10x level:

- Content upgrades for every blog post
- Free tools to help solve major marketing problems that intersect with our product
- Competition-free content people are desperate not to miss

Now, let's dig into how we use each tactic, what makes them work, and how you can use them in your marketing context.

CONTENT UPGRADES

A content upgrade is a companion resource to content like blog posts. Often, they are things like templates, calculators, worksheets, or any other document that helps your audience put what you're teaching them into practice. To use them to build an email list, we gate them behind an email opt-in form. So, they get the resource by paying with an email address.

This has become pretty standard practice in content marketing. However, at CoSchedule, we routinely craft such comprehensive content upgrades that we believe people would be willing to pay for them. For example, here's an eight-piece content upgrade bundle for a single blog post. It's filled with PDFs, spreadsheet templates, and editable worksheets:

1. PDF: Email list building tips template to help beginners get started
2. PDF: Email list building guide to help you implement every tactic you learn throughout this blog post.
3. Worksheet: Email subject line guide to help you increase your open rates
4. PDF: 500 words to use in your blog titles (and therefore, your email subject lines)
5. Spreadsheet: Email subject line A/B test spreadsheet template to help you continually improve your subject lines
6. PDF: Best time to send email guide to help you reach most of your subscribers according to best practices
7. PDF: Best day to send email Google Analytics custom report to help you use your own data to know the days of the week when your audience opens your email
8. Custom Report: Best time to send email Google Analytics custom report to help you send emails at the absolute best times when your audience clicks through to read your content

These included guides, spreadsheets, templates, and custom Google Analytics reports are dedicated to helping our readers do absolutely everything we're about to teach them.

A content upgrade bundle

As of writing this, we have more than 220 content upgrades available in our blog posts and our Marketing Resource Library.* Our content upgrades are a core component of meeting our standard of performance of actionability. They're always custom designed to contour the content we're creating. And in total, our content upgrades are responsible for well over one hundred thousand email subscribers.

The best part about killer content upgrades is that as long as you're actually showing people how to solve real problems, the upgrades practically write themselves. All you need to do is format your how-to

---

* You can find hundreds of free marketing resources in CoSchedule's Marketing Resource Library by visiting https://coschedule.com/resources

solutions in a spreadsheet, editable document, or even a printable PDF. If you're providing actionable value, a content upgrade is a natural result.

I know what you're thinking: "I barely have time to write a blog post, much less create a content upgrade." But what if you just created one fewer post per week and used that time to create a content upgrade? That trade would be worth it, because your list will grow faster even though you're publishing one less piece per week. That's a pretty great deal. You could even follow Pat Flynn's lead and create one content upgrade per month that's incorporated into every post. This is super efficient, super smart, and undeniably effective.

The bottom line here is you should weigh content upgrades as heavily important in your content mix. They allow your value to travel farther, make your content more actionable, and help grow email lists. They're well worth the investment, and too important to skip.

TOOLS

After content upgrades, our most effective list-building drivers have been free tools. Our top three tools for list building have been Headline Analyzer, the Click To Tweet Wordpress Plugin, and Social Message Optimizer. Here are the email subscribers each tool has produced.

Headline Analyzer

I shared the story of our Headline Analyzer in Chapter Five, "10x Projects." But I want to mention it again here, because in just twenty-four months it's contributed about 20 percent of our total list growth.

Subscribers Generated: 55,040
Timeframe: 24 months

Click To Tweet WordPress Plugin

In 2013, we built a social sharing plugin called "Click To Tweet" for WordPress. It's a smart little tool that allows anyone with a Word-

Press blog to craft readymade tweets for their readers to share with just a click or tap. We gave it away for free, and today, it's used on over ten thousand websites. This has also helped build our email list, because when you give away stuff that's this good, people want to know what else you have to offer.

Subscribers Generated: 7,407
Timeframe: 1.5 years

Social Message Optimizer

Our Social Message Optimizer is a free tool that helps marketers write better messages that boost engagement, build trust, drive traffic, and spark conversions. It allows users to type in their message, select which social network it's written for, and then let our sophisticated algorithm score it. It helps them capture more eyeballs with their messages, getting even more likes, comments, shares, and clicks. It does all this by optimizing according to proven best practices and real data from 6.9 million social media messages analyzed by our team.

Subscribers Generated: 1,806
Timeframe: 8 months

COMPETITION-FREE CONTENT

Next, we've also invested heavily in competition-free content outside of blogging and tools. We have created free courses, an ultimate indexable guide, webinars, and an ebook.

Free Marketing Courses

Here's the deal: we've shared a lot of actionable marketing advice and in-depth how-to content over the years. Our team has published hundreds of articles, hosted scores of webinars, recorded videos, and hosted sixty-plus podcast episodes packed with marketing wisdom. The millions of visitors, downloads, and views tell the story of an audience that craves our content.

So, at the beginning of 2017, we asked ourselves, "What's the next step?" Thus, our free online Marketing Strategy and Social Media Strategy courses were born.* Each course offers six lessons packed with worksheets, templates, videos, and guides to create a marketing or social media strategy from scratch in just two weeks. Each student exchanges an email address for access to the course.

Subscribers Generated: 14,732

Timeframe: 10 months

Live Webinars

We've offered webinars for everything from marketing strategy to influencer partnerships to product demonstrations. While they're not a unique platform, the numbers make them worth considering. According to a 2016 "Webinar Benchmarks Report" that analyzed 12,780 webinars:†

- Webinars attract an average of 233 attendees
- Webinar viewers watch an average of 50 minutes
- Watchtime has increased by 31.5 percent since 2010
- Of global attendees, 20 percent downloaded content, 7 percent submitted questions, and 31 percent responded to polls

Our results have mirrored those of the study.

Subscribers Generated: 3,395

Timeframe: 14 months

Social Media Strategy Ebook

For us, social media strategy is a content core topic. So, we curated our very best content on the subject, wrote some brand new stuff, and packaged it into a 114-page ebook called Social Media Strategy.

---

* You can enroll in both marketing courses for free at: https://coschedule.com/marketing-courses

† https://bizibl.com/marketing/download/2016-webinar-benchmarks-report

It's a guide to help marketers:

- Get organized and take control of their social media strategy
- Listen to and connect with their audience's needs to create content that boosts engagement
- Figure out a social media editorial calendar that will quadruple traffic

It's available as a free download in exchange for an email address.*

Subscribers Generated: 2,473

Timeframe: 16 months

Marketing Strategy Ultimate Guide

Like social media strategy, marketing strategy as a whole is a perennially popular topic. So, our demand generation team laid out their framework for crafting a marketing strategy that includes everything from measuring ROI to results-based budgeting. It's a gold mine for marketing managers tasked with creating a lean strategy that will get results. This ultimate guide is a microsite organized in ten chapters. The content itself is 100 percent free and ungated—meaning you don't even have to enter an email address to read it. However, we have multiple worksheets and templates throughout that help marketers put their newfound knowledge into action. We give them access to these resources in exchange for an email address. What's most impressive is that this guide generated 1,042 email signups in just ten days.

Subscribers Generated: 1,587

Timeframe: 2 months

* Grab your free copy at https://coschedule.com/social-media-strategy

BUILDING AND ENGAGING A JAW-DROPPING EMAIL LIST

Now, content upgrades, free tools, and investing in competition-free content are simply three of the ways we've grown our email list to a quarter-million subscribers strong. You can test similar methods that fit within your competition-free content framework. To bring 10x email promotion in for a landing, here are a few more best practices we follow. Each of these should also become part of your email list-building—and engagement—strategy.

HOW PRETTY SHOULD YOUR EMAIL BE?

Here's a basic question: what should your emails look like? Should they be well designed and super professional looking? Or should they be plain, with just text and some links?

HTML-enhanced email vs. plain-text email

When we at CoSchedule tested several HTML-enhanced emails for the ones we use to announce new blog posts, we found that our plain-text versions increased the number of opens by 3.5 percent. With this small change, our emails immediately started sending more traffic to our content. A few percentage points may seem like small beans. But when your list is more than 250,000 strong, that's 7,500 more people opening our emails. And seriously, regardless of how big your list is, 3 percent is 3 percent!

Additionally, plain-text emails look more authentic and less spammy than HTML-enhanced emails. HubSpot came to the same conclusion in their research, hinting that email filters may be strong enough to weed out over-enhanced emails.* This is an incredibly easy test to run for your own email sends. Here's another benefit: plain text emails are a lot quicker to create and require zero design time, as well.

5 SUBJECT LINE BEST PRACTICES

Now, let's head north of the body content. Email inboxes are busy, highly competitive places. So, before we dive further into list-building tactics, it's important to remember that email promotion involves actually getting people to open, read, and engage with your emails, as well. Naturally, the email subject line will be on the front lines of your quest for email opens. This is because a subject line has just one goal: to get people to open your email. Without opens, you have no clicks. And without clicks, you have no conversions. So, here are five best practices to stand out and capture interest as quickly as possible.

One: Numbers Are Your Friends

According to A/B testing performed by the email platform Campaign Monitor, subject lines with numbers saw a 57 percent better open rate than those without.† To give even more context, they suggest: "The key to success with this formula is the number you use. If you are suggesting effort a reader needs to expend (like steps in

---

* https://blog.hubspot.com/marketing/plain-text-vs-html-emails-data
† https://www.campaignmonitor.com/blog/email-marketing/2014/09/subject-line-formulas/

a process for instance), then using a low number works better as it suggest the process is quicker and easier. However, if you are providing value to the reader (like a number of ways to increase email subscribers) then a higher number will work better as it increases the reader's perception of the value your email will provide them."

Two: Characters Count

Character and word count matter because there is limited real estate available for your subject lines. Typically, desktops show roughly sixty characters and mobile devices about twenty-five to thirty.* So, think through where your email subscribers will first see your email. Will it be on a smartphone or a desktop? In a study called "The Art and Science of Effective Subject Lines," Return Path found that emails with subject lines between sixty-one and seventy characters long were read most, at a rate of 17 percent.

Three: 10 Phrases That Increase Open Rates

Much like emotionally resonant words for article headlines, there are words and phrases that boost open rates. Here are ten to test in your coming email campaigns:†

1. thanks
2. golden
3. iphone
4. breaking
5. advice
6. course
7. breaking
8. exclusive

* https://returnpath.com/wp-content/uploads/2015/04/
RP-Subject-Line-Report-FINAL.pdf
† http://content.adestra.com/hubfs/2015_Reports_and_
eGuides/2015_Subject_Line_Report.pdf

9. review

10. top stories

Four: 10 Phrases That Decrease Open Rates

While there are email open-rate heroes, there are also villains. Here are ten phrases to avoid for optimal open rates:*

1. get rid of

2. secret of

3. shocking

4. what you need to know

5. won't believe

6. quickest

7. aim

8. call

9. put

10. 2 for 1

Five: A/B Testing

Today, every email service worth its salt will include the ability to split test your subject lines. At CoSchedule, we conduct A/B tests religiously. An A/B test, or split test, is a method of comparing two versions of the same content against one another to analyze which performs best. For instance, you might be promoting a piece of content about a new tool your company is launching. To conduct your own, start by simply asking yourself, "What do we want to learn?" For example, do you want to know if including a number in your subject lines increases opens? Are you testing for emojis? Or even the effectiveness of capitalization? Define what you want to learn, then split test accordingly.

* https://returnpath.com/wp-content/uploads/2015/04/
RP-Subject-Line-Report-FINAL.pdf

Bonus: Email Subject Line Tester

Create click-worthy subject lines with the free Email Subject Line Tester tool (https://coschedule.com/email-subject-line-tester). It will help you write email subject lines that drive more opens, more clicks, and more conversions.

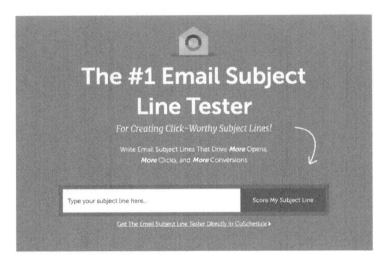

LANDING PAGES

If you have any digital marketing experience, you've undoubtedly heard of landing pages. They are web pages designed for one purpose: conversions. Typically, the reason will either be to get a visitor to click through to another page, or to convert into an email subscriber, lead, or customer. They are designed so that the visitor can only take one action, meaning there is no top-level navigation or other links to distract them. There's simply one action to be taken on the page.

Our most popular landing page is dedicated to giving away the social media strategy ebook I described earlier in exchange for an email address. It's a key search term for us, and the ebook intersects perfectly with the value CoSchedule provides as the social media calendar that takes what our audience reads to the next level. Now, your landing pages will differ based on the action you're calling your visitors to take, and the content you're providing. But overall, they're a fantastic way to build an email list.

As you approach building your own landing pages, here are some wins we've found that you should consider implementing:

One Clear Call to Action

First, your landing page should have one purpose, meaning one clear CTA. In this case, a CTA is a compelling directive for your audience to take one specific action—not pick from a variety of choices. A landing page isn't the place to give your audience options. It's a page intensely focused on compelling the visitor to take an action.

Provide Real Value

Key to compelling visitors to take action is providing actual value on the page! A landing page isn't just a big ad. Treat it as you would any piece of 10x content.

Quid Pro Quo

Landing pages are ideal for lead magnets. So, continue riding the value train and exchange a quality resource for that email address. It's a win–win when you deliver on value. Remember, it's not simply about getting the opt-in; it's about creating a relationship so they'll actually open the emails you send in the months to come.

Keyword Driven

Finally, landing pages need keywords, too. They can rank on search engines, so give them some SEO love. Do your research using Brian Dean's Skyscraper Technique and optimize your content for SEO impact.

BUNDLE YOUR FREEBIES

If you're in the content upgrade game (which you should be), then get smart with how you repurpose yours. For example, let's say you're in banking, and you've created a free tool for calculating a mortgage payment as a content upgrade. Chances are, that's going to be a content core topic for you. That means you'll be talking about mortgages from multiple angles over the course of time.

So, don't offer your calculator only once! Instead, bundle it with other related content upgrades to give away a "kit" or "bundle." This provides serious layers of value with no additional effort. The reality is, every visitor won't read every single piece of content on your website, or visit all of your landing pages. This means if you simply use a content upgrade one time, it's being underutilized.

Instead of providing one free piece of awesome content in exchange for an email address, why not two? We asked ourselves that question and put it to the test. We've tested this extensively and found the more bonus content we give away in exchange for an email address, the higher the conversion rate. The bigger our bundle of freebies, the more people subscribe.

For example, when we gave away just one checklist, our average conversion was 3.38 percent. Not bad, right?

But when we switched to providing content bundles of fifteen and scheduled the welcome popup to show up once every five days, conversions jumped to more than 6 percent.

If fifteen seems like a lot, don't sweat it. Simply start with what you have. If you have three related giveaways, put 'em together and see what happens. Measure your results and test if this method works for you. Just remember, your results won't come from copying our bundling technique. They'll come from producing competition-free content that fits within your content core. This method will simply add accelerant to the bonfire of growth you're creating via content.

Experiment with Giveaway Content Types

Next, some content types are just more effective than others. Here's what we've learned our audience likes:

- *Templates.* We focus on highly actionable content, so tools to put newfound knowledge into practice make perfect sense.
- *Tear sheets, worksheets, checklists, and guides.* This follows the same theory as templates. The reader has learned something new. So, each resource type typically

summarizes the big ideas and offers a few bonus points to help our audience get the results they want.

- *Infographics.* Infographics, as discussed last chapter, are an excellent way to distill information and communicate the highlights visually.
- *Custom Google Analytics reports.* If you have a website, you should have Google Analytics set up. No exceptions. However, it can feel overwhelming for someone new to such a powerful and complex tool—especially if they have a non-technical background. So, when we're teaching our audience to measure website performance in specific ways, we create custom Google Analytics reports they can download and use without having to set them up manually.
- *Photoshop CC actions.* CoSchedule is a badass social media tool. So, we create a ton of content around social media scheduling, how to write killer messages, and how to effectively use visuals. We also know lots of marketers want to use design well, but may have designers who are very busy. To remove the hurdle, we created a custom Photoshop CC action that automatically resizes images to work perfectly for Facebook, Twitter, LinkedIn, and Google+.
- *Slide decks.* If you do webinars, you have slide decks. If you have slide decks, you have insightful content to give away in exchange for an email address. These are excellent companion resources for kits and bundles, as well.
- *Editable Word, Excel, and PowerPoint documents.* While these often qualify as templates, they're worth calling out in their own right. Microsoft owns considerable market share in the business and consumer worlds. So, chances are your audience uses, and is familiar with, the Microsoft software suite. This means your content upgrades will be ready to use straight out of the box for people. These are often popular search terms to optimize for, as well.

Your audience may also prefer bonus content in the form of videos, spreadsheets, white papers, or something we haven't even explored. The point is this: In your first few months, publish lots of different types of content upgrades and measure your results. Repeat your success, and stop creating stuff that performs poorly.

START WITH WHAT YOU HAVE

You need to build an audience you own, and email is, hands down, the way to do that. If you have already begun building an email list, excellent. Use the frameworks in this chapter to catalyze its growth. And if you don't have one today, get one; MailChimp is free to start with! The barrier to entry and continued use is extraordinarily low.

Here's the truth. If your email list isn't at the center of the ROI you are generating for your business, news flash: you are doing it wrong. Your email list should be a constant driver of business, and if it isn't, you need to take it more seriously.

So, what do you have right now you can repurpose into content upgrades? Are there any internal resources or tools your team uses that may benefit your audience? If so, leverage them to build your email list. And use juicy CTAs to drive conversion rates sky-high . . . which is exactly what you're going to learn at the beginning of Phase Four in the *10x Marketing Formula*.

Your 10x Toolbox
Put this chapter into action with your 10x Toolbox by visiting https://coschedule.com/10x-toolbox

Free Tool: Email Subject Line Tester
Create click-worthy subject lines with the free Email Subject Line Tester tool. It will help you write email subject lines that drive more opens, more clicks, and more conversions, by visiting https://coschedule.com/email-subject-line-tester

PHASE FOUR: ANALYZE

The fourth phase of the 10x Marketing Formula
will help you optimize your content to convert
an audience into customers. And finally, you
will learn to focus on and measure everything
against your One Metric that Matters (1MTM)—
the metric most directly tied to revenue growth.

CHAPTER THIRTEEN

CONVERSION PSYCHOLOGY

Muscle atrophy happens when muscles waste away, losing strength and size. The primary reason this happens is through a lack of physical activity. If the muscle isn't exercised, it shrinks. Today, I think many marketers exhibit a form of marketing atrophy: weak calls to action. What should be strong, decisive, and robust, is weak and even nonexistent.

Here's what happened. Somewhere along the way, many marketers got this terrible idea drilled into them. They knew content marketers were supposed to be helpful, but they fell for the notion that being helpful means never actually selling one's product or service.

Yes, the content marketer's job is to be helpful. So, if you're not in business to be helpful to customers, then get out of freaking business. But you know what? Being helpful will nearly always involve positioning your product or service.

At some point, many of us forgot that our companies were helpful. However, we also believe our companies can actually provide value, right? If they couldn't, why would we work there in the first place?

Duh.

The truth is, if your company is in business, it is already helpful. It doesn't need the marketing team's help. Your job is to make that value a reality for prospective customers. You're connecting your company's proven solutions with your prospect's solvable pain. But for some reason, many marketers feel bad trying to sell. Somehow, we've come to believe that trying to sell is "advertising," and that advertising equals "bad." So we feel too salesy to actually pitch, promote, and *market*! It's okay that your company uses content as a vehicle for building trust with potential customers. What's not okay is if you *don't* sell with it.

Listen, I get it. Content marketers love the soft-sell to provide value, and that's great, but if you never turn the corner and position your product: (1) you're not really marketing anything, and (2) you're not actually being helpful. I've heard marketers all over the world say: "Garrett, we're having trouble proving our value as content marketers to our boss and company."

Do you know why? Because they've been told that good content marketing is the opposite of advertising. Therefore, they believe it isn't about sales. But here's the rub: sales are what their boss cares about—and so does yours. You have to find a way to generate business value, and that means getting away from the idea that content marketing and real CTAs are incompatible.

To be a 10x marketer, you must sell with your content. This means transcending the role of simple media creator. To an extent, it's true that companies should be media creators, but it's not the entire reality. The marketer's job isn't simply to produce content. Rather, it's to produce content that produces business results. And to produce results, you have to convert traffic into customers.

Conversion psychology is all about what makes people buy, try, and click. Why do they take the actions that marketers want them to? Are there common triggers that spark engagement? Are there psychological levers any marketer can pull?

Just imagine if you could get your customers to say "Thank you!" for your CTAs? That's not marketing fiction. It happens. Check it out.

Cali Dalynn Bock
@CaliBock

`( Follow )` ∨

@CoSchedule Just wanna let you guys know
your content is on point. So informative and
soft-salesy that before I knew it, I scrolled all
the way to your bottom-page CTA and
jumped in #contentmarketing #sales

5:27 PM - 15 Nov 2017

In this chapter, you're going to learn how to write CTAs that work
so well people will literally thank you for them. And the first step is
to remember your content core. A CTA is most effective when your
content marries the value your company provides with what your
prospective customer wants. The second, then, becomes closing the
deal with a good CTA.

To find repeatable success, we'll dissect what makes people say
"Yes!" We'll work through how you can build conversion ammo of your
own, outline the purpose of CTAs, and wrap it up with four kinds of
CTAs you can use to increase your conversions.

Simple. Focused. Straightforward. (Just like a good CTA.)

10X MARKETING INTERVIEW:
JOANNA WIEBE ON WHY PEOPLE CLICK, TRY, AND BUY

In my opinion, there's no better place to start with conversion psychology
than Joanna Wiebe. Joanna is the creator of Copy Hackers, cofounder of
Airstory, and an absolute authority on copywriting and conversions. So,
she's the perfect person to help us understand the psychology behind why
people click, try, and buy. I interviewed her exclusively for this chapter
because her expertise as a conversion copywriter is exactly the skill set
you'll need to acquire for this phase of your 10x marketing journey.*

---

* Listen to the full interview at coschedule.com/10x-toolbox

"CONVERSION COPYWRITING USES ALL OF THIS TO GET PEOPLE TO SAY 'YES,' USING ONLY YOUR WORDS."

—JOANNA WIEBE,
CREATOR OF COPY HACKERS

First, what exactly is conversion copywriting? As Joanna explains, "Conversion copywriting combines the user experience online with the psychology of decision making." Instead of being something fancy and new, it's a return to the fundamentals. Yes, it's copywriting and content that is peppered with new ideas and insights. But, there are also changeless factors of human perceptions, motivations, and behaviors infused into its heartbeat.

Joanna sums it up like this: "Conversion copywriting uses all of this to get people to say 'yes,' using only your words. And then measures to see if it actually worked or not."

"Conversion copywriting uses all of this to get people to say 'yes,' using only your words."

The 10x difference between traditional copywriting and conversion copywriting is that while traditional copy is meant simply to inform, conversion copy is written to get people to say yes. This distinction is important as we learn the magic of conversion psychology. Think about it like the difference between a journalist and a marketer. A journalist writes copy to inform. A marketer writes copy to convert.

5 STAGES OF AWARENESS

However, there is nuance here, fueled by what Joanna calls the "five stages of awareness." The principle is that every person in your audience, on your site, or in your email list is in their own stage, which is measured in relationship to their belief in your product or service as the best solution to their pain. Here are the five stages:

1. Unaware
2. Pain Aware
3. Solution Aware
4. Product Aware
5. Most Aware

Here's how you can think of these stages practically.

1. Person is unaware.
A visitor is likely to be unaware if they haven't identified their pain or your role as a solution. This stage requires top-of-the-funnel content to move them to the next stage of awareness.

2. Person is feeling the pain.
A visitor is likely to be pain aware if they're feeling pain, but haven't yet identified the solutions that exist for that pain. Imagine that you've started experiencing sharp pain in your knees while walking. At this point, you won't know how to solve it; you're simply aware that it exists.

3. Person knows there's a cure for the pain.
A visitor is likely to be solution aware when they've felt the pain and discovered that solutions exist for it. However, they still don't know that your solution either exists or is a match to solving their problem.

4. Person knows you can solve their pain.
Here, they are product aware if they know that your product is one of the solutions to their pain. This means they're shopping. They're stacking you up against the competition. To return to our friend with the knee pain, he or she is trying to decide if it's time to see a doctor, take some ibuprofen, or simply buy a knee brace for $19.98.

5. Person knows you are the best solution.
This is the coveted, bottom of the funnel stage! They are most aware when they know your solution is the best to solve their pain. Getting people to say yes in this stage is relatively easy. However, the hard part is actually moving them to this stage! Generally speaking, the more aware someone becomes, the deeper in the funnel they're likely to be.

GETTING TO "YES" WITH THE 5 STAGES OF AWARENESS

Motivating people to say yes to your offer, no matter how big or how small, is a matter of understanding both what's inside them and which stage of awareness they are in. This way, you can demystify their thought processes and invite them to enter the next stage of awareness.

You start by asking, "What brought them to me today?" What's going on in their life that they would need what you have to give? Do they have a pain they're trying to solve that intersects with your product? (Think content core, here!) Are they trying to decide on the best product or service for their context? The more you understand where they're at and why they've come to you, the better you can progressively draw them into further stages of awareness.

So, how do you move your visitors, audience, or email subscribers from one stage to the next? This is where it's time to get serious about your CTAs. For instance, if a visitor is in the pain aware stage, where they're feeling the hurt but don't know how to fix it, it makes sense to offer something like an ebook that'll help them solve the pain while simultaneously becoming aware of your product as a long-term, or ultimate, solution. So, should you send emails or publish content that offers an ebook and includes a straightforward CTA like "Download the Free Ebook"? Should you employ persuasion tactics like social proof, scarcity, or fear of missing out?

This is where it's time to get even more savvy.

CALLS TO VALUE VS. CALLS TO ACTION

Joanna explains that,

> Once you get visitors to the bottom of the funnel, great. That's where persuasion tactics work really well. That's actually where a lot of conversion tests play best, because the motivation stuff is taken care of, right? People are motivated by that point, and all you have to do is move them from them mentally saying yes, to actually saying yes— which is such a small river to have to cross.

The marketing world loves persuasion techniques . . . Like, "Oh, let's throw that little bit of glitter on the page." And when it comes down to it, they only work sometimes, and bigger, stronger, smarter, really old-school stuff continues to do most of the heavy lifting, from what I've seen. And we have to think more about that.

What Joanna is getting at is that you must realize the difference between calls to action and calls to value (CTVs). A CTA is calling the audience to take a focused action like "Download Free Ebook," "Buy X Product," or something similar. A CTA stresses clarity and simplicity. This is no time to get clever. However, until you have moved them to the "most aware" stage, you're not yet calling them to action—you're calling them to the next stage of value.

A CTV completes the phrase, "I want to . . ." So, a CTV is written to the promise of value an action holds, rather than focusing on the action itself. Joanna returns to the ebook download as an example.

The phrase "Download Free Ebook" is a CTA. However, if the visitor isn't ready to purchase, then your goal should be focusing on the value the next stage provides. Naturally, your audience would be asking themselves, "What value does this ebook promise me? What am I going to get?" The CTA "Download Free Ebook" tells them they're going to get a free ebook. But why do they want a free ebook right now?

"A CTA stresses clarity and simplicity. This is no time to get clever."

Imagine the ebook is about how to quickly craft a content strategy. In this case, the value is to save time, effort, and brain power on creating something they know they need—a content strategy. Knowing what to publish, when to publish it, and why it matters to their audience is expressive of their pain here. So, the value of the ebook is better communicated like this: "Create a Content Strategy in 10 Minutes."

THE 5 STAGES OF AWARENESS

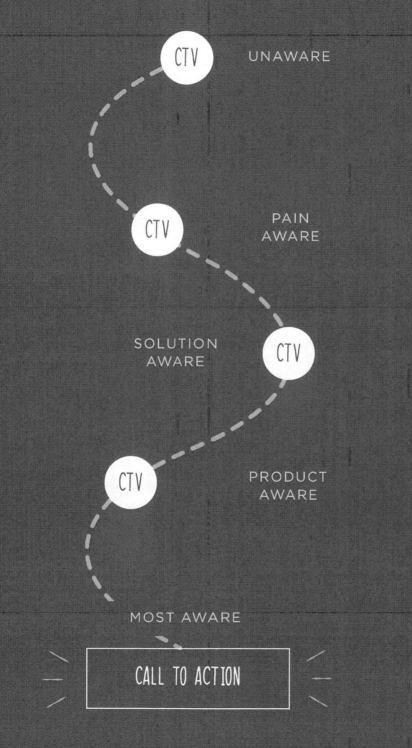

UNAWARE

PAIN
AWARE

SOLUTION
AWARE

PRODUCT
AWARE

MOST AWARE

CALL TO ACTION

If we zoom out and look at the five stages of awareness as an integrated flow, you're really creating a string of CTVs that lead your audience to the "most aware" stage. This is the place where they're ready for the CTA, and it's time to close the deal. This is 10x marketing at its finest.

People click, try, and buy because the perceived value is greater than the cost. But understanding their current thought process in relation to your product is the linchpin of conversions. In essence, you're drawing them deeper into your content core. In turn, their motivation to say yes continually builds. This is because your value perfectly meets both their needs and their willingness to commit at each stage in the funnel, thus taking the relationship further.

RESEARCH-FUELED CTAS AND CTVS

The best CTAs and CTVs will use the actual words your customers use when looking for solutions to their current stage of awareness. To get these golden phrases requires customer research. However, some of the best ways for doing great customer research aren't fancy, expensive ones at all. There are myriad places online you can mine for customer language.

How to Use Google for Audience Research

Let's begin with how to use Google for research and listening. Your first stop should be Google. Simply type in the keywords related to your topic and look for both the content that currently ranks and the autocomplete searches. The top-ranking pages will help you understand the problems your audience is experiencing (from their point of view) and the words they use to describe them. This content will help you discern what's called "searcher intent," or the reason behind someone's search. What exactly were they trying to solve when they typed in those phrases?

Next, the autocomplete phrases help by suggesting alternative, or related, phrasing for a query. This will also help you find customer phrasing and language surrounding a search term. Additionally, these words and phrases are the ones visitors will use when searching for a solution. You, with your competition-free content, want to be that solution.

Blog Comments

While you're reviewing the top search results for keywords, you'll find another research method at your disposal. Blog post and article comments are a treasure trove of audience insight. This is a great way to gather freely available qualitative data. In the comments section, not only will you read your audience's actual words, but you'll uncover their specific questions as, well.

You can define both *how* they're speaking and *what gaps* in education or execution remain after encountering content. And not only that, but you can read how your competition is responding. With just a few searches, a bit of scrolling, and some reading, you have insight that's often as valuable as a survey.

As you read through these sections, I suggest also copying key phrases and questions that stand out to you. For example, let's say you work for an agency and are researching customer language around a service you offer: "social media management." In this case, not only are you competing with other agencies offering the same service, but you're also competing with self-serve tools that help with the same job.

A quick scroll into the comments section on a Social Media Examiner article titled "5 Social Media Management Tools to Save

Time" shows a common thread readers are looking for.* The readers' comments suggest they have frustrations with current tools and are unclear as to why they should choose one tool over the other.

With just a cursory perusal you can lift verbatim statements like "I'm frustrated with [X Tool] because the drawbacks outweigh the benefits." In that single sentence you can learn:

1. *Customer pain:* frustration with their current social media management tool
2. *Which competing solution is failing:* X Tool
3. *Why the solution is failing:* drawbacks outweigh the benefits

The comment continues, " I need to know what other options are out there, how they compare to each other, differences and what platform I can use, XYZ . . ."

In just a few moments of research you already have insight into the customer's pain, language, and intention behind visiting the keyword you're writing about. This gives you serious ammo for both creating competition-free content to drive traffic *and* how the topic will fit within your content core.

As an example, we can adapt this target audience language into this CTV with confidence: "Stop being frustrated with your current tools, and download your free toolkit now!" The key is pinpointing the pain (frustration), its source (current tools), and your solution (free toolkit).

Social Media User Groups

Much like blog post comments as a listening technique, social media user groups on platforms like Facebook and LinkedIn are also invaluable. There are targeted groups for nearly every niche in the world. To make the most of them, simply join, listen, and engage

* https://www.socialmediaexaminer.com/5-social-media-management-tools-to-save-time/

with those who fit the bill of your target audience. Understand that I'm not suggesting you spam the group to promote your services. You're simply there to learn.

In keeping with our social media management angle, there happens to be a Facebook group entitled "Social Media Managers." As of writing this, it's also an active group, with 277 posts today and 452 members added in the last week.

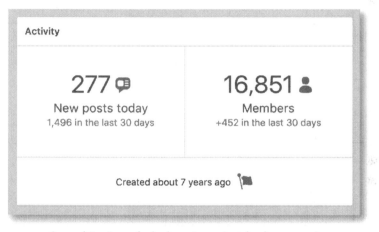

Source: https://www.facebook.com/groups/socialmediamanagers/

Active groups like this are the most likely candidates to be worth your time. Once you join, there will be anywhere from hundreds to thousands of conversations for you to study. A quick way to find what you're looking for is with the "Find" command, which will help you jump straight to the instances your keyword or phrase has been mentioned.

Question Platforms

Social media networks have not been exhausted yet! Platforms like Quora and Reddit also offer learning opportunities. In case you're unfamiliar, Quora is a social network that allows users to ask questions of experts on given topics or simply to the community at large. Questions will routinely get hundreds of answers, and then provide sub-threads to learn from, as well. And Reddit, of course, is a massive news aggregator and discussion site where similar intel can be found. Here, the principle is the same. Search for keyword-related questions and subject matter to lift language and fresh angles you may not have considered.

One-on-One Customer Interviews

While those research methods allow you to look outside of your current audience and customer base, don't neglect talking to the people who already know, like, and trust you. Customer interviews are a powerful way to learn exactly how your customers express their needs, describe your solutions, and think. Simply put, you're looking to have a conversation to hear their language.

When you grab key phrases your customers actually use, you can connect directly with them—and people like them. Rather than falling prey to jargon or product babble, your value will be communicated with crystal clarity. When you can harness their actual words, you can grab attention and infuse your CTVs and CTAs with compelling copy.

When I'm able to talk one on one with my customers via user groups, surveys, or even phone conversations, there are five research questions I always like to ask:

1. What prompted you to start looking for a solution like {our product}?
2. Why did you choose {our product}?
3. What is the most significant difference {our product} is making in your business today?
4. How would you {briefly} describe {our product} to someone else?
5. What is the single greatest benefit {our product} provides?

The answers to these questions will set the tone for your CTVs and CTAs, and therefore let you speak directly to the customer using their own language. Being able to describe the benefit of your product or service this way is both extremely valuable and appealing. It's also a brilliant way of learning how to best connect with your audience at each of the five stages of awareness. You can then tailor your messaging to their unique place in the funnel. However, what's most important here is to get comfortable asking for the sale. And the closer you can marry your messaging and value with the way they express their needs, the more confidently you can call them to either action or value.

A SAMPLE CTV

Let's illustrate this point by adapting some of our actual customer feedback from a one-on-one interview about our product, with one of our customers whose social media agency scaled because of how CoSchedule increased their productivity:

"For me, it's come down to the fact that I've been able to take on more clients and make more money."

In our customer's case, they were managing more than thirty social profiles—one by one. Ouch. That's a lot of time, login credentials, and headache. To leverage this statement, let's pretend I'm writing a CTV for visitors in the pain aware stage of awareness. They're experiencing the pain of being bottlenecked by managing loads of social media accounts manually.

Here's a CTV that will use a verbatim statement to move our visitors from pain aware to solution aware:

"Take on more clients and make more money with these free social media management workflows."

From here, the content upgrade's job would be to give away the workflows that are baked right into CoSchedule. Our workflows will certainly increase productivity, but the resource will point toward the next stage in using our automation features.

A SAMPLE CTA

Next, let's craft a CTA using another verbatim customer statement:

> *"I'm a visual person, so seeing our content mapped out in front of me really helps me know what I have planned. When I have it ready to go, I can focus on other things. It's a great feeling."*

Imagine I'm creating content for visitors in the solution aware stage of awareness. In this case, the pain I'm addressing is lacking a quick-reference, bird's-eye view of your content roadmap. Sure, you've done the hard work of planning and making a content schedule, but are you supposed to carry that plan around in your head with you? Or leave it scattered across multiple tabs on a spreadsheet? No way!

So, let's craft a CTA to invite the visitor to a free trial of CoSchedule:

> *"Get a bird's-eye-view of your entire content schedule in seconds"*
> [Get Started Free]

The possibilities are endless. However, you can write tighter, more effective CTAs when you inject the rocket fuel of customer research. If you want to attract more customers, there is simply no replacement for talking to the people who have already bought. Now, I am going to use the term CTA from here on out for clarity—but interpret everything against the five stages of awareness and choose either a CTV or CTA depending upon context.

HOW TO STRUCTURE EVERY PAGE FOR CONVERSIONS

To create fertile soil for conversions, you must combine content with intent and structure. First, let's look more deeply at intent. This comes up every time we redesign our blog at CoSchedule. As we've touched on briefly before, you have to start thinking about every page on your website as your homepage. This includes your blog posts and landing pages, too.

If you're doing any kind of SEO work at all, people are going to find your content and landing pages through search. In turn, this means your content becomes the very first encounter they have with your brand. This is the same with social promotion, as well. If you want your website to generate profitable customer action, every page must have one job assigned to it. And it will be a CTA tailored to your content core. Your reader should be presented with one clear action to take.

Ask yourself this question: "If this is the first and only time this person will visit our site, and we can only get them to do one thing on this page, what would it be?" Then, analyze said page and ask this follow-up question: "Do the content and CTAs on this page work together to drive toward that action?" If this isn't happening, you have an instant opportunity for improvement!

"If you want your website to generate profitable customer action, every page must have one job assigned to it."

You must include CTAs in every piece of content. Remember, the myth of content marketing is that you simply need to create quality content to attract clicks, win conversions, and magically get those credit cards swiping. However, this seldom works if you neglect asking for the sale. You must include a clear and compelling CTA on every page to close the deal.

KILL YOUR SIDEBAR

Next, let's look at structure. Your page design should also be driven by CTAs. According to a Nielsen Norman Group study, the average user leaves a web page in less than ten seconds.* This means you only have a few blinks of an eye to clearly communicate the value your page offers the visitor. So anything you do to distract from the one purpose your page has is harming performance.

One of the most frequent offenders of this code is sidebar content. Sidebars are littered with stuff like:

- Category lists
- Podcast promotions
- "Limited-time" offers
- Upcoming webinars
- A search box...
- An upcoming conference
- Recent posts
- Popular posts
- Recent comments
- And on and on

Let me make this simple: delete all of it! There is nothing crazier to me than content creators who literally take out ads on their own content. And that's what these are, a bunch of ads. This stuff is nothing but a distraction for your readers.

Instead, all content should drive toward desired audience behavior. Whatever the action is, that's the only CTA you should find on a given page. And I'll guarantee that you don't hope your content drives people to click on a list of categories to choose from!

Abolish the sidebar.

I dig in on this point because we used to make this silly sidebar mistake. But when we determined that the one major action we wanted

---

* https://www.nngroup.com/articles/how-long-do-users-stay-on-web-pages/

people to take was signing up for our email list, we deleted all the extraneous junk from our pages and focused on one CTA—and it worked.

So now, when you land on a CoSchedule blog post, all you'll find is content. We simply offer the content our readers came for plus a relevant CTA, usually centered around giving them a value-added resource using the bookends technique (more on that below). This is what happened when we made this change:

- Our pageviews grew by more than 400 percent
- Our email subscriptions rose by more than 1,000 percent
- And to date, our qualified leads have increased by more than 9,000 percent

This happened all because of one word: focus. We got rid of the distractions and asked for the conversion more aggressively. If you aren't focused on the profitable action you want to generate, neither will your audience be.

CHOOSE YOUR LEVEL OF CTA

We've talked a lot about conversions and focus and CTAs. Now, let's get into the nuts and bolts of how to present and deliver these CTAs we've been working so hard to build. While it's true your CTAs need to be laser focused, they can vary in approach. Here, we'll look at four ways you can present your CTAs: inline finesse, inline content upgrades, punch-in-the-eye, and the bookends technique.

SIMPLICITY AND INLINE FINESSE

Sleek and unobtrusive, applying some inline finesse may be just the right touch. This is the simplest form of delivery of a CTA, but it can be as effective as any other. An inline CTA is a call to action within the flow of your body copy. It can be either hyperlinked text, like this example:

Plus, with social scheduling tools like Best Time Scheduling and ReQueue, you can set and forget all your social promotion. Sign up for a free 14-day trial and or request a demo and take your company's blogging workflow to the next level.

Inline CTA example from the CoSchedule blog

Or a contextually relevant combination of copy and graphics, like this example from CrazyEgg:

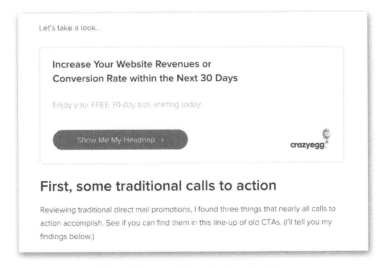

Inline CTA example from the CrazyEgg blog

While either can be effective, AWeber found something interesting when they ran extensive A/B split testing on text-based CTAs versus buttons. Over the course of dozens of tests, the text-based CTAs outperformed the buttons 53 percent of the time.[*] From this research, they concluded that their audience had become used to seeing the buttons,

---

[*] https://blog.aweber.com/case-studies/buttons-vs-text-links.htm

so they'd tuned them out. Because they were already reading the copy, however, it meant they actually read the CTA rather than breezing by it.

If you have a consistent readership on your blog or your email list, consider running a test of your own. See if your results follow AWeber's. And seamlessly weave inline CTAs into your copy.

OFFER CONTENT UPGRADES INLINE

Content upgrades are delicious bonus resources readers can download in exchange for an email address. Offering them inline in your content makes them extremely relevant. After all, if you're teaching your audience how to solve a problem, prepare a resource to help them do exactly that, place that resource in the most relevant place in your content, and you'll be collecting emails like crazy.

Example from the CoSchedule blog

Placing the content upgrade means both describing it and offering it as a download. On our blog, we like to show it as a graphic. Notice that our copy also describes exactly what's inside the content upgrade and how it fulfills the promise the post has made. In this example, there are six benefits the user will receive, and the upgrade's value is described thoroughly.

PUNCH THEM IN THE EYE (LIKE NEIL PATEL)

If you've ever read an article, listened to a podcast, or watched a video by Neil Patel, you know he's a straightforward guy. He's also an aggressive marketer who knows his stuff. As the cofounder of companies like KISSmetrics and Hello Bar, growth runs through his veins—and especially through his content.

Neil is a CTA champion. But his approach is a little different from those of many of the timid, soft-selling marketers we talked about at the beginning of the chapter. Subtlety isn't his strong suit. Instead, Neil opts for the "Punch 'em in the eye" method. Right now, when you land on NeilPatel.com, you see this:

From neilpatel.com

Hmm . . . I wonder what Neil wants you to do?

All other page navigation is located in the footer. This page has one purpose: drive people into using his clever lead-generation form. Neil uses this method in his content, as well. When his readers get to the end of his articles, what do they find? Three more CTAs:

- Sticky Header: Do you want more traffic?
- Sidebar: Do you want more traffic?
- Inline Graphic: If you liked this blog post, then you'll love this . . . (Surprise! This takes you to the same CTA form as the others.)

From an article on neilpatel.com

Neil simply never quits punching people in the eye. But guess what? It works.

Now, I think we need to address the elephant in the room here: marketers are frequently allergic to such strong methods. Just like they are often allergic to sending more email, they justify this reticence by imagining, "Well, I'm taking it easy on my customers and giving them a break from the noisy world of email and popups."

After all, that's what our audience wants, right? They want to visit a web page unaccosted by CTAs. They want to open their inbox in the morning and see it gloriously free of content from brands.

All right. Time for the tough love. Get real and stop over thinking it. Whether you like it or not, your competitors are willing to use these methods. And not only that, but the data say they work! So, why wouldn't you want to take the plunge, too? The reality is that the brand that asks for the sale is the one that gets the results. And no, it won't damage your brand—just like that spelling error won't kill you, either.

If you makes you feel better there are a few things you can do:

Get Out the Measuring Tape

Make sure you measure results so that you know it's worth it. Tools like Optimizely or Visual Website Optimizer are good places to start. They will allow you to test two versions of your page—for example, one with CTAs and one without. From there, you will be able to measure the difference in performance and move forward with the winner.

Get a Savvy Designer

Hire a good designer who understands conversations. There are plenty of "classy" ways to handle such direct messages that can actually enhance your users' experience. For example, the CoSchedule blog balances the punch-them-in-the-face approach with beautiful design. Everything feels like it belongs.

Have a Cookie

Use cookies (or smart plugins) to detect returning visitors. If they have previously completed the CTA or popup, you can suppress those interactions for a cleaner experience. At CoSchedule, we use these cookies to detect the customer's stage of awareness, so we adjust our aggressiveness and messaging accordingly.

Leaving so Soon?

Use exit-intent technology. If you are absolutely terrified of bumming out your visitors with aggressive popups, then consider showing popups only when the user is showing signs of leaving the page. This allows for the best reading experience while still slipping in your CTAs. Even better—combine this with your cookies and avoid popups altogether if the reader has already responded to one of your CTAs in the text.

Rely on Text

Don't forget that if nothing else, you should be working simple CTAs into the text of your blog posts. These are subtle and have been shown to convert better than buttons anyhow, so what do you have to lose?

Remember the pivotal question: "If this is the only time someone will be visiting your page, what is the one thing you want them to do?" Assume every visit is your only shot to move that person into the next stage of awareness. As a 10x marketer, are you willing to squander what may be your one and only chance?

Nope. So don't be afraid to throw a friendly, value-added punch every now and again. (Or every single time.)

9,360 PERCENT GROWTH WITH THE BOOKENDS TECHNIQUE

Last, we'll look at what we've dubbed the "bookends technique." The name isn't all that clever. It simply describes the structure of a page relative to our CTAs. Because each page has one goal, the idea is to bookend our content with CTAs that drive customer action toward it.

Let's dissect an example. One of our most popular blog posts is called "What 20 Studies Say About The Best Times To Post On Social Media." Spoiler alert: it's all about when to schedule social media messages! It's intensely helpful, and packed with buckets of actionable data, infographics, and downloadable resources. However, our main goal on that page is to encourage visitors to become trial users and take CoSchedule for a test drive.

The CTAs are inline and specifically targeted at the social scheduling features baked into the platform: ReQueue and Best Time Scheduling.

The first CTA exists to inform the reader, "Hey, if you don't want to read this 5,000-word post, you can have our tools do all of this super important, yet labor intensive, stuff for you."

The first bookend CTA

Then comes the body copy. It delivers on every promise. Using insights from twenty studies and proprietary data, we share the optimal times to share messages on every major social media network. And not only do we give times, but we break it down, too, accounting for time zones and message type, and even giving away custom Google Analytics reports to test for yourself. This is incredible stuff. In fact, this post attracts more than 150,000 unique pageviews every month.

However, as we discussed in Chapter Eleven, "10x Social Promotion," manually scheduling your messages for the optimal times is 10 percent work when a smart tool does it better than you can. So, at the end of the post, we offer the CTA a second time. It's phrased differently, but the action is the same.

The second bookend CTA

When we started using the bookends technique across our blog, we achieved a 9,360 percent increase in trial signups. That is 10x growth at its finest. All because we were willing to ask.

DON'T FORGET ABOUT YOUR PSYCHOLOGY

We've covered a ton of ground in this this chapter. But the key is this: "Don't psych yourself out!" Most content marketers underutilize CTAs, which is silly, because they work. There are lots of ways to lessen their "annoyance" quotient. Perhaps the best is to focus on which stage of awareness people are at. When you correctly diagnose where they are in relation to becoming a customer, you can surgically make mouth-watering offers that are perfectly suited to their needs at that moment.

We have further advanced our CTA strategy over the years to better accommodate the stage each customer is in. We built a custom tool that allows us to detect a visitor's activity on our site using cookies. If they are a brand new visitor, our CTA is to sign up for our email list. If they've already opted in, we allow them to download our resources without entering an address—which is a great experience for them. But, we also switch our CTAs to invite them into a trial account of CoSchedule.

While your CTAs don't need to get that techy and advanced, they will grow in sophistication to meet your audience in their stage of awareness. This works so well because rather than trying to dupe people into giving you their email addresses, phone numbers, or money, you're giving them exactly what they want and need at the moment.

This is truly the secret to asking for the sale and getting to the "Yes!"

Your 10x Toolbox

Put this chapter into action with your 10x Toolbox by visiting https://coschedule.com/10x-toolbox

10x Marketing Interview:
Joanna Wiebe on Why People Click, Try, and Buy
Creator of Copy Hackers and Aistory, Joanna Wiebe, and I unpack the psychology behind conversions. Joanna explains the five stages of awareness, and how to use calls to action and calls to value to turn visitors into customers. You will have access to the full audio interview plus transcript.

CHAPTER FOURTEEN

ONE METRIC THAT MATTERS

Author and financial mastermind Dave Ramsey has a system that's helped thousands of people climb out of financial debt—sometimes millions of dollars of debt, a true 10x accomplishment. There are seven "baby steps" he guides people through to get there:*

> *Baby Step 1: $1,000 cash in a beginner emergency fund*
> *Baby Step 2: Use the debt snowball to pay off all your debt but your house*
> *Baby Step 3: A fully funded emergency fund of 3 to 6 months of expenses*
> *Baby Step 4: Invest 15% of your household income into retirement*
> *Baby Step 5: Start saving for college*
> *Baby Step 6: Pay off your home early*
> *Baby Step 7: Build wealth and give generously*

---

* https://www.daveramsey.com/baby-steps/

As people in the program progress from one step to the next, their goal shifts. Those in debt don't start by focusing on building wealth and generous giving. Instead, they start all the way back at step one: get $1,000 in the bank as a starter safety net.

While the long-term goal is huge—financial independence and the ability to invest buckets of money into worthy causes—it's reverse-engineered in steps and stages. This is how startups and marketing teams alike should view their goal-setting and analytics activities. Bottom line: your goal metric should reflect the stage your team or company is at. I call this your "one metric that matters" (1MTM).

FOCUS AND DISCIPLINE

Dave Ramsey's debt snowball works because it encourages two things: focus and discipline. People working the system focus on one step, and one chunk of debt, at a time. They pour all of their efforts and extra cash into one immediate goal after another, eventually leading them to their ultimate goal of living debt free. The 1MTM framework operates in exactly the same way.

Focus

One metric that matters forces you and your team to focus with laser-beam intensity on the one thing that matters most. This is different from typical analytics methods, which usually dilute focus across popcorn KPIs—meaning we look at our analytics dashboard and grab the numbers that corroborate the story we *want* to tell. Having one primary metric will keep our eyes locked onto the focal point, the one part of the business we have decided to value more highly than any other.*

---

* Note: This doesn't mean the rest of your other analytics are useless. They are still very useful. They simply aren't the one metric that matters. In the *10x Marketing Formula*, we want one metric to be your North Star. At the same time, the other analytics in your purview become diagnostic tools. They should help you understand why, or why not, the metric is improving. They will help you diagnose what works and what doesn't. In sum, they still matter, but aren't the one metric that matters most.

Discipline

Dave Ramsey says to take one baby step at a time, and one step only. This creates discipline. Disciplining ourselves to focus on one metric makes us 100 percent accountable to increasing it. Plus, it becomes a singular lens through which we evaluate all projects. We will instantly know if a strategy or method is good or not depending on how well it serves our one metric. Either it will serve to improve our one metric, or it will not.

Focus and discipline ultimately allow for the necessary behavioral changes to take place. To achieve 10x results, your mindset and methodologies need to change, as well. In their book *Lean Analytics* authors Alistair Croll and Benjamin Yoskovitz explain: ". . . if you want to change behavior, your metric must be tied to the behavioral change you want."[*] For our purposes, I'll paraphrase to this: "If you want to change results, your metric must be tied to the results you want."

Imagine it like this. A marketing manager is busy trying to increase her company's social following, website traffic, email list growth, and sales-qualified leads at the same time. She's awash in metrics, dashboards, and competing priorities. This is an impossible scenario—but one in which many marketing managers find themselves.

"If you want to change results, your metric must be tied to the results you want."

However, if the same marketer looks at the data, she may find that *all* of those metrics grow as long as she brings in more traffic. A-ha! So, if that's true, all this lucky marketer needs to do is focus on bringing in more traffic. Therefore, traffic becomes her 1MTM. As she increases this metric, the rest of the metrics will take care of themselves.

---

[*] Croll, Alistair, and Benjamin Yoskovitz. Lean Analytics: Use Data to Build a Better Startup Faster. Sebastopol, CA: O'Reilly, 2013. 11.

We're looking for the gas pedal to supercharge growth. And your 1MTM is that gas pedal. If you put all of your effort into one basket, and then set it on that gas pedal, you're going to get a 10x return.

Do you remember the content hacker's KPI formula? This is where it comes into its own.

1MTM + Goal + Timeline = Content Hacker

SETTING APPROPRIATE METRICS

Just because you're focused on a certain metric right now doesn't mean that's all you will pursue this year, this quarter, or even this month. Instead, you will learn to choose the metric that's most appropriate for your stage of growth. This means your metric will be ever-evolving as you get better, bigger, and more successful.

"You need to start with a goal that's realistic for where you're at."

Startups are a perfect template for this analytical evolution. In the early stages, a startup is scrappy and starving. Even if they have a solid injection of cash from investors, they are still unproven, and results are forthcoming. They've sold the vision, and now it's time to deliver. In a way, they're like the college kid who's living on student loans. They can burn through the borrowed money and blow it on things like the newest Xbox and chicken wings. Or, they can use their cash for the essentials (like beans, rice, and ramen noodles) while they pursue their 1MTM: graduation. Their goal is appropriate to their stage.

THREE STAGES OF GROWTH

A helpful framework involves looking at your marketing team or company in one of three phases. I call them startup, growth, and scale.

Long term, the goal is 10x revenue growth, or to make sales leads rain from the ceiling. To do this, you need to start with a goal that's realistic for where you're at. As you incrementally set stage-appropriate goals, you work toward 10x growth of each metric along the way.* The beauty of these stages is that any content or digital marketing team can use these stages to evaluate themselves, as well. Here's how they work:

1. Stage one: You need traffic

2. Stage two: You need an audience

3. Stage three: You need to figure out business value

These phases are prescriptive for any size company or marketing team. A pitfall to avoid here is something big companies or established teams often fall into: trying to skip stages. Even if your company is large and your marketing team well established, you need to be realistic with your stage. Often, large companies with recognition assume they will magically get traffic and a loyal audience will materialize. The reality is, it's frequently harder than they expect. Large companies often get traffic, but just as often fail to build an audience. Despite that, they jump to the scale stage right away—and experience dismal results. Even the biggest teams need to follow and master all three stages in sequence. So, respect the stage you're in today.

---

* Download your own Growth Stage Maturity Matrix for free at https://coschedule.com/10x-toolbox

At CoSchedule, we have found these to be the necessary evolution for a 10x marketing team. Stages one and two will be the same for every team, regardless of size. And stage three is more flexible, where you can start doing your own thing. But it's mission critical to begin with traffic. Let's break down each stage and its goal.

Startup Stage: Get Traffic

Your team needs to know how to get traffic anytime and all the time. Imagine a retail store with beautiful products, stunning displays, and helpful staff waiting to provide a great experience. Everything in the store may be world class, but if no one ever comes through the front doors, its excellence is wasted and won't generate results. You can't sell to people who aren't there. To get results, you must have traffic.

Choose your 1MTM: Pageviews, new visitors, unique visitors, or search hits are all good options. Your 1MTM is traffic related in stage one.

Growth Stage: Build an Audience

After you have mastered getting traffic, you need to turn visitors into a loyal audience. You must create a following that is interested in learning more from you. In stage two, it's time to turn your traffic into an audience.

Choose your 1MTM: Email subscribers, social followers, or community members. Your 1MTM is audience related in stage two.

Scale Stage: Drive Business Value

Once your team drives consistent traffic that converts steadily into new audience members, it's time to focus on business value. This is where you learn to monetize the following you have worked so hard to build. However, it will not happen in a consistent, reliable, and predictable flow if you try to skip stages one and two.

THE STAGES OF GROWTH

STARTUP

○ TRAFFIC

GROWTH

● LOYAL AUDIENCE

SCALE

● DRIVE BUSINESS VALUE

 NEW CUSTOMERS
- PROFITABLE
- CUSTOMER
- ACTION

At CoSchedule, we've cycled through a few different 1MTMs in stage three. We focused for more than a year on trial signups, and now have shifted focus to sales leads. This stage will evolve as your results grow. However, this stage will focus relentlessly on driving business value.

Choose your 1MTM: Paid customers, new subscribers, trial users, or qualified leads. Your 1MTM is business-value related in stage three.

WHEN TO PROGRESS

As you work through each stage, a key question will emerge: "How will our team know when to move to the next stage?" After all, if you're unsure of when to move on, you may transition too early and hamstring your results. However, if you wait too long, you're likely leaving results on the table.

Here's a simple way to know when it's time to graduate. Create a specific goal for each stage. For example, if your team is in stage one, your goal might be to reach 250,000 pageviews per month. This makes it easy. Once you can do that, you can move to stage two. Then, set a similarly clear goal and work the process.

WHAT ARE YOU AFRAID OF?

To make these stages work for you, you need to honestly assess which stage you're in. Then, as I illustrated, you need to set a clear goal to determine when it's time to move to the next stage. You will be tempted to jump right to stage three in order to drive value. If you shortcut stages one and two, I promise you will be disappointed in your results. The *10x Marketing Formula* is a process. You have to use the right tools and the right timeline to build your 10x marketing machine. However, I do understand this is a risk, and may feel scary.

Most marketers think focusing exclusively on driving traffic or email list building is too simple. The thought process is something like: "We're professionals, damnit! It has to be more complicated than this, right?!"

Wrong!

To them it feels shallow, or even beside the point. They'll say things like, "But how do we know if it is the right kind of traffic?" Questions like this are fine, but if you don't know how to drive traffic and build a loyal audience, you will be unable to drive meaningful business value anyway. Plus, if you can drive traffic on demand, you will, by the law of averages, be able to prove business value. Think of stages one and two as weapons, or key skills. Once you master them, you will be able to deploy, adapt, and improve them as you go. First learn to get traffic. Then, over time, learn what the right traffic is (using data) and then tweak the formula to get it.

For example, at CoSchedule we learned that for every hundred thousand pageviews, 5 percent converted into a trial signup no matter what we did. So, in stage one, our sole focus of "drive pageviews" was a guaranteed way to drive business value (even though we weren't focusing on it directly).

At the beginning, our mindset was also that traffic as our 1MTM was "good enough for now." We knew it would be a pivotal component of our long-term success. We also realized it wouldn't be our exclusive focus forever. We knew we would evolve. Both have proven true, and they will for you, as well.

HOW TO HELP YOUR TEAM USE 1MTM

The 1MTM framework is all encompassing. It becomes the end to which all activities build. And this is true not simply of individual contributors, but of your team as a whole. To help them use the framework requires two things: adoption and communication.

Adopting 1MTM

Now, you may be ready to wholeheartedly embrace the 1MTM framework. However, some people on your team may not be so warm to the idea. Often, when I discuss this concept with other marketers, they scoff. They say, "You're telling me we're not supposed to use all of this incredible data available to us?"

That's not what I'm asserting. Instead, I am saying that despite all of that data, your team needs to have one high-level goal that they consistently use to measure their success. This doesn't mean that you can't look at other metrics or data points. They aren't automatically off limits. That would be like saying Joe Maddon's Cubs shouldn't worry about strikeouts if their 1MTM is a World Series victory. It's nonsensical.

Instead, it means you should view other metrics through the lens of your 1MTM. Each one then becomes a supporting data point. Use these other metrics as tools for understanding how to get better at growing your 1MTM. I call them "diagnostic metrics." If your 1MTM isn't growing, these metrics should help you understand why not and what you can do about it. This obstacle to adoption is easily overcome when it's understood that your team won't forsake all data. Instead, it's a way to laser-focus on the most important growth, your 1MTM.

Embracing and owning a single metric as a team also has gives you the ability to create deeper ownership. When everyone knows what you're driving toward, they're empowered to make ad-hoc decisions to help your team get there. Everyone will know how to help move things forward in any given context because they can measure all of their work against growing the 1MTM.

Remember the individual KPI scorecards from Chapter Nine? These scorecards will help everyone track how they are helping the team grow your 1MTM. Ensure everyone has a clear KPI and a deadline, and then give them total control over how they will accomplish their KPI goal. Their scorecard will then break down exactly what contribution they are responsible for by day, week, and month.

Communicating 1MTM

To foster this kind of team adoption and ownership requires steady communication. And this will mean ensuring your team has total clarity on the one thing you're trying to achieve. So you must be clear on the metric, goal, timeline, and how to measure it. If you're a manager or team leader, it's great for you to adopt the 1MTM framework, but if your team doesn't understand or communicate it, you're missing a key ingredient.

If you're a 10x team, you're already doing daily scrums or standup meetings. This is a perfect time to talk about your progress every morning. Additionally, your team should make it the focus of conversation for your weekly retros. Essentially, your team should eat and breath this metric. For this phase of the *10x Marketing Formula* to work requires total focus and obsession.

CHOOSE YOUR TOOLS

As you master each stage, you will also measure your progress along the way. After all, whenever you're talking about metrics, you're inherently talking about measurement. We've worked hard to define the right marketing tool stack for our team. Obviously, our needs have changed over time. However, as we've found, the one constant to choosing the right tools is understanding what you want to measure before choosing them.

The Wrong Approach

Often, marketers survey analytics tools and pick the one with the nicest looking charts or the one that can populate the most stats. They then build reports and design their marketing goals around the things the tool allows them to track. In turn, they chase tool-driven metrics that *don't matter*. This is the wrong approach because it dilutes our ability to focus on the 1MTM.

The Right Approach

Rather, what marketers need is a simple way to measure their 1MTM. Here's the right approach:

1. *Set your 1MTM:* What stage are you in?
2. *Define your goal:* What specific number will you hit before advancing to the next stage?
3. *Find a simple way to measure your 1MTM:* What tool allows you to measure and track your 1MTM?
4. *Track progress and incorporate this into your daily team meetings:* How is your 1MTM growing, and are you keeping your team focused on it?

At CoSchedule, we frequently use a single report generated in KISSmetrics to track our 1MTM. These reports can be hard to build, and might require a web developer, but they allow us incredible focus on our 1MTM. For instance, here is a report called "Content To Trial Signup." This report tracks exactly which content, or pages, are producing the most trial signups, which was our 1MTM at the time.

From there, this all-important report is input into a Google Spreadsheet so our team can refer to it constantly in meetings and as they work.

	Date Range	Unique visits	Signup Page Visits	Trial Signups	Pageviews	Email Subscribers	Notes
2	Week 1	91,000	2,200	1,000	240,000	4,000	Changed homepage CTA for demo
3	Week 2	93,500	2,300	1,100	235,000	3,800	
4	Week 3	95,000	2,500	1,200	250,000	4,200	Launched ads for course/ Launched Social Message Optimizer tool
5	Week 4	96,750	2,450	1,300	255,000	4,250	Launched course
6	Week 5	98,000	2,550	1,400	260,000	4,400	Course
7	Week 6	100,250	2,600	1,500	265,000	4,450	Memorial Day Weekend
8	Week 7	101,000	2,750	1,600	270,000	4,500	
9	Week 8	104,000	3,000	1,700	275,000	4,750	

Notice, there are diagnostic metrics that accompany our team's trial signup numbers. Metrics like traffic, trial signup type, and email subscribers provide further context for our team. Each either influences or correlates to our 1MTM.

Once the right 1MTM tool is selected, additional analytics packages and tools can be added. But, keep in mind, these are going to be diagnostic tools to help you understand why your 1MTM is growing (or not). They will be supplementary, clarifying, and 1MTM-boosting tools that sharpen focus rather than blurring it.

THE BOTTOM LINE ON METRICS

Here's the deal. Today, most marketers don't have a data problem—they have a filtering problem. There is an endless sea of data to be gathered, from heatmaps to affinity categories and every granular detail in between. And that data is only as useful as your ability to put it to work. However, this issue is solved with the 1MTM framework.

Take heatmaps, for example. They are an excellent diagnostic tool, especially when focused on improving email signups and are considering ideal placement of your CTAs. A tool like this may help you find the most prime real estate. Useful? Of course! But only when it actually serves your 1MTM. If you're looking to grow your email list with better CTA placement, this information is gold—but it isn't a 1MTM on its own.

Notice the tool's purpose is not more data. It's about how that data can be used to serve your 1MTM. Without the 1MTM framework, heatmaps tend to be really interesting, but not particularly helpful. Use tools like this wisely.

Focus is discipline applied to activity. This means focusing on your 1MTM at every stage of growth will require new degrees of discipline. The discipline to say no to distractions. The discipline to ignore irrelevant data. The discipline to keep all efforts driving toward increasing that one metric.

Just like the rest of the *10x Marketing Formula*, 1MTM isn't a magic bullet. The only way it works is if you actually do the work. Metrics and analysis are an integral part of the entire process, but only if used as a lens to focus activity on 10x work—and as a scalpel to cut out the 10 percent stuff immediately. A good 1MTM will automatically differentiate your 10x opportunities from your 10 percent improvements. Simply ask yourself, "Will this opportunity improve our 1MTM?" If the answer is no, move on.

"Focus is discipline applied to activity."

Both you and your team have the potential to achieve 10x growth on revenue, profit, or sales leads—whatever it is, it's up to you. All you need to do is focus relentlessly on your 1MTM, the true path to guaranteed marketing results.

Your 10x Toolbox

Put this chapter into action with your 10x Toolbox by visiting https://coschedule.com/10x-toolbox

Template: Growth Stage Maturity Matrix
This template helps you identify which stage of growth your team is in. As well, you will define your 1MTM and goal KPI.

THE 10X MARKETING TOOLBOX

You become what you measure, so why not solve for what actually matters?
    — Avinash Kaushik, Digital Marketing Evangelist, Google

In Section Three, you'll find the final resources you need to become a 10x marketer. Every movement needs a manifesto. Every creator needs tools. Here, you'll find both.

CHAPTER FIFTEEN

THE 10X MARKETING MANIFESTO

Legend has it that in the year 2001, a group of free-thinking software engineers met at the top of a mountain (literally) and wrote something called the Agile Manifesto for Software Development.* The product of their work goes something like this:

> *We are uncovering better ways of developing software by doing it and helping others do it. Through this work we have come to value:*
>
> - *Individuals and interactions over processes and tools*
> - *Working software over comprehensive documentation*
> - *Customer collaboration over contract negotiation*
> - *Responding to change over following a plan*
>
> *That is, while there is value in the items on the right, we value the items on the left more.*

---

* https://martinfowler.com/articles/agileStory.html

Of course, this manifesto became the bedrock for the agile methodology we all know and understand today. It's a great story, and you can still read the manifesto in its original form here: http://agilemanifesto.org

They were my type of people. Technology nerds who loved their craft and weren't willing to settle for the old ways of doing things. They sensed something was wrong with the way software was made, so they decided to do something about it. And, true to form, they didn't start with anything fancy. They started with an MVP called "Lightweight methods." It was only later that it became known as agile.

In sum, this is what I have tried to do in the *10x Marketing Formula*. Now, I don't claim to be as brilliant as these guys. This was a team of seventeen professionals in the mountains. I'm just one founder with an eye for marketing on the open plains of North Dakota (yes, North Dakota). Hardly a consensus. Nonetheless, consider this my contribution in the race for results-oriented marketing.

THE 11 TRAITS OF A 10X MARKETER

Now, I won't be so bold as to write my own manifesto . . . But if I were to try, here are the eleven characteristics of the 10x marketer I would hope to present:

> *10x marketers... work in a "Results or die!" oriented business. No 10 percenters allowed.*

> *10x marketers... are creative problem solvers, but not creatives. We value wins, not laughs.*

> *10x marketers... know it isn't about working a plan; it's about working ideas to produce results.*

10x marketers… understand that growth requires failure. Strength is in progress, not perfection.

10x marketers… always think and prioritize 10x. They forget 10 percent.

10x marketers… always have a badass editorial calendar fueled by 10x projects.

10x marketers… know ideas are only as good as their ability to execute them.

10x marketers… consistently create the best content on the whole damn internet.

10x marketers… run teams that learn and adapt, not mindlessly execute "the plan."

10x marketers… consistently see and test their assumptions against actual results.

10x marketers… always orbit and grow their one metric that matters.

WHY THIS WILL WORK

10x marketers thrive on a mantra of "Results or die!" No matter how large or small our team, we think like a scrappy startup, act like a scrappy startup, and market like a scrappy startup. And you've just learned the formula for becoming the person who blazes your own dirt path. You have the recipe for creating strategic shortcuts—but it's only yours if you use it.

The formula is all-encompassing. It's not a marketing strategy buffet where you pluck an idea or two. Instead, it's an integrated whole that must be implemented in totality for you to achieve 10x results.

STRATEGIC
SHORTCUTS

Because it's not fancy, you may be tempted to set some of it aside or dismiss its potential impact. That would be a mistake. The *10x Marketing Formula* works precisely because it is simple. There are zillions of marketing books out there touting intricate planning methods and theories. However, they're a pain to implement. This means they flat out don't get done.

The formula works precisely because it isn't a strict plan to follow. Rather, it's built on frameworks and principles you can use at a moment's notice. They will help you quickly focus on the right things and improve the instincts of you and your team. This is where the formula will contribute most greatly to your success.

YOUR 10X MARKETING FRAMEWORKS

Competition-free content helps you immediately stand out and add value to your target audience in a way only you can. Your content core topics enable your team to connect the dots between what your customers care about and the value your business has for them. The 10x vs. 10 percent framework makes it dead simple to prioritize projects with tenfold growth potential over the piddly, 10 percent improvements (like correcting typos!). And with your 10x calendar, you can map out your 10x projects to ensure they are continually shipped on an aggressive timeline.

Along the way, the content you create will be 10x better than anything on the topic, which is so important, because every page on your website is your homepage. This content will also be informed by your minimum viable marketing (MVM) process, which will allow your team to validate assumptions, test ideas, and find the projects and campaigns that will yield 10x ROI.

Your social media promotion will be tremendously effective because of savvy smart-o-mation, giving you back precious hours to focus on 10x work. And the email list-building principles are evergreen, so you can steadily grow and monetize your list. All the while, you will learn the skill of driving traffic to your site (among others) as you put the one metric that matters (1MTM) framework and three stages of growth into action. And you will continuously convert your audience into customers by understanding how to call them to action (and to value) based upon their stage of awareness.

These frameworks are where the power is! It doesn't flow from following a detailed map, but from reacting with the right instincts. And through the application of these principles, that is exactly what you and your team will develop.

WHEN PLANS FAIL

You see, plans fail and circumstances change unpredictably. Instincts will make or break you.

In his book *Outliers*, Malcolm Gladwell tells the story of two pilots navigating Korean Air flight 801 through heavy rain. On the approach to land, they were unable to see the runway. However, a signal on the ground seemed to indicate the runway was just ahead of them. But the flight engineer knew better, and urged the captain to pull up.

The captain and the first officer ignored the engineer and kept on course, following their process. Alarms began to bark as the plane came closer and closer to the ground. But still, no runway came into view. The flight engineer again suggested that the captain pull up and try again. Finally, the captain agreed. But it was too late. Seconds later Korean Air flight 801 slammed into the side of a mountain, tragically killing 228 of the 254 passengers aboard.

The crazy thing about this tragic story is that the plane didn't crash because of poor flying. In fact, the pilots were following the protocols they were trained in. Rather, what they failed to realized is that the situation had changed. They were flying in uncharted territory; and something new was required that their training hadn't provided them. Flexibility. Namely, the ability to think on their feet, defy instructions, and improvise in this new context. The real problem was they'd never developed the skills to do this.

This is a similar situation to one in which many marketing teams find themselves today. Content marketing came with plenty of instructions. The problem is they aren't enough to keep your airplane in flight. You will need need some fresh principles with which to operate. And that is what I've aimed to provide in this book.

ARE YOU WILLING?

The *10x Marketing Formula* isn't a detailed process, because those don't work. It's a framework, mindset shift, and attitude that says, "Screw it. We want 10x results, and we're going to cut the crap and make sure we get there."

Your marketing results are not dictated by blind execution of a complicated plan. Instead, they're tied to your willingness to risk failure, learn from it, and relentlessly execute the 10x frameworks you have learned. Perfection is a toxic illusion, a poison pill, an edenic fantasy. If things don't work, you'll admit it and move on.

You will pursue growth, never non-failure. Tenfold growth, not 10 percent improvements. Go big or go back to marketing school. At their core, 10x teams embrace simple frameworks over complex processes. And always move one big metric tied to growth—the 1MTM.

"They're tied to your willingness to risk failure, learn from it, and relentlessly execute the 10x frameworks you have learned."

In the same breath, it must be said that the *10x Marketing Formula* won't magically print ROI. The only thing that can produce results is good marketing—and that is wholly dependent on you, the marketer. The principles are both portable and powerful, but they will only work if you do!

Now, it's commendable if you have some new tricks up your marketing sleeves. After all, we've showcased plenty of content hacks and unique marketing tactics from some of the world's best marketers. But, be careful to take away more than a few new tricks to try out. Tricks and hacks may help for a while, but the linchpin to success with the *10x Marketing Formula* is fresh ideas and strategies developed specifically for your team, industry, company, and context.

If you're willing to lead your team with a 10x mindset and operate like a scrappy, results-or-die! startup, then you're ready for the *10x Marketing Formula*. Good luck!

CHAPTER SIXTEEN

THE 10X MARKETING FORMULA APPLIED

If you made it this far, you've experienced a revolution in your marketing mindset, methodologies, and most importantly, results. You've accomplished a lot.

You found your competition-free content niche and zeroed in on your content core. You've discovered 10x projects, planned how you'll execute them, and know how to communicate and collaborate with your team.

Your team should also have experienced a renaissance. I hope they're energized by the clarity of lean 10x workflows. By fresh ways to create and measure 10x content. And of course, their newfound freedom to fail (and therefore learn). The true hallmarks of a 10x team will be their desire to move quickly and fail fast. Their conversations will center around results—not just campaigns. Around KPIs—not just projects.

That means at this point, you know everything you and your team need to do to get 10x results. The logical next step is to apply what you've learned. And as you begin to implement the *10x Marketing Formula*—even with your 10x projects, your 10x calendar, your 10x workflows, and beyond—you'll likely come across many apparent roadblocks that would prevent you from moving forward.

At this stage, the biggest 10x opportunity you have is eliminating the 10 percent busywork that lurks around almost every marketing activity.

WHAT THE 10X MARKETING FORMULA BUILT

As I've thought about how to best help you forge ahead, it seems appropriate to share the example of how we've applied the *10x Marketing Formula* within our marketing team here at CoSchedule.

From the start, we carefully built a 10x marketing team, hiring only the people we believed would be exceptional culture fits. They're talented, they're smart, and they love to move fast. They've prioritized the right projects, created the right content, defined the right workflows, and embraced the minimum viable marketing mantra. Even with a world-class team and processes, though, we've still run into roadblocks—but not the kind you might think.

Like so many marketers, we would spot opportunities for wins, but lacked the systems to implement them without getting sucked into the 10 percent sludge. For example, we created 10x workflows for every piece of content following the same process you learned in Chapter Seven:

1. Write down everything that needs to be done.
2. Remove unnecessary tasks from your list.
3. Combine similar tasks.
4. Give each task a definition of done.
5. Assign responsibility for each task.
6. Determine when each task should be done.
7. Estimate how long each task should take.

We had a team more than willing to make the process work. We knew through research, examples, and studies that each step was backed by data. So we knew this was the best way to execute as efficiently as possible.

The next step was to actually delegate the tasks, which meant notifying each team member of their responsibilities, reminding them before their tasks were due so the work would be completed on time, and enabling collaboration on the content they were creating. The thing was, it was nearly impossible to execute that process without a tool designed to help us apply every component of our workflow.

What we needed was a method to:

1. Create and save workflows for the content we'd create over and over again, like blog posts (so we wouldn't have to rewrite them every time we used them).

2. Assign each task to a specific team member, complete with the due date and clear understanding of expectations, and let them know automatically the moment the task was assigned (so we wouldn't have to manually message each team member in a separate system).

3. Remind the team before tasks were due (so everyone would be held accountable and get their work done on time without feeling like we were dealing with fire drills the day before pieces were meant to publish).

4. Keep communication around each piece within context of that specific content (so we wouldn't feel lost in email inboxes with endless CC threads).

Our 10x workflow existed, but we needed to remove a lot of the 10 percent, tedious, manual busywork tacked onto the creation of every piece. That's how the *10x Marketing Formula* influenced the idea behind CoSchedule itself.

Now, the process is streamlined to remove inefficiencies, which allows us to focus on 10x projects and content, rather than trivial minutiae. We trust in the process, we trust the tool to keep us accountable, and we focus on the things that will actually generate results instead of keeping us herding cats.

Similarly, we wanted to capture every opportunity from the social media following we've worked so hard to build. So we researched the obvious, easy wins to increase our reach with a few hypotheses:

Hypothesis One

If we post at the times when most of our audience is active on each network, more of them will see our content and ultimately come back to our website. So we researched and found the best times to post on the major social networks.

- Facebook: 1 p.m., 3 p.m., and 9 a.m.;
- Twitter: 5–6 p.m., 12 p.m., and 3 p.m.;
- Pinterest: 8–11 p.m. (with 9 p.m. at peak), 2–4 a.m. and 2–4 p.m., and 1–3 p.m.;
- LinkedIn: 5–6 p.m., 7–8 a.m., and 12 p.m.;
- Google+: 9 a.m., 11 a.m., and 12–1 p.m.;
- Instagram: 8–9 a.m., 2 a.m., and 5 p.m.

However, the problem was trying to remember all of those eighteen best times and planning our days to post manually around that cadence. (Incidentally, this is the same problem the marketer in Chapter Eleven faced—he was stuck in the "It's only time" trap!)

Hypothesis Two

If we share our blog posts to social media more than once, more of those followers will see them so we'll get more traffic. So we posted more and refined our very early posting cadence to this:

- Facebook: the same day as publish and the following month;
- Twitter: the same day as publish and later that same day, the day after publish, the following week, the following month, then two months later;
- Pinterest: the same day as publish and two weeks later;
- LinkedIn: the same day as publish and three weeks later;
- Google+: the time of publish, the following week, and the following month.

This was really hard to make possible considering the sheer amount of content we were publishing, in addition to remembering the best times to post on these networks. Let's just say it was a lot of balls to juggle at once.

Hypothesis Three

If we reshare our best-performing social media messages, we will get bigger results from our future shares. This will also eliminate the need to write brand new content and fill in gaps (or missed opportunities) for each network's accepted best practices for daily number of shares. So we researched how often to post on each network each day and discovered we should:

- Facebook: post at least once per day (and sometimes twice);
- Twitter: post fifteen times per day;
- Pinterest: post eleven times per day;
- LinkedIn: post once every business day;
- Google+: post twice per day;
- Instagram: post at least once every day.

The problem was that we didn't have one place to see all the messages we planned to share on these networks. Not to mention the overwhelming feeling we were just getting by, and missing chances to capture value our research was helping us uncover.

All of that research led us to one conclusion: *we needed a tool to help us manage our social media.* Unfortunately, a tool didn't exist that fulfilled all of our 10x social promotion requirements. So again, the *10x Marketing Formula* influenced the functionality we built into CoSchedule to help our own marketing team execute more efficiently.

The need to post to all of our social networks at the best times gave birth to the Best Time Scheduling feature. This feature literally translated all of our marketers' research into a system that not only automatically posts to every network at the best time, but also spaces the messages apart so we don't spam our followers by posting all at once.

Next, the challenge of sharing a blog post to social media more than once inspired us to build a feature called Social Templates, which essentially helps our team follow a standardized posting schedule for every piece of content. This makes sure we share content well after the initial time of publish (think of our forty-day posting schedule I shared in Chapter Eleven).

When we discovered we were missing opportunities to reshare our best-performing social media messages to fill in the gaps in our daily posting frequencies, we decided to build Social Analytics to help us find our best-performing messages. Then we built a social media automation feature called ReQueue to easily reshare those top performers to fill in the gaps.

And for one final example, we knew if we consolidated our toolset and did everything in our power to eliminate copy/pasting, we would have more time to create 10x content and actually achieve 10x results. To do that, we:

1. Pulled together a list of the tools we were using for marketing.
1. Created a tool requirements checklist to help us find the tool that would fit our needs.

The thing was, there really wasn't a project management tool that integrated with the social networks we were using. And there wasn't a social media scheduling tool that helped us manage our WordPress blog. And there wasn't an editorial calendar tool that helped us collaborate efficiently as a team. And down the line the problems went.

So again, the *10x Marketing Formula* influenced the functionality we built into CoSchedule to help our team manage blog posts, social media, workflows, collaboration, and a whole lot more, all in one place.

In short, we built CoSchedule so we could market the 10x way. It's mission control for every detail of our marketing. In one place, we're in effortless command. To market the 10x way meant a move from a disconnected mess to a tight, incredibly powerful 10x calendar.

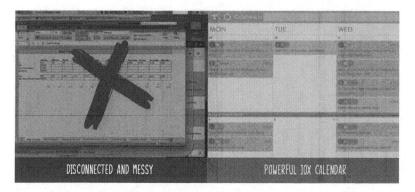

DISCONNECTED AND MESSY   POWERFUL 10X CALENDAR

We could not have achieved 10x results without a marketing platform that transcends the disconnected way of doing things. And the parallel between the evolution of CoSchedule and our implementation of the *10x Marketing Formula* is identical.

Now, you may be thinking, "That's great. I'm glad you're happy with the product you built! We'll stick it out with our current way of doing things while we test the waters of the formula." But key to your success is knowing that the formula isn't something to append to your current marketing plan. Instead, it should become the heartbeat of your entire marketing program. If you're going to become a 10x marketer, embrace that it's designed to live at the center of absolutely every activity.

We carefully vetted our current marketing tools and those available against the requirements of 10x marketing. I highly recommend you do the same. Really, it's as simple as asking and answering these questions:

1. What activities does the *10x Marketing Formula* require our team to do?
2. What tools (or platform) may help us execute these activities?
3. What tools remove as much tedious 10 percent busywork as possible?

As a final word of wisdom, ensure that your answers to these questions determine the budget for your tools—rather than your budget determining your tools. The marketing stack that allows you to implement the *10x Marketing Formula* with as little friction as possible will amplify your ability to generate revenue.

WHAT'S NEXT?

Now, you may have a final, lingering question. We've spent the entire book exploring how to become a 10x marketer. But, how do you know when you've actually become one?

Here's how you'll know when you've arrived: when you achieve 10x results, your team talks regularly about moving quickly and failing fast, and you've finished this book!

In essence, it's a belief that arriving is just the beginning. Because 10x marketers aren't one-hit wonders. They are the content hackers who bleed "results-or-die!" They're the ones who never settle for what worked yesterday. Who aren't content to play the copycat marketing game. And those who master the skills laid out in this book.

The *10x Marketing Formula* is your blueprint for growth—*not just for today*, but for the rest of your career. Retrain your brain to think this way, guide your team to develop these new instincts, and for the love of marketing, never draft another marketing plan again!

I want to invite you into a new era of marketing success. And I hope you'll consider trying the product the *10x Marketing Formula* helped us build. I also want to personally invite you to join our private 10x Marketing LinkedIn group by visiting http://cos.sc/10x-marketing-leadership Here you will find your new peer group, a community of leaders focused on 10x growth above all else.

Now, take this book, the 10x Toolbox resources our team has created for you, and chase results like your career depends on it. Because, in the end, it really does. Work like you've only got three months to live. From now on, it's 10x or lights out, results or die!

But don't worry. Now you know exactly what to do.

APPENDIX

Well done on finishing the *10x Marketing Formula*! You know have the blueprint for creating competition-free content that stands out and gets 10x results.

I'm excited for the tenfold growth you have the potential of achieving in the near future. To help you on your way, I created this final section to be a quick guide and refresher on each phase and stage of the formula. You can refer to this guide for an overview of all the resources included in your free 10x Toolbox.

Every tool is available by visiting *https://coschedule.com/10x-Toolbox*

MINDSET: CONTENT HACKING

A content hacker is a results-or-die! marketer who merges agile growth tactics with high-converting content to achieve rapid 10x growth. The content hacker ethos is: one part marketing, one part engineering, one part high risk, and a whole lot of high reward.

10X TOOLBOX RESOURCE

10x Marketing Interview: Noah Kagan and the Proactive Dashboard: Founder of Sumo.com and AppSumo, Noah Kagan, and I talk growth hacking, embracing failure, and testing fifty-two growth ideas per year. He explains their team's use of proactive dashboards to track progress against their goal and own the process. You will have access to the full audio interview plus transcript.

PHASE ONE: PLAN

Your 10x marketing journey starts here. In Phase One, you will outline what your content will look like and discover exactly how that content delivers the core value your business offers to your target customers. This phase forms the nucleus of your content strategy.

Stage One: Competition-Free Content

Competition-free content is content that adds tremendous value to your customers and audience that only you can produce. It is content so uniquely valuable, it makes your competition look like they didn't even try. It's the key to content that stands out and gets results.

10X TOOLBOX RESOURCE

Worksheet: Competition-Free Content Niche: This worksheet will help you identify and outline your own competition-free content niche.

Stage Two: Content Core

Your content core connects the dots between what your customers care about and what you have to offer them. It contrasts with "parallel topics," which drive traffic, but fail to bring business results. Content core topics intersect your target customers' needs with the value your products or services provide.

Worksheet: Finding Your Content Core: This worksheet will help you connect your customers' needs with your business value.

Worksheet: Content Core Customer Interviews: This worksheet includes five content core questions to ask in target customer interviews.

PHASE TWO: EXECUTE

In Phase Two, you will execute the highest-growth projects of your career. This phase of the formula helps you: brainstorm 10x projects to achieve tenfold results, map them out onto your 10x calendar, create lean workflows that skyrocket efficiency, create the best content in your niche, and build an agile 10x team.

Stage Three: 10x Projects

A 10x project is one that can positively impact a large number of people in your audience and produce big revenue returns for your business. We contrast 10x projects with 10 percent improvements.

Template: 10x Project Ideas and Prioritization: This is a template for you and your team to brainstorm, score, and prioritize your 10x ideas.

Stage Four: 10x Calendar

A 10x calendar is a badass editorial calendar fueled by 10x projects, absent of 10 percent work. Your 10x calendar will become mission control for all marketing activities.

Template: 10x Calendar: This is a simple editorial calendar template for you to map out your 10x projects.

10x Marketing Interview: Pat Flynn and the $300,000 Launch: Pat Flynn and I talk about how he and his team at Smart Passive Income used their 10x calendar to power an online course launch that resulted in $300,000 of revenue. You will have access to the full audio interview plus transcript.

Stage Five: 10x Workflows

10x workflows are pre-approved, lean, and include high standards of performance that create smartly organized processes to streamline productivity. They cut redundant tasks, define what "done" looks like, and define how long each task should take.

10X TOOLBOX RESOURCE

Sample: 10x Blog Post Workflow: This is a sample of our 10x blog post workflow. Combine the process laid out in this chapter with the real-world example of what it looks like.

Stage Six: 10x Content

10x content is content so superior to everything else on a given topic it renders all other pieces irrelevant. With 10x content, you will add unmatched value to your users and get results.

10X TOOLBOX RESOURCES

10x Marketing Interview: Jeff Goins and the Content Scorecard: In this interview, author and speaker Jeff Goins explains how his team developed the content scorecard—a tool he says transformed their results. You will have access to the full audio interview plus transcript.

Template: 10x Content Scorecard: This template helps you score your content before it's ever published. It's a dead simple way for ensuring consistent quality and measuring potential impact before a piece is published.

10x Marketing Interview: Brian Dean and the Skyscraper Technique: SEO expert Brian Dean and I discuss his "Skyscraper

Technique." It's a brilliant method for creating the best content on a given topic. You will have access to the full audio interview plus transcript.

Checklist: The Skyscraper Technique Checklist: This is a checklist for using Brian's Skyscraper Technique for content research and creation.

Free Tool: Headline Analyzer: The Headline Analyzer is a free tool that will help you write headlines that drive traffic, shares, and search results. It is available absolutely free at https://coschedule.com/headline-analyzer

Stage Seven: 10x Team

10x teams embrace a process that acknowledges guessing, embraces failure, thrives on learning, and consistently pursues the best results over activity. They rigorously apply agile marketing principles with small, low-risk experiments to move fast, learn quickly, and find what works (and what doesn't).

10X TOOLBOX RESOURCE

10x Marketing Interview: Andrea Fryrear on "What is an agile marketing team?": In this interview, founder of Marketing Sherpas Andrea Fryrear dives deep into how marketing teams can appropriate and apply agile methods. You will have access to the full audio interview plus transcript.

PHASE THREE: PUBLISH

In phase three, you will adopt the minimum viable marketing process (MVM) to test your assumptions, de-risk projects, and ship those projects quickly. You will also learn to how to use intelligent social automation for 10x social promotion, as well as build and monetize an email list.

Stage Eight: Minimum Viable Marketing

Minimum viable marketing is a process for testing your assumptions about the results a project or idea will generate. Assumptions are extremely risky because they're so often wrong, which dooms your ideas to failure. MVM helps you quickly validate them and minimize risk of investing in projects likely to fail.

10X TOOLBOX RESOURCE

10x Marketing Interview: Ash Maurya and Lean Principles Applied: Author of Scaling Lean, Ash Maurya, and I talk about the confluence between minimum viable products and 10x marketing. You will have access to the full audio interview plus transcript.

Stage Nine: 10x Social Promotion

10x social promotion is a framework for combining intelligent automation (smart-o-mation) with robust, engagement-increasing social media methods. Create awesome stuff, then never shut up about it.

10X TOOLBOX RESOURCE

Photoshop CC Action: Social Media Image Photoshop CC Action: This Photoshop CC action will automatically size graphics for social networks Facebook, Twitter, Google+, and LinkedIn.

Infographic: Best Times To Post Infographic: This infographic is a quick reference guide to the optimal times to post on every social network. (Tip: You can automate this process with CoSchedule's Best Time Scheduling feature.)

Google Analytics Custom Report: Best Times To Post On Social Media: This custom Google Analytics report will show you the best times to post to your social accounts based on traffic for each network.

Free Tool: Social Message Optimizer: The Social Message Message Optimizer is a free tool that uses a powerful algorithm to help you optimize your social messages for every social network. It is available absolutely free at https://coschedule.com/social-message-optimizer

10x Marketing Interview: John T. Meyer on Visual Storytelling: Co-founder of Lemonly, John T. Meyer, and I discuss how his company used visual storytelling and microcontent for a 960 percent return on investment. You will have access to the full audio interview plus transcript.

Stage Ten: 10x Email Promotion

10x email promotion is the mindset and methodologies required to prioritize, build, and monetize a massive email list. This is a priority in the 10x Marketing Formula because you own the list you build, while you rent your social media following.

10X TOOLBOX RESOURCE

Free Tool: Email Subject Line Tester: Create click-worthy subject lines with the free Email Subject Line Tester tool. It will help you write email subject lines that drive more opens, more clicks, and more conversions, by visiting https://coschedule.com/email-subject-line-tester

PHASE FOUR: ANALYZE

The fourth phase of the *10x Marketing Formula* will help you optimize your content to convert an audience into customers. And finally, you will learn to focus on and measure everything against your one metric that matters (1MTM)—the metric most directly tied to revenue growth.

Stage Eleven: Conversion Psychology

Conversion psychology helps 10x marketers crawl into the minds of their customers, understand the five stages of awareness in the conversion funnel, and write compelling calls to value and calls to action.

10x Marketing Interview: Joanna Wiebe on Why People, Click, Try, and Buy: Creator of Copy Hackers and Aistory, Joanna Wiebe, and I unpack the psychology behind conversions. Joanna explains the five stages of awareness funnel, and how to use calls to action and calls to value to turn visitors into customers. You will have access to the full audio interview plus transcript.

Stage Twelve: One Metric That Matters

1MTM is a framework for focus, analysis, and ultimate results using three stages of growth. Your 1MTM becomes your team's North Star of activity and success.

Template: Growth Stage Maturity Matrix: This template helps you identify which stage of growth your team is in. As well, you will define your 1MTM and goal KPI.

ABOUT THE AUTHOR

Garrett Moon is the CEO and co-founder at CoSchedule, the web's most popular marketing calendar and the fastest-growing startup in North Dakota. Ranked as the best business tool built by a startup on Entrepreneur.com, CoSchedule helps more than ten thousand marketing teams stay organized in more than one hundred countries around the world. In 2016, CoSchedule was named one of the top five startups in Tech.Co's Startup of the Year Competition.

As a thought leader, Garrett has been blogging and speaking about content marketing, social media marketing, and startup business for more than seven years. He's been featured on sites like *Entrepreneur*, *Forbes*, *Social Media Examiner*, and *Content Marketing Institute*, and is an invited speaker at some of the world's most popular marketing conferences, including INBOUND and Content Marketing World.

 @garrett_moon   linkedin.com/in/garrettmoon/